Natural Disaster Management

Natural Disaster Management

Anshuman Sharma

RANDOM PUBLICATIONS
NEW DELHI (INDIA)

Natural Disaster Management

ISBN 978-93-5111-493-2

Published in 2015 in India by

RANDOM PUBLICATIONS

4376-A/4B, Gali Murari Lal, Ansari Road
New Delhi-110 002
Phone : +9111-43580356, 011-23289044, 011-43142548
e-mail: sales@randompublications.com,
info@randompublications.com, randomexports@gmail.com

Reprinted 2019

Type Setting by : Friends Media, Delhi-110089
Digitally Printed at: Replika Press Pvt. Ltd.

Preface

A natural disaster is the consequence or effect of a natural, hazardous event, occurring when human activities and natural phenomenon (a physical event, such as a volcanic eruption, earthquake, hurricane, tsunami, landslide, etc.) become enmeshed. Natural disasters result in catastrophic consequences for living things in the vicinity. The enormous havoc and dislocation caused by natural disasters have become a great burden particularly on the highly populated and poverty stricken developing countries causing perpetual misery to thousands of lives and livestock. Over the past 20 years alone, these extreme natural disasters have resulted in the loss of life of more than 3 million people and have affected over 800 million people all over the world, causing damage to property to the tune of 50-100 billion dollars, 50 per cent of which is due to floods and cyclones.

Disaster management is the organization and management of resources and responsibilities for dealing with all humanitarian aspects of emergencies, in particular preparedness, response and recovery in order to lessen the impact of disaster. Even though extreme natural events such as floods, drought, cyclones and earthquakes are not totally under human control, prediction of occurrence of some of these events with a good degree of certainty is possible, thanks to the developments in space technology. Instead of collectively taking up the challenge of preventing or at least mitigating the effects of such disasters, providing aids after the events which are both inadequate and untimely has only resulted in perpetuating the misery of the worst affected, silently suffering victims of disasters.

The present book provides practitioners, educators and students with a comprehensive overview of the players, processes and special issues involved in the management of natural disasters. It will also serve as a reference to governmental and other agencies involved in international disaster management activities.

Author

Contents

1

Introduction

The term disaster can be defined as "a natural or man-made event that negatively affects life, property, livelihood or industry often resulting in permanent changes to human societies, ecosystems and environment."

As the definition suggests, disasters are highly disruptive events that cause suffering, deprivation, hardship, injury and even death, as a result of direct injury, disease, the interruption of commerce and business, and the partial or total destruction of critical infrastructure such as homes, hospitals, and other buildings, roads, bridges, power lines, etc. Disasters can be caused by naturally occurring events, such as earthquakes, hurricanes, flooding, or tornadoes, or they can be due to man-made events, either accidental (such as an accidental toxic spill or nuclear power plant event), or deliberately caused (such as various terrorist bombings and poisonings).

Certain types of natural disasters are more likely to occur in particular parts of the world. For instance, areas near coastline, lakes or rivers are more likely to experience flooding problems than are land-locked areas. However, most every place you could live is prone to one type of natural disaster or another. No place is absolutely safe from natural disaster. And, of course it goes without saying, that no place is safe from the threat of terrorism and other man-made disaster events.

It may be impossible to avoid disasters, but it isn't impossible to plan ahead of time so as to minimize the impact that any given disaster might have on you or your family's health, safety and property. There are steps you can take ahead of time, including, purchasing the proper types of insurance, preparing a disaster kit and supplies, making a disaster plan and rehearsing it with your family, and staying informed so that you can do your best to get out of the way of predictable dangerous occurrences, that can help you, your family, and your property stay as safe as possible.

Defining Natural Disasters

Natural disasters are tremendous forces of nature that have been known to destroy cities and towns all over the world. Some of the most well-known natural disasters that happen every year are: avalanches, earthquakes, volcanic eruptions, floods, tsunamis, tornadoes, droughts, heat waves, hailstorms, and hurricanes (also known as cyclones and typhoons). They can happen at any time of any day, thus everyone needs to know how to be prepared and how to react when they occur.

The effects of natural disasters can be devastating. They can result in loss of life and physical damage to one's body or to one's property. Natural disasters can also result in economic damage. With all the damage the natural disaster can do to a country, the affected governments will have to pay to reconstruct buildings and infrastructure. The economic damage would most likely leave these governments with a huge debt.

Natural disasters are large and destructive forces that ravage the Earth. These disasters can kill millionsof people and destroy entire cities. Examples of natural disasters are hurricanes, tsunamis,earthquakes, volcanic eruptions, avalanches, landslides, mudslides, typhoons, or tornadoes. These disasters cannot be prevented, but a person who is prepared may be able to reduce loss of property and loss of life. Simple actions such as planning escape routes, having an emergency supply kit, and having a plan of what to do during the disaster can save lives.The intention of this website is to inform viewers about the dangers of natural disasters so that with this information theycan be prepared if a disaster strikes. Through thefour main sections of the website, a viewer will not only learn about many aspects of natural disasters, but also how to protect themselves when a disaster strikes.

Types of Natural Disasters

Natural disasters come in many different shapes and forms. They cause tragedies and dilemmas all over the world. Some disasters cause flooding and water complications; while others can cause buildings to collapse.

Natural disasters can take hundreds of lives, homes, and businesses each year.

There are many different types of natural disasters. Below are a few of the many disasters that take place in the world every year.

Avalanches

An avalanche is a sudden, rapid flow of snow down a slope, occurring when either natural triggers, such as loading from new snow or rain, or artificial triggers, such as explosives or backcountry skiers, overload the snowpack. The influence of gravity on the accumulated weight of newly fallen uncompacted snow or on thawing older snow leads to avalanches which may be triggered by earthquakes, gunshots and the movements of animals. Avalanches are most common during winter or spring but glacier movements may cause ice avalanches during summer. Avalanches cause loss of life and can destroy settlements, roads, railways and forests. From a geophysical perspective, avalanches are an example of a non-critical, punctuated equilibrium system. Typically occurring in mountainous terrain, an avalanche can mix air and water with the descending snow. Powerful avalanches have the capability to entrain ice, rocks, trees, and other material on the slope. Avalanches are primarily composed of flowing snow, and are distinct from mudslides, rock slides, and seraccollapses on an icefall. In contrast to other natural events which can cause disasters, avalanches are not rare or random events and are endemic to any mountain range that accumulates a standing snowpack. In mountainous terrain avalanches are among the most serious objective hazards to life and property, with their destructive capability resulting from their potential to carry an enormous mass of snow rapidly over large distances.

Avalanches are classified by their morphological characteristics and are rated by either their destructive potential, or the mass of the downward flowing snow. Some of the morphological characteristics used to classify avalanches include the type of snow involved, the nature of the failure, the sliding surface, the propagation mechanism of the failure, the trigger of the avalanche, the slope angle, slope aspect, and elevation. The size of an avalanche, its mass and its destructive potential are rated on a logarithmic scale, typically of 5 categories, with the precise definition of the categories depending on the observation system or geographic region in which the avalanche occurs.

Earthquakes

An earthquake is the result of a sudden release of energy in the Earth's crust that creates seismic waves. At the Earth's surface, earthquakes manifest themselves by vibration, shaking and sometimes displacement of the ground. The vibrations may vary in magnitude. Earthquakes are caused mostly by slippage within geological faults, but also by other events such as volcanic activity, landslides, mine blasts, and nuclear tests. The underground point of origin of the earthquake is called the focus. The point directly above the focus on the surface is called the epicenter. Earthquakes by themselves rarely kill people or wildlife. It is usually the secondary events that they trigger, such as building collapse, fires, tsunamis (seismic sea waves) and volcanoes, that are actually the human disaster. Many of these could possibly be avoided by better construction, safety systems, early warning and evacuation planning.

Some of the most significant earthquakes in recent times include:

— The 2004 Indian Ocean earthquake, the third largest earthquake in recorded history, registering a moment magnitude of 9.1-9.3. The huge tsunamis triggered by this earthquake cost the lives of at least 229,000 people.

— The 2011 Tôhoku earthquake and tsunami registered a moment magnitude of 9.0. The death toll from the earthquake and tsunami is over 13,000, and over 12,000 people are still missing.

— The 8.8 magnitude February 27, 2010 Chile earthquake and tsunami cost 525 lives.

— The 7.9 magnitude May 12, 2008 Sichuan earthquake in Sichuan Province, China. Death toll at over 61,150 as of May 27, 2008.

— The 7.7 magnitude July 2006 Java earthquake, which also triggered tsunamis.

— The 7.6-7.7 magnitude 2005 Kashmir earthquake, which cost 79,000 lives in Pakistan.

Volcanic Eruptions

Volcanoes can cause widespread destruction and consequent disaster through several ways. The effects include the volcanic eruption itself that may cause harm following the explosion of the volcano or the fall of rock. Second, lava may be produced during the eruption of a volcano. As it leaves the volcano, the lava destroys many buildings and plants it encounters. Third, volcanic ash generally meaning the cooled ash—may form a cloud, and settle thickly in nearby locations. When mixed with water this forms a concrete-like material. In sufficient quantity ash may cause roofs to collapse under its weight but even small quantities will harm humans if inhaled. Since the ash has the consistency of ground glass it causes abrasion damage to moving parts such as engines. The main killer of humans in the immediate surroundings of a volcanic eruption is the pyroclastic flows, which consist of a cloud of hot volcanic ash which builds up in the air above the volcano and rushes down the slopes when the eruption no longer supports the lifting of the gases. It is believed that Pompeii was destroyed by a pyroclastic flow. A lahar is a volcanic mudflow or landslide. The 1953 Tangiwai disaster was caused by a lahar, as was the 1985 Armero tragedy in which the town of Armero was buried and an estimated 23,000 people were killed.

A specific type of volcano is the supervolcano. According to the Toba catastrophe theory 70 to 75 thousand years ago a super volcanic event at Lake Toba reduced the human population to 10,000 or even 1,000 breeding pairs creating a bottleneck in human evolution. It also killed three quarters of all plant life in the northern hemisphere. The main danger from a supervolcano is the immense cloud of ash which has a disastrous global effect on climate and temperature for many years.

Floods

A flood is an overflow of an expanse of water that submerges land. The European Union (EU) Floods Directive defines a flood as a temporary covering by water of land not normally covered by water. In the sense of "flowing water", the word may also be applied to the inflow of the tide.

While the size of a lake or other body of water will vary with seasonal changes in precipitation and snow melt, it is not a significant flood unless such escapes of water endanger land areas used by man like a village, city or other inhabited area.

Floods can also occur in rivers, when flow exceeds the capacity of the river channel, particularly at bends or meanders. Floods often cause damage to homes and businesses if they are placed in natural flood plains of rivers. While flood damage can be virtually eliminated by moving away from rivers and other bodies of water, since time out of mind, people have lived and worked by the water to seek sustenance and capitalize on the gains of cheap and easy travel and commerce by being near water. That humans continue to inhabit areas threatened by flood damage is evidence that the perceived value of living near the water exceeds the cost of repeated periodic flooding.

The word "flood" comes from the Old English flood, a word common to Germanic languages. Deluge myths are mythical stories of a great flood sent by a deity or deities to destroy civilization as an act of divine retribution, and are featured in the mythology of many cultures. Some of the most notable floods include:

— The Huang He (Yellow River) in China floods particularly often. The Great Flood of 1931 caused between 800,000 and 4,000,000 deaths.
— The Great Flood of 1993 was one of the most costly floods in United States history.
— The 1998 Yangtze River Floods, in China, left 14 million people homeless.
— The 2000 Mozambique flood covered much of the country for three weeks, resulting in thousands of deaths, and leaving the country devastated for years afterward.
— The 2005 Mumbai floods which destroyed 1094 people.
— The 2010 Pakistan floods, damaged crops and infrastructure, claiming many lives.

Tropical cyclones can result in extensive flooding and storm surge, as happened with:

— Bhola Cyclone, which struck East Pakistan (now Bangladesh) in 1970,
— Typhoon Nina, which struck China in 1975,
— Hurricane Katrina, which struck New Orleans, Louisiana in 2005, and
— Cyclone Yasi, which struck Australia in 2011

Limnic Eruptions

A limnic eruption, also referred to as a lake overturn, is a rare type of natural disaster in which carbon dioxide (CO_2) suddenly erupts from deep lake water, suffocating wildlife, livestock and humans. Such an eruption may also cause tsunamis in the lake as the rising CO_2 displaces water. Scientists believe landslides, volcanic activity, or explosions can trigger such an eruption. Lakes in which such activity occurs may be known as limnically active lakes or exploding lakes. Some features of limnically active lakes include:

— CO_2-saturated incoming water
— A cool lake bottom indicating an absence of direct volcanic interaction with lake waters
— An upper and lower thermal layer with differing CO_2 saturations
— Proximity to areas with volcanic activity

Scientists have recently determined, from investigations into the mass casualties in the 1980s at Lake Monoun and Lake Nyos, that limnic eruptions and volcanic eruptions, although indirectly related, are actually separate types of disaster events

To date, this phenomenon has been observed only twice. The first was in Cameroon at Lake Monoun in 1984, causing the asphyxiation and death of 37 people living nearby. A second, deadlier eruption happened at neighbouring Lake Nyos in 1986, this time releasing over 80 million cubic meters of CO_2 and killing between 1,700 and 1,800 people, again by asphyxiation.

Due to the nature of the event, it is hard to determine if limnic eruptions have happened elsewhere. However, a third lake—Lake Kivu—containing massive amounts of dissolved CO_2 exists on the border between the Democratic Republic of the Congo and Rwanda. Sample sediments from the lake were taken by Professor Robert Hecky from the University of Michigan which showed that an event caused living creatures in the lake to go extinct approximately every thousand years, and caused nearby vegetation to be swept back into the lake.

The Messel pit fossil deposits of Messel, Germany, show evidence of a limnic eruption there in the early Eocene. Among the victims are perfectly preserved insects, frogs, turtles, crocodiles, birds, anteaters, insectivores, early primates and paleotheres.

Once an eruption occurs, a large CO_2 cloud forms above the lake and expands to the neighbouring region. Because CO_2 is denser than air, it has a tendency to sink to the ground while pushing breathable air up. As a result, life forms that need to breathe oxygen suffocate once the CO_2 cloud reaches them, as there is very little oxygen in the cloud. The CO_2 can make human bodily fluids very acidic, potentially causing CO_2 poisoning. As victims gasp for air they actually hurt themselves more by inhaling the CO_2 gas.

At Lake Nyos, the gas cloud descended from the lake into a nearby village where it settled, killing nearly everyone. In this eruption, some people as far as 25 km (16 mi) from the lake died. A change in skin colour on some bodies led scientists to think that the gas cloud may have contained a dissolved acid such as hydrogen chloride as well, but that hypothesis is disputed. Many victims were found with blisters on their skin. This is believed to have been caused by pressure ulcers, which are likely to have formed from the low levels of oxygen present in the blood of those asphyxiated by the carbon dioxide. Thousands of cattle and wild animals were also asphyxiated, but no official counts were made. On the other hand, vegetation nearby was mostly unaffected except for that which grew immediately adjacent to the lake. There the vegetation was damaged or destroyed by a 5-meter (16.4 ft.) tsunami from the violent eruption.

Tsunamis

A tsunami is a series of water waves caused by the displacement of a large volume of a body of water, typically an ocean or a large lake. Earthquakes, volcanic eruptions and other underwater explosions (including detonations of underwater nuclear devices), landslides, glacier calvings, meteorite impacts and other disturbances above or below water all have the potential to generate a tsunami.

Tsunami waves do not resemble normal sea waves, because their wavelength is far longer. Rather than appearing as a breaking wave, a tsunami may instead initially resemble a rapidly rising tide, and for this reason they are often referred to as tidal waves. Tsunamis generally consist of a series of waves with periods ranging from minutes to hours, arriving in a so-called "wave train". Wave heights of tens of metres can be generated by large events. Although the impact of tsunamis is limited to coastal areas, their destructive power can be enormous and they can affect entire ocean basins; the 2004 Indian Ocean tsunami was among the deadliest natural disasters in human history with over 230,000 people killed in 14 countries bordering the Indian Ocean.

The Greek historian Thucydides suggested in 426 B.C. that tsunamis were related to submarine earthquakes, but the understanding of a tsunami's nature remained slim until the 20th century and much remains unknown. Major areas of current research include trying to determine why some large earthquakes do not generate tsunamis while other smaller ones do; trying to accurately forecast the passage of tsunamis across the oceans; and also to forecast how tsunami waves would interact with specific shorelines

Tsunami can be generated when the sea floor abruptly deforms and vertically displaces the overlying water. Tectonic earthquakes are a particular kind of earthquake that are associated with the Earth's crustal deformation; when these earthquakes occur beneath the sea, the water above the deformed area is displaced from its equilibrium position. More specifically, a tsunami can be generated when thrust faults associated with convergent or destructive plate boundaries move abruptly, resulting in water displacement, owing to the vertical component of movement involved. Movement on normal faults will also cause displacement of the seabed, but the size of the largest of such events is normally too small to give rise to a significant tsunami.

Blizzards

A blizzard is a severe snowstorm characterized by strong winds. By definition, the difference between blizzard and a snowstorm is the strength of the wind. To be a blizzard, a snow storm must have sustained winds or frequent gusts that are greater than or equal to 56 km/h (35 mph) with blowing or drifting snow which reduces visibility to 400 meters or ¼ mile or less and must last for a prolonged period of time — typically three hours or more. Snowfall amounts do not have to be significant. Ground blizzards require high winds to stir up already fallen snow.

Blizzards can bring near-whiteout conditions, and can paralyse regions for days at a time, particularly where snowfall is unusual or rare. The 1972 Iran blizzard, which caused approximately 4000 deaths, was the deadliest in recorded history. Significant blizzards include:

— The Great Blizzard of 1888 in the United States

— The 2008 Afghanistan blizzard

— The North American blizzard of 1947

— The 1972 Iran blizzard resulted in approximately 4,000 deaths and lasted for 5 to 7 days.

Cyclonic Storms

In meteorology, a cyclone is an area of closed, circular fluid motion rotating in the same direction as the Earth. This is usually characterized by inward spiraling winds that rotate anticlockwise in the Northern Hemisphere and clockwise in the Southern Hemisphere of the Earth. A cyclone is a synonym for hurricane . Most large-scale cyclonic circulations are centered on areas of low atmospheric pressure. The largest low-pressure systems are cold-core polar cyclones and extratropical cyclones which lie on the synoptic scale. Warm-core cyclones such as tropical cyclones, mesocyclones, and polar lows lie within the smaller mesoscale. Subtropical cyclones are of intermediate size. Upper level cyclones can exist without the presence of a surface low, and can pinch off from the base of the Tropical Upper Tropospheric Trough during the summer months in the Northern Hemisphere. Cyclones have also been seen on extraterrestrial planets, such as Mars and Neptune.

Cyclogenesis describes the process of cyclone formation and intensification. Extratropical cyclones form as waves in large regions of enhanced mid-latitude temperature contrasts called baroclinic zones. These zones contract to form weather fronts as the cyclonic circulation closes and intensifies. Later in their life cycle, cyclones occlude as cold core systems.

Weather fronts separate two masses of air of different densities and are associated with the most prominent meteorological phenomena. Air masses separated by a front may differ in temperature or humidity. Strong cold fronts typically feature narrow bands of thunderstorms and severe weather, and may on occasion be preceded by squall lines or dry lines. They form west of the circulation center and generally move from west to east. Warm fronts form east of the cyclone center and are usually preceded by stratiform precipitation and fog. They move poleward ahead of the cyclone path. Occluded fronts form late in the cyclone life cycle near the center of the cyclone and often wrap around the storm center.

Tropical cyclogenesis describes the process of development of tropical cyclones. Tropical cyclones form due to latent heat driven by significant thunderstorm activity, and are warm core. Cyclones can transition between extratropical, subtropical, and tropical phases under the right conditions. Mesocyclones form as warm core cyclones over land, and can lead to tornado formation. Waterspouts can also form from mesocyclones, but more often develop from environments of high instability and low vertical wind shear.

Droughts

A drought is an extended period of months or years when a region notes a deficiency in its water supply. Generally, this occurs when a region receives consistently below average precipitation. It can have a substantial impact on the ecosystem and agriculture of the affected region. Although droughts can persist for several years, even a short, intense drought can cause significant damage and harm the local economy.

This global phenomenon has a widespread impact on agriculture. The United Nations estimates that an area of fertile soil the size of Ukraine is lost every year because of drought, deforestation, and climate instability. Lengthy periods of drought have long been a key trigger for mass migration and played a key role in a number of ongoing migrations and other humanitarian crises in the Horn of Africa and the Sahel.

Periods of drought can have significant environmental, agricultural, health, economic and social consequences. The effect varies according to vulnerability. For example, subsistence farmers are more likely to migrate during drought because they do not have alternative food sources. Areas with populations that depend on as a major food source are more vulnerable to drought-triggered famine.

Drought can also reduce water quality, because lower water flows reduce dilution of pollutants and increase contamination of remaining water sources. Common consequences of drought include:

— Diminished crop growth or yield productions and carrying capacity for livestock
— Dust bowls, themselves a sign of erosion, which further erode the landscape
— Dust storms, when drought hits an area suffering from desertification and erosion
— Famine due to lack of water for irrigation
— Habitat damage, affecting both terrestrial and aquatic wildlife
— Malnutrition, dehydration and related diseases
— Mass migration, resulting in internal displacement and international refugees
— Reduced electricity production due to reduced water flow through hydroelectric dams
— Shortages of water for industrial users
— Snake migration and increases in snakebites
— Social unrest
— War over natural resources, including water and food
— Wildfires, such as Australian bushfires, are more common during times of drought

Well-known historical droughts include:

— 1900 India killing between 250,000 and 3.25 million.

— 1921-22 Soviet Union in which over 5 million perished from starvation due to drought

— 1928-30 northwest China resulting in over 3 million deaths by famine.

— 1936 and 1941 Sichuan Province China resulting in 5 million and 2.5 million deaths respectively.

— As of 2006, states of Australia including South Australia, Western Australia, New South Wales, Northern Territory and Queensland had been under drought conditions for five to ten years. The drought is beginning to affect urban area populations for the first time. With the majority of the country under water restrictions.

— In 2006, Sichuan Province China experienced its worst drought in modern times with nearly 8 million people and over 7 million cattle facing water shortages.

— 12-year drought that was devastating southwest Western Australia, southeast South Australia, Victoria and northern Tasmania was "very severe and without historical precedent".

Hailstorms

Hail is a form of solid precipitation. It consists of balls or irregular lumps of ice, each of which is referred to as a hail stone. Hail stones on Earth consist mostly of water ice and measure between 5 millimetres (0.20 in) and 200 millimetres (7.9 in) in diameter, with the larger stones coming from severe thunderstorms. Hail is possible within most thunderstorms as it is produced bycumulonimbi (thunderclouds), and within 2 nautical miles (3.7 km) of the parent storm. Hail formation requires environments of strong, upward motion of air with the parent thunderstorm and lowered heights of the freezing level. Hail is most frequently formed in the interior of continents within the mid-latitudes of Earth, with hail generally confined to higher elevations within the tropics.

There are methods available to detect hail-producing thunderstorms using weather satellites and weather radar imagery. Hail stones generally fall at higher speeds as they grow in size, though complicating factors such as melting, friction with air, wind, and interaction with rain and other hail stones can slow their descent through Earth's atmosphere. Severe weather warnings are issued for hail when the stones reach a damaging size, as it can cause serious damage to man-made structures and, most commonly, farmers' crops. Any thunderstorm which produces hail that reaches the ground is known as a hailstorm. Hail has a diameter of 5 millimetres (0.20 in) or more. Hail stones can grow to 15 centimetres (6 in) and weigh more than 0.5 kilograms (1.1 lb).

Unlike ice pellets, hail stones are layered and can be irregular and clumped together. Hail is composed of transparent ice or alternating layers of transparent and translucent ice at least 1 millimetre (0.039 in) thick, which are deposited upon the hail stone as it cycles through the cloud, suspended aloft by air with strong upward motion until its weight overcomes the updraft and falls to the ground. Although the diameter of hail is varied, in the United States, the average observation of damaging hail is between 2.5 cm (1 in) and golf ball-sized (1.75 in). Stones larger than 2 cm (0.75 in) are usually considered large enough to cause damages. The Meteorological Service of Canada will issue severe thunderstorm warnings when hail that size or above is expected.

Heat Waves

A heat wave is a prolonged period of excessively hot weather, which may be accompanied by high humidity. There is no universal definition of a heat wave; the term is relative to the usual weather in the area. Temperatures that people from a hotter climate consider normal can be termed a heat wave in a cooler area if they are outside the normal climate pattern for that area. The term is applied both to routine weather variations and to extraordinary spells of heat which may occur only once a century. Severe heat waves have caused catastrophic crop failures, thousands of deaths from hyperthermia, and widespread power outages due to increased use of air conditioning. Heat waves often occur during the Dog Days of summer; indeed the French term canicule, denoting the general phenomenon of a heat wave, derives from the Italian canicula applied to the star Sirius, also known as the "Dog Star." Some regions of the globe are more susceptible to heat waves than others, typically inland desert, semidesert, and Mediterranean-type climates.

Tornadoes

A tornado is a violent, dangerous, rotating column of air that is in contact with both the surface of the earth and a cumulonimbus cloud or, in rare cases, the base of a cumulus cloud. They are often referred to as a twister or a cyclone, although the word cyclone is used in meteorology in a wider sense, to name any closed low pressure circulation. Tornadoes come in many shapes and sizes, but are typically in the form of a visible condensation funnel, whose narrow end touches the earth and is often encircled by a cloud of debris and dust. Most tornadoes have wind speeds less than 110 miles per hour (177 km/h), are approximately 250 feet (80 m) across, and travel a few miles (several kilometers) before dissipating. The most extreme tornadoes can attain wind speeds of more than 300 mph (480 km/h), stretch more than two miles (3 km) across, and stay on the ground for dozens of miles (more than 100 km). Well-known historical tornadoes include:

— The Tri-State Tornado of 1925, which killed over 600 people in the United States;

— The Daulatpur-Saturia Tornado of 1989, which killed roughly 1,300 people in Bangladesh.

Fires

A wildfire is any uncontrolled fire in combustible vegetation that occurs in the countryside or a wilderness area. Other names such as brush fire, bushfire, forest fire, desert fire, grass fire, hill fire, squirrel fire, vegetation fire, and veldfire may be used to describe the same phenomenon depending on the type of vegetation being burned. A wildfire differs from other fires by its extensive size, the speed at which it can spread out from its original source, its potential to change direction unexpectedly, and its ability to jump gaps such as roads, rivers and fire breaks. Wildfires are characterized in terms of the cause of ignition, their physical properties such as speed of propagation, the combustible material present, and the effect of weather on the fire.

Wildfires occur on every continent except Antarctica. Fossil records and human history contain accounts of wildfires, as wildfires can occur in periodic intervals. Wildfires can cause extensive damage, both to property and human life, but they also have various beneficial effects on wilderness areas. Some plant species depend on the effects of fire for growth and reproduction, although large wildfires may also have negative ecological effects.

Strategies of wildfire prevention, detection, and suppression have varied over the years, and international wildfire management experts encourage further development of technology and research. One of the more controversial techniques is controlled burning: permitting or even igniting smaller fires to minimize the amount of flammable material available for a potential wildfire. While some wildfires burn in remote forested regions, they can cause extensive destruction of homes and other property located in the wildland-urban interface: a zone of transition between developed areas and undeveloped wilderness

Effects of Natural Disasters

Natural disasters can be as devastating as causing massive destruction of populated areas to causing minimal damage. Some of the most dangerous natural disasters do not happen here on Earth, but occur in space. Natural disasters that happen in space are gamma ray bursts, supernovas, asteroids, and black holes. A black hole is dense enough that light cannot escape its gravitational pull. If one were to drift close to Earth, the planet could be drawn toward it and be sucked into it. Most of these space disasters could cause total destruction of human life. If not total destruction, they could possibly destroy some of the earth's magnetic field which is essential for protecting the planet from solar flares. Some endangering threats have already been discovered. One asteroid, Apophis, is expected to come close to Earth in 2036, but there is only a 0.001% chance of it actually hitting Earth.

Other natural disasters are sometimes harmless. Solar flares are blocked by the earth's magnetic field and are not harmful to Earth. Some landslides and other natural disasters are too small to injure any human or animal life, or occur in unpopulated areas.However, there are some serious natural disasters that occur on Earth such as: volcanoes, earthquakes, tsunamis, and hurricanes. These disasters cause thousands of deaths every year and will continue to affect the earth's population for years to come. Ways must be found to minimize the effects of these disasters on society.

Preparation and Mitigation

Natural disasters affect everyone alike. However, the nature of impact varies based on their vulnerability which is physical, social and/or attitudinal and the coping capacities of those affected. There has been an increase in the number of natural disasters over the past few years, and with it, increasing loss on account of urbanization and population growth, as a result of which the impact of natural disasters is felt to a large extent.The occurrence of disaster related deaths are on a rise and the Asian region accounts for 98.85 per cent of overall deaths during the year 2008 which is significantly higher compared to other regions of the world.

Globally, each time a disaster occurs; there is physical, educational, economic and psychological impact and the Indian sub-continent is no exception to it. Around 85 per cent of India's geographical area is prone to natural hazards such as cyclones, floods, earthquakes, landslides and droughts besides localized hazards. Traditionally, India has been reactive in its approach towards disasters; with precious resources being spent on relief, rehabilitation and reconstruction. Of late, there has been a major shift in its approach. The focus has shifted to pre-disaster aspects like prevention, mitigation and preparedness as it is felt that appropriate mitigation measures can substantially, if not completely, mitigate the impact of disasters.

To reduce the impact of disasters, the Hyogo Framework for Action 2005, priority 3 (UNISDR's) ensures the "Use knowledge, innovation and education to build a culture of safety and resilience at all levels." Key activities include:

a) Information management and exchange

b) Education and training

c) Research and

d) Public awareness

Education for disaster management is a trans-disciplinary exercise aimed at developing knowledge, skill and values at all level. Some of the recent disasters that have affected the education sector in India are the Gujarat earthquake where 971 students and 31 teachers were killed, 1,884 schools collapsed; Tamil Nadu Fire incident where 93 children died in a fire due to explosion of a cooking gas cylinder; North Pakistan, Kashmir earthquake where 17,000 students died at school, and 10,000 school buildings destroyed.

To build in a culture of safety and resilience at all levels in the education sector, there is a need to carry out a large number of initiatives. Some of the ongoing initiatives of Government of India with support from various stakeholders are:

a) *Inclusion of disaster management in the curriculum:* To reduce vulnerability, the Central Board for Secondary Education (CBSE), with support from Ministry of Home Affairs (MHA) and Human Resource

Development (MHRD), Government of India and United Nations Development Programme (UNDP) have incorporated Disaster Management as part of its frontline curriculum in Social Science for class VIII, IX, X and XI. The success of this initiative at the national level has encouraged the State Education Boards of the country to have the subject as part of its curriculum.

b) *Training of teachers:* The subject of Disaster Management being a new subject, a need was felt to train the teachers who could in turn facilitate the transaction of the subject in the classrooms. To cater to the growing need, the National Council of Education Research and Training with support from United Nations Development Programme (UNDP) have developed self learning training modules which focus on 'Health, Safety and Well Being of School Children'. A large number of teachers have been trained at the national, state and local level by the Government with support from various stakeholders like NGOs, corporate, academic institutions etc.

c) *Awareness campaigns:* Print, electronic and folk media have been has been widely utilized to generate awareness amongst the school community and parents. Posters, short video clippings on various hazards focusing on preparedness and mitigation measures have been developed by Government, UN agencies and NGOs. Games, puzzles, colouring activity books have also been developed to generate awareness on hazards specially targeting the primary children and children out of schools. Street plays and magic shows have also been used to create awareness amongst teachers and students and parents.

Looking at the need of the hour, and to build a culture of safety at all levels, the National Disaster Management Authority (NDMA) of Government of India with support from Non Governmental Organizations, corporate, academic institutions etc. need to develop guidelines for schools which should reflect issues related to the education sector namely child rights and emergencies, integrating Disaster Risk Reduction with development, inclusion of DM as curricular and co-curricular activities, structural and non structural safety of educational institutions, training and capacity development at various levels etc.

Disaster preparedness includes all of the activities that are carried out prior to the advance notice of a catastrophe in order to facilitate the use of available resources, relief, and rehabilitation in the best possible fashion.

Disaster preparedness starts at the local community level; if local resources were insufficient, it would branch out to the national level, and if needed, the international level. Disaster mitigation is the ongoing effort to lessen the impact disasters have on people and property. Fewer people and communities would be affected by natural disasters with the use of this process. Because of the varying degree of each natural disaster, there are different mitigation strategies for each. Outlined in the following tables are some important recommendations for protection against disaster.

Disaster management is the process of addressing an event that has the potential to seriously disrupt the social fabric of the community. Disaster management is similar to disaster mitigation, however it implies a whole-of-government approach to using community resources to fight the effects of an event and assumes the community will be self-sufficient for periods of time until the situation can be stabilized. Through disaster management, we cannot completely counteract the damage but it is possible to minimize the risks through early warning, provide developmental plans for recuperation from the disaster, generate communication and medical resources, and aid in rehabilitation and post-disaster reconstruction.

The exchange of correct information following the event is important, in order to ensure the resources necessary to support response and recovery activities. The 72 hours following a major event is the most difficult time because of a lack of coordination among relief organizations. Problems that interrupt rather than coordinate the rescue efforts of all groups involved often occur because of hasty decision-making under complicated circumstances and the large number of organizations, which are unsure of their roles during operations.

Disaster prevention is concerned with policies and programs to prevent the recurrence of natural disasters and covers the long-term aspect of such disasters. The small price to pay for any method of prevention and protection pays off in the long run. An example of this is the Anheuser-Busch facility. In the early 1980s, Anheuser-Busch invested $15 million to protect its facilities from an earthquake. In 1994, an earthquake whose epicenter was 12 miles away from the facility hit, however because of the prevention the company took, it saved an estimated $300 million in damages.

Programs that follow and track disasters have improved throughout the years. In the 1970s, only the specialized departments of large companies, universities, and the government covered disasters. Desktop systems and computer communications emerged as a technology for linking emergency professionals on a global basis in the eighties. With the 1990s, computer equipment became more powerful and is now an essential component of disaster operations worldwide. Today Earth observation satellites provide basic support in pre-disaster preparedness programs: in-disaster response, monitoring activities, and post-disaster reconstruction.

As the population increases, it is expected that economic and societal costs of disasters will increase every year. The need to prevent property damage, disaster costs, injury and deaths is increasing because it is expected in the next 15 years that even more Americans will live and work in regions of natural disaster risks. With the established and anticipated disaster programs, communities can prepare and recover faster, however we must not forget the severity of any disaster and we must remember to be prepared for all of them.

References

Alexander D. (2002). *Principles of Emergency planning and Management.* Harpended: Terra publishing.

Bankoff, G. Frerks, G. Hilhorst D. (*eds.*) (2003). *Mapping Vulnerability: Disasters, Development and People.*

Lee Davis (2008). "*Natural Disasters*". Infobase Publishing.

Luis Flores Ballesteros. "What determines a disaster?" 54 Pesos Sep 2008:54 Pesos 11 Sep 2008.

Wisner, B. Blaikie, P. Cannon, T. and Davis I. (2004). *At Risk - Natural hazards, people's vulnerability and disasters.* Wiltshire: Routledge.

2

Avalanches: Control and Rescue

An avalanche is a sudden, drastic flow of snow down a slope, occurring when either natural triggers, such as loading from new snow or rain, or artificial triggers, such as snowmobilers, explosives or backcountry skiers, overload the snowpack.

Avalanche is a mechanical phenomenon: The influence of gravity on the accumulated weight of newly fallen uncompacted snow or on thawing older snow leads to avalanches which may be triggered by earthquakes, gunshots and the movements of animals. Typically occurring in mountainous terrain, an avalanche can mix air and water with the descending snow. Powerful avalanches have the capability to entrain ice, rocks, trees, and other material on the slope. Avalanches are primarily composed of flowing snow, and are distinct from mudslides, rock slides, and serac collapses on an icefall.

Avalanches are not rare or random events and are endemic to any mountain range that accumulates a standing snowpack. Avalanches are most common during winter or spring but glacier movements may cause ice avalanches during summer. In mountainous terrain, avalanches are among the most serious objective hazards to life and property, with their destructive capability resulting from their potential to carry an enormous mass of snow rapidly over large distances. Avalanches cause loss of life and can destroy settlements, roads, railways and forests.

Avalanches are classified by their morphological characteristics and are rated by either their destructive potential, or the mass of the downward flowing snow. Some of the morphological characteristics used to classify avalanches include the type of snow involved, the nature of the failure, the sliding surface, the propagation mechanism of the failure, the trigger of the avalanche, the slope angle, slope aspect, and elevation. The size of an avalanche, its mass and its destructive potential are rated on a logarithmic scale, typically of 5 categories, with the precise definition of the categories depending on the observation system or geographic region in which the avalanche occurs.

Formation

Most of the time, avalanches are caused by external stress on the snowpack; natural events are not random or spontaneous events. Natural triggers of avalanches include additional precipitation, rapid warming, rock fall, ice fall, and other impulse loads; however, even when environmental conditions are consistent, the seasonal snowpack will evolve over time and develop stresses, often from the downslope creep of the snowpack. Artificial triggers of avalanches include skiers, snowmobiles, and controlled explosive work. The triggering stress usually causes an avalanche at the location where force is directly applied to the snowpack (local trigger), but can in some cases cause avalanche formation at a different location nearby (remote trigger). Remotely triggered avalanches occur when a disturbance is transmitted from one location in the snowpack to another location in the snowpack. Small avalanches sometimes trigger much larger avalanches: for example, a small avalanche may apply significant overburden pressure to the snowpack, disturbing deeper weaknesses, and a larger avalanche may form as a result. This phenomenon is referred to as "stepping down".

A number of the forces acting on a snowpack can be readily determined. For example, there is little problem in calculating the weight of the snow, which provides information about the load on a weak layer. However, other factors are much more difficult to determine. It is very difficult to estimate the shear, ductile and tensile strengths within the snowpack or relative to the ground below. These strengths vary with the hardness of the snow, type of snow crystal, the number of bonds per unit volume, and the strength of contact interfaces between the layers. The thermo-mechanical properties of the snow crystals in turn depend on the local conditions such as ambient air temperature that control moisture transport inside the snowpack. One of the aims of avalanche research is to develop and validate computer models that can describe the evolution of the seasonal snowpack over time. A complicating factor is the chaotic interaction of terrain and weather, which causes significant spatial and temporal variability of the depths, crystal forms, and layering of the seasonal snowpack.

Classification

The nature of the failure of the snowpack is used to morphologically classify the avalanche. To this point, there are two main types of avalanches: loose snow avalanches and slab avalanches, and either type of avalanche can involve dry or wet snow. For this reason, professionals refer to avalanches as "dry loose snow avalanches", "wet loose snow avalanches", "dry slab avalanches", and "wet slab avalanches". The primary distinction between wet and dry avalanches is the presence of liquid water in the snow at the time of avalanche formation.

Loose Snow Avalanches

Loose snow avalanches, most common in steeper terrain, often occur in freshly fallen, low-density surface snow, or in older surface snow that has been softened by strong solar radiation. In loose snow avalanches, the release usually starts at a point and the avalanche gradually widens as it travels down the slope and entrains more snow. The characteristic shape of a loose snow avalanche is usually described as resembling a teardrop. Large, loose snow avalanches may cause slab avalanches.

Slab Avalanches

Slab avalanches form frequently in new snow, wind deposited snow, and, less frequently, in old snow, and have the characteristic appearance of a block of snow cut out from its surroundings by fractures. Elements of slab avalanches include the following: a crown fracture at the top of the start zone, flank fractures on the sides of the start zones, and a fracture at the bottom called the stauchwall. The crown and flank fractures are vertical walls in the snow delineating the snow that was entrained in the avalanche from the snow that remained on the slope.

Slab avalanches, which account for around 90% of avalanche-related fatalities, form when the application of dynamic forces causes catastrophic structural failure inside a weakness below a slab of snow. Energy for fracture propagation is provided by gravity as the slab falls onto the weak layer. This cascade of failures causes one layer of snow to delaminate from the layer of snow below, enabling gravity to pull the delaminated slab downhill. Fracture propagation can be widespread, sometimes traveling for hundreds of meters, and in some cases kilometers, and can involve snow depths ranging from 10 centimeters to five or six meters. Avalanches that form when the failure occurs between the base of the snowpack and the ground are known as full depth slab avalanches.

Among the largest and most powerful of avalanches, dry slab avalanches can exceed speeds of 300 km/h, and masses of 10,000,000 tonnes; their flows can travel long distances along flat valley bottoms and even uphill for short distances. A powder snow avalanche is a turbulent cloud of snow and air that forms when an avalanche travels over an abrupt change in slope angle, such as a cliff band. Powder snow avalanches may also form when the powder cloud of a dry slab avalanche continues moving after the core of the avalanche has stopped.

There are two main types of slab avalanches, "soft slab avalanches", and "hard slab avalanches". Both types of avalanches are denoted by debris morphology: the debris from a soft slab avalanche is highly granular, resembling a slurry of snowballs and ice grain paste, and the debris from a hard slab avalanche is angular, often featuring pieces of the original slab that did not break up during descent. Avalanches that descend significant vertical or horizontal distances may create debris that is not suitable for classification purposes.

Elements of Avalanches

Doug Fesler and Jill Fredston developed a conceptual model of the three primary elements of avalanches: terrain, weather, and snowpack. Terrain describes the places where avalanches occur, weather describes the meteorological conditions that create the snowpack, and snowpack describes the structural characteristics of snow that make avalanche formation possible.

Terrain

Avalanche formation requires a slope where snow can accumulate, yet has enough steepness for the snow to accelerate once set in motion by the combination of mechanical failure (of the snowpack) and gravity. The angle of the slope that can hold snow, called the angle of repose, depends on a variety of factors such as crystal form and moisture content. Some forms of drier and colder snow will only stick to lower angle slopes; while wet and warm snow can bond to very steep surfaces. In particular, in coastal mountains, such as the Cordillera del Paine region of Patagonia, deep snowpacks collect on vertical, and overhanging, rock faces. The angle of slope that can allow moving snow to accelerate depends on a variety of factors such as the snow's shear strength, which is itself dependent upon crystal form, and the configuration of layers and inter-layer interfaces.

The snowpack on slopes with sunny exposures is strongly influenced by sunshine. Diurnal cycles of thawing and refreezing can stabilize the snowpack by promoting settlement. Strong freeze thaw cycles result in the formation of surface crusts during the night, and the formation of unstable surface snow during the day. Slopes in the lee of a ridge or other wind obstacle accumulate more snow and are more likely to include pockets of deep snow, wind slabs, and cornices, all of which, when disturbed, may result in avalanche formation. Conversely the snowpack on a windward slope is often much shallower than on lee slopes.

The start zone of an avalanche must be steep enough to allow snow to accelerate once set in motion, additionally convex slopes are less stable than concave slopes, because of the disparity between the tensile strength of snow layers and their compressive strength. The composition and structure of the ground surface beneath the snowpack influences the stability of the snowpack, either being a source of strength or weakness. Avalanches are unlikely to form in very thick forests, however boulders and sparsely distributed vegetation can create weak areas deep within the snowpack, through the formation of strong temperature gradients. Full-depth avalanches (avalanches that sweep a slope virtually clean of snow cover) are more common on slopes with smooth ground cover, such as grass or rock slabs.

Generally speaking, avalanches follow drainages down slope, frequently sharing drainage features with summertime watersheds. At and below tree line, avalanche paths through drainages are well defined by vegetation boundaries called trim lines, which occur where avalanches have removed trees and prevented regrowth of large vegetation. Engineered drainages, such as the avalanche dam on Mount Stephen in Kicking Horse Pass, have been constructed to protect people and property, by redirecting the flow of avalanches. Deep debris deposits from avalanches will collect in catchments at the terminus of a run out, such as gullies, and river beds.

Slopes flatter than 25 degrees or steeper than 60 degrees typically have a lower incidence of avalanche involvement. Human triggered avalanches have the greatest incidence when the snow's angle of repose is between 35 and 45 degrees; the critical angle, the angle at which human-triggered avalanches are most frequent, is 38 degrees. But when the incidence of human triggered avalanches are normalized by the rates of recreational use hazard increases uniformly with slope angle, and no significant difference in hazard for a given exposure direction can be found. The rule of thumb is: A slope that is flat enough to hold snow but steep enough to ski has the potential to generate an avalanche, regardless of the angle.

Avalanche Paths

Avalanche paths in alpine terrain may be poorly-defined because of limited vegetation. Below treeline, avalanche paths are often delineated by vegetative trim lines created by past avalanches.

Avalanches and avalanche paths share common elements: a start zone where the avalanche originates, a track along which the avalanche flows, and a runout zone where the avalanche comes to rest. The debris deposit is the accumulated mass of the avalanched snow once it has come to rest in the runout zone. For the image at left, many small avalanches form in this avalanche path every year, but most of these avalanches do not run the full vertical or horizontal length of the path. The frequency with which avalanches form in a given area is known as the return period.

Snowpack Structure and Characteristics

The snowpack is composed of ground-parallel layers that accumulate over the winter. Each layer contains ice grains that are representative of the distinct meteorological conditions during which the snow formed and was deposited. Once deposited, a snow layer continues to evolve under the influence of the meteorological conditions that prevail after deposition.

For an avalanche to occur, it is necessary that a snowpack have a weak layer (or instability) below a slab of cohesive snow. In practice the formal mechanical and structural factors related to snowpack instability are not directly observable outside of laboratories, thus the more easily observed properties of the snow layers (e.g. penetration resistance, grain size, grain type, temperature) are used as index measurements of the mechanical properties of the snow (e.g. tensile strength, friction coefficients, shear strength, and ductile strength). This results in two principal sources of uncertainty in determining snowpack stability based on snow structure: First, both the factors influencing snow stability and the specific characteristics of the snowpack vary widely within small areas and time scales, resulting in significant difficulty extrapolating point observations of snow layers across different scales of space and time. Second, the relationship between readily observable snowpack characteristics and the snowpack's critical mechanical properties has not been completely developed.

While the deterministic relationship between snowpack characteristics and snowpack stability is still a matter of ongoing scientific study, there is a growing empirical understanding of the snow composition and deposition characteristics that influence the likelihood of an avalanche. Observation and experience has shown that newly fallen snow requires time to bond with the snow layers beneath it, especially if the new snow falls during very cold and dry conditions. If ambient air temperatures are cold enough, shallow snow above or around boulders, plants, and other discontinuities in the slope, weakens from rapid crystal growth that occurs in the presence of a critical temperature gradient. Large, angular snow crystals are an indicator weak snow, because such crystals have fewer bonds per unit volume than small, rounded crystals that pack tightly together. Consolidated snow is less likely to slough than loose powdery layers or wet isothermal snow; however, consolidated snow is a necessary condition for the occurrence of slab avalanches, and persistent instabilities within the snowpack can hide below well-consolidated surface layers. Uncertainty associated with the empirical understanding of the factors influencing snow stability leads most professional avalanche workers to recommend conservative use of avalanche terrain relative to current snowpack instability.

Weather

Avalanches can only occur in a standing snowpack. Typically winter seasons at high latitudes, high altitudes, or both, have weather that is sufficiently unsettled and cold enough for precipitated snow to accumulate into a seasonal snowpack. Continentality, reflected by the distance from the moderating effects of oceans, is another important factor. The evolution of the snowpack is critically sensitive to small variations within the narrow range of meteorological conditions that allow for the accumulation of snow into a snowpack. Among the critical factors controlling snowpack evolution are: heating by the sun, radiational cooling, vertical temperature gradients in standing snow, snowfall amounts, and snow types. Generally, mild winter weather will promote the settlement and stabilization of the snowpack; and conversely very cold, windy, or hot weather will weaken the snowpack.

At temperatures close to the freezing point of water, or during times of moderate solar radiation, a gentle freeze-thaw cycle will take place. The melting and refreezing of water in the snow strengthens the snowpack during the freezing phase and weakens it during the thawing phase. A rapid rise in temperature, to a point significantly above the freezing point of water, may cause avalanche formation at any time of year.

Persistent cold temperatures can either prevent new snow from stabilizing or destabilize the existing snowpack. Cold air temperatures on the snow surface produce a temperature gradient in the snow, because the ground temperature at the base of the snowpack is usually around °C, and the ambient air temperature can be much colder. When a temperature gradient greater than 10 °C change per vertical meter of snow is sustained for more than a day, angular crystals called depth hoar or facets begin forming in the snowpack because of rapid moisture transport along the temperature gradient. These angular crystals, which bond poorly to one another and the surrounding snow, often become a persistent weakness in the snowpack. When a slab lying on top of a persistent weakness is loaded by a force greater than the strength of the slab and persistent weak layer, the persistent weak layer can fail and generate an avalanche.

Any wind stronger than a light breeze can contribute to a rapid accumulation of snow on sheltered slopes downwind. Wind slab forms quickly and, if present, weaker snow below the slab may not have time to adjust to the new load. Even on a clear day, wind can quickly load a slope with snow by blowing snow from one place to another. Top-loading occurs when wind deposits snow from the top of a slope; cross-loading occurs when wind deposits snow parallel to the slope. When a wind blows over the top of a mountain, the leeward, or downwind, side of the mountain experiences top-loading, from the top to the bottom of that lee slope. When the wind blows across a ridge that leads up the mountain, the leeward side of the ridge is subject to cross-loading. Cross-loaded wind-slabs are usually difficult to identify visually.

Snowstorms and rainstorms are important contributors to avalanche danger. Heavy snowfall will cause instability in the existing snowpack, both because of the additional weight and because the new snow has insufficient time to bond to underlying snow layers. Rain has a similar effect. In the short-term, rain causes instability because, like a heavy snowfall, it imposes an additional load on the snowpack; and, once rainwater seeps down through the snow, it acts as a lubricant, reducing the natural friction between snow layers that holds the snowpack together. Most avalanches happen during or soon after a storm.

Daytime exposure to sunlight will rapidly destabilize the upper layers of the snowpack if the sunlight is strong enough to melt the snow, thereby reducing its hardness. During clear nights, the snowpack can re-freeze when ambient air temperatures fall below freezing, through the process of long-wave radiative cooling, or both. Radiative heat loss occurs when the night air is significantly cooler than the snowpack, and the heat stored in the snow is re-radiated into the atmosphere.

Dynamics of Avalanches

When a slab avalanche forms, the slab disintegrates into increasingly smaller fragments as the snow travels downhill. If the fragments become small enough the outer layer of the avalanche, called a saltation layer, takes on the characteristics of a fluid. When sufficiently fine particles are present they can become airborne and, given a sufficient quantity of airborne snow, this portion of the avalanche can become separated from the bulk of the avalanche and travel a greater distance as a powder snow avalanche. Scientific studies using radar, following the 1999 Galtür avalanche disaster, confirmed the hypothesis that a saltation layer forms between the surface and the airborne components of an avalanche, which can also separate from the bulk of the avalanche.

Driving a (non-airborne) avalanche is the component of the avalanche's weight parallel to the slope; as the avalanche progresses any unstable snow in its path will tend to become incorporated, so increasing the overall weight. This force will increase as the steepness of the slope increases, and diminish as the slope flattens. Resisting this are a number of components that are thought to interact with each other: the friction between the avalanche and the surface beneath; friction between the air and snow within the fluid; fluid-dynamic drag at the leading edge of the avalanche; shear resistance between the avalanche and the air through which it is passing, and shear resistance between the fragments within the avalanche itself. An avalanche will continue to accelerate until the resistance exceeds the forward force.

Modelling

Attempts to model avalanche behaviour date from the early 20th century, notably the work of Professor Lagotala in preparation for the 1924 Winter Olympics in Chamonix. His method was developed by A. Voellmy and popularised following the publication in 1955 of his Ueber die Zerstoerungskraft von Lawinen.

Voellmy used a simple empirical formula, treating an avalanche as a sliding block of snow moving with a drag force that was proportional to the square of the speed of its flow:

$$\text{Pref} = \frac{1}{2}\rho v^2$$

\He and others subsequently derived other formulae that take other factors into account, with the Voellmy-Salm-Gubler and the Perla-Cheng-McClung models becoming most widely used as simple tools to model flowing (as opposed to powder snow) avalanches.

Since the 1990s many more sophisticated models have been developed. In Europe much of the recent work was carried out as part of the SATSIE (Avalanche Studies and Model Validation in Europe) research project supported by the European Commission which produced the leading-edge MN2L model, now in use with the Service Réstitution Terrains en Montagne (Mountain Rescue Service) in France, and D2FRAM (Dynamical Two-Flow-Regime Avalanche Model), which was still undergoing validation as of 2007.

Avalanche Control

Avalanche control or avalanche defense activities reduce the hazard avalanches pose to human life, activity, and property. Avalanche control begins with a risk assessment conducted by surveying for potential avalanche terrain by identifying geographic features such as vegetation patterns, drainages, and seasonal snow distribution that are indicative of avalanches. From the identified avalanche risks, the hazard is assessed by identifying threatened human geographic features such as roads, ski hills, and buildings. Avalanche control programs address the avalanche hazard by formulating prevention and mitigation plans, which are then executed during the winter season. The prevention and mitigation plans combine extensive snow pack observation with three major groups of interventions: active, passive, and social sometimes more narrowly defined as "explosive", "structural", and "awareness", according to the prevalent techniques used. Avalanche control techniques either directly intervene in the evolution of the snow pack, or lessen the effect of an avalanche once it has occurred. For the event of human involvement, avalanche control organizations develop and train exhaustive response and recovery plans.

Risk and Hazard Assessment

Risk assessment geographical surveys for potential avalanche terrain by studying topography, vegetation, and seasonal snow distribution. Hazard assessment geographical surveys for the consequences of avalanche by studying exposure of urbanization, industrialization, transportation, recreational activities, and the distribution of human use of the potential avalanche terrain identified in the risk assessment.

Prevention and Mitigation

Prevention and mitigation begins with observing the snow pack to forecast the risk of avalanche occurrence. The forecast risk then determines the necessary interventions to reduce the hazard posed by an avalanche.

Observation and Forecasting

Snow pack observation studies the layering and distribution of the snow to estimate the instabilities of the snow pack and thus the risk of an avalanche occurring in a particular terrain feature. In areas of heavy human use the snow pack is monitored throughout the winter season to assess its evolution under the prevailing meteorological conditions. In contrast to heavily used avalanche terrain where forecasting is the goal of snow observation, in remote terrain, or terrain that is infrequently visited, snow pack observation elucidates the immediate instabilities of the snow pack.

Active Interventions

Active techniques reduce the risk of an avalanche occurring by promoting the stabilization and settlement of the snow pack through three forms of intervention: disrupting weak layers in the snow pack, increasing the uniformity of the snow pack, and lessening the amount of snow available in snow pack for entrainment in an avalanche; this can be accomplished either by triggering smaller less hazardous avalanches, or by directly influencing the structure of the layering of the snow pack. Active avalanche control can be broadly classified into either mechanical or explosive methods. Mechanical methods are typically used in either remote terrain, smaller terrain, or less hazardous terrain; while explosive methods are used in accessible large high hazard terrain, or terrain with industrial, commercial recreational, urbanized, and transportation usage.

In the smallest terrain features the simplest method of avalanche control is a mechanical intervention that disrupts weak snow layers by directly walking through them, a technique referred to as boot packing. For larger features this method can be extended by mechanized redistribution of snow using large tracked vehicles called snow groomers. These two mechanical interventions can only be safely done as the snow is deposited and before it develops any instabilities. In terrain that can only be sporadically accessed, or in a highly developed snow pack that is too deep for boot packing, ski stabilization techniques are used. The first technique of ski stabilizing is a method of entering a slope called ski cutting. In this method a skier attempts to trigger a small avalanche by breaking the tensile support of the upper snow pack through a quick traverse along the top of the slope, the skier can be belayed on a rope to further protect them from being caught in an avalanche. A snow pack can then be further settled out, or stabilized, by further down slope ski traffic through it. Finally knotted cord can be used to saw through the roots of cornices, causing the cornice to drop onto the snow pack of the slope below. This has the combined effect of reducing the objective hazard posed by the cornice, and providing a large impact force on the snow pack.

Explosive techniques involve the artificial triggering of smaller less destructive avalanches, by detonating charges either above or on the snow surface. The explosives may be deployed by manually hand tossing and lowering, by bombing from a helicopter, or by shelling with a small howitzer, recoilless rifle, or air gun. In balancing the hazard to personnel with the effectiveness of the deployment method at accessing and triggering avalanche terrain, each method has its drawbacks and advantages. Among the newest methods, strategically placed remote controlled installations that generate an air blast by detonating a fuel-air explosive above the snow pack in an avalanche starting zone, offer fast and effective response to avalanche control decisions while minimizing the risk to avalanche control personnel;

a feature especially important for avalanche control in transportation corridors. For example the Avalanche Towers (Sprengmast) installed in Switzerland, Austria, and Norway use solar powered launchers to deploy charges from a magazine containing 12 radio controlled charges. The magazines can be transported, loaded, and removed from the towers by helicopter, without the need for a flight assistant, or on site personnel.

Explosive control has proved to be effective in areas with easy access to avalanche starting areas and where minor avalanches can be tolerated. It is mostly unacceptable, however, in areas with human residence and where even a small probability of a larger avalanche is unacceptable.

Permanent Interventions

Permanent techniques slow, stop, divert, or prevent snow from moving; either completely or to enough of an extent that the destructive forces are significantly lessened. Permanent techniques involve constructing structures and modifying terrain for purposes classified as:

— Snow retention structures (snow racks, avalanche snow bridges, snow nets), used in the upper path of probable avalanche paths

— Avalanche barriers: The main part of the avalanche barriers is based on a high tensile strength steel wire mesh, extending across the slope and reaching to the surface of the snow. The supporting effect created by the retaining surface prevents possible creeping within the snow cover and sliding of the snow cover on the terrain surface. Breaking-away of avalanches is thus prevented at the starting zone, while occurring snow movements are restricted to the extent that they remain harmless. The forces resulting from the snow pressure are absorbed by the snow nets and carried off over the swivel posts and anchor ropes into the anchor points.

— Snow redistribution structures (wind baffles, snow fences)

— Snow deflection structures used to deflect and confine the moving snow within the avalanche track.. They should not deflect the avalanche sharply, because in the latter case they may be easily overrun by snow.

— Snow retardation structures (e.g. snow breakers), mostly used in small-slope parts of the avalanche track, to enhance the natural retardation

— Snow catchment structures

— Direct protection of important objects and structures, e.g., by snow sheds (avalanche sheds).

A single intervention may fulfill the needs of multiple classes of purpose, for example Avalanche dams, ditches, earth mounds, and terraces are used for deflection, retardation, and catchment. Other passive methods include:

— reforestation, up the natural tree line — forests serve all the functions of artificial avalanche defenses: retention, redistribution, retardation and catchment

— snow caves, as well as recessed, dug out, and snow walled quinzhees and bivouac shelters are used to temporarily protect bivouacking climbers and skiers by providing them with breathing space in the event of burial by avalanches.

— Architectural streamlining and wedge shaping buildings, such as those found in the historic high mountain villages of the Alps..

Social Interventions

To mitigate the hazard of avalanches, social interventions reduce the incidence and prevalence of human avalanche involvement by modifying the behavior of people, so that their use of avalanche terrain is adapted to prevent their involvement in avalanches. Avalanche control organizations accomplish this by targeting awareness and education programs at communities that frequent avalanche terrain. Surveys of avalanche accidents have observed that most avalanches that involve people are caused by people, and of those victims many were unaware of the risk of avalanche occurrence. To address this observation, introductory awareness and education programs provide instruction in the avoidance of hazardous avalanche involvement through the recognition of avalanche terrain, the observation of snow pack instabilities, and the identification of human activities that cause avalanches. Avalanche control organizations also publicly disseminate forecasts, bulletins, warnings, and reports of avalanche activity to assist communities of avalanche terrain users.

Response and Recovery

Avalanche control organizations plan for, and respond, to avalanches. Typical responses span from clearing transportation corridors of avalanche debris, to repairing industrial and recreational facilities, to search, rescue, and recovery. To improve the outcome of human avalanche involvement avalanche control organizations offer training and education to both professionals and recreational amateurs in avalanche preparedness.

Professional Preparedness

Professional responses to avalanches are targeted at avalanches involving the general unprepared public. When avalanches are forecast to occur, avalanche terrain to which the general unprepared public is exposed will be closed, and after the avalanches have occurred the area is cleared of debris, and repaired. When unexpected avalanches occur that involve the general unprepared public, avalanche control organizations respond with large professionally organized search teams involving probe lines, and trained search and rescue dogs.

Amateur Preparedness

Recreational response to avalanches involves the rapid formation of an ad hoc search and rescue team. The ad hoc search and rescue teams rely on all the participants having prepared for a potential avalanche by carrying the correct search and rescue equipment, and undergoing the appropriate training.

Avalanche Rescue

There are several ways to prevent avalanches and lessen their power and destruction. They are employed in areas where avalanches pose a significant threat to people, such as ski resorts and mountain towns, roads and railways. Explosives are used extensively to prevent avalanches, especially at ski resorts where other methods are often impractical. Explosive charges are used to trigger small avalanches before enough snow can build up to cause a large avalanche. Snow fences and light walls can be used to direct the placement of snow. Snow builds up around the fence, especially the side that faces the prevailing winds. Downwind of the fence, snow buildup is lessened. This is caused by the loss of snow at the fence that would have been deposited and the pickup of the snow that is already there by the wind, which was depleted of snow at the fence. When there is a sufficient density of trees, they can greatly reduce the strength of avalanches. They hold snow in place and when there is an avalanche, the impact of the snow against the trees slows it down. Trees can either be planted or they can be conserved, such as in the building of a ski resort, to reduce the strength of avalanches.

Artificial barriers can be very effective in reducing avalanche damage. There are several types. One kind of barrier (snow net) uses a net strung between poles that are anchored by guy wires in addition to their foundations. These barriers are similar to those used for rockslides. Another type of barrier is a rigid fence like structure (snow fence) and may be constructed of steel, wood or pre-stressed concrete. They usually have gaps between the beams and are built perpendicular to the slope, with reinforcing beams on the downhill side. Rigid barriers are often considered unsightly, especially when many rows must be built. They are also expensive and vulnerable to damage from falling rocks in the warmer months. Finally, there are barriers that stop or deflect avalanches with their weight and strength. These barriers are made of concrete, rocks or earth. They are usually placed right above the structure, road or railway that they are trying to protect, although they can also be used to channel avalanches into other barriers. Occasionally, earth mounds are placed in the avalanche's path to slow it down.

Safety in Avalanche Terrain

Terrain management

Terrain management involves reducing the exposure of an individual to the risks of travelling in avalanche terrain by carefully selecting what areas of slopes to travel on. Features to be cognizant of include not undercutting slopes (removing the physical support of the snow pack), not travelling over convex rolls (areas where the snow pack is under tension), staying away from weaknesses like exposed rock, and avoiding areas of slopes that expose one to terrain traps (gulleys that can be filled in, cliffs over which one can be swept, or heavy timber into which one can be carried).

Group management

Group management is the practice of reducing the risk of having a member of a group, or a whole group involved in an avalanche. Minimize the number of people on the slope, and maintain separation. Ideally one person should pass over the slope into an area protected from the avalanche hazard before the next one leaves protective cover. Route selection should also consider what dangers lie above and below the route, and the consequences of an unexpected avalanche (i.e., unlikely to occur, but deadly if it does). Stop or camp only in safe locations. Wear warm gear to delay hypothermia if buried. Plan escape routes. In determining the size of the group balance the hazard of not having enough people to effectively carry out a rescue with the risk of having too many members of the group to safely manage the risks. It is generally recommended not to travel alone, because there will be no-one to witness your burial and start the rescue. Additionally, avalanche risk increases with use; that is, the more a slope is disturbed by skiers, the more likely it is that an avalanche will occur. Most important of all practise good communication within a group including clearly communicating the decisions about safe locations, escape routes, and slope choices, and having a clear understanding of every members skills in snow travel, avalanche rescue, and route finding.

Risk Factor Awareness

Risk factor awareness in avalanche safety requires gathering and accounting for a wide range of information such as the meteorological history of the area, the current weather and snow conditions, and equally important the social and physical indicators of the group.

Leadership

Leadership in avalanche terrain requires well defined decision making protocols that use the observed risk factors. These decision making frameworks are taught in a variety of courses provided by national avalanche resource centres in Europe and North America. Fundamental to leadership in avalanche terrain is honestly assessing and estimating the information that was ignored or overlooked. Recent research has shown that there are strong psychological and group dynamic determinants that lead to avalanche involvement.

Even small avalanches are a serious danger to life, even with properly trained and equipped companions who avoid the avalanche. Between 55 and 65 percent of victims buried in the open are killed, and only 80 percent of the victims remaining on the surface survive. (McClung, p.177).

Research carried out in Switzerland based on 422 buried skiers indicates how the chances of survival drop:

— Very rapidly from 92 percent within 15 minutes to only 30 percent after 35 minutes (victims die of suffocation)

— Near zero after two hours (victims die of injuries or hypothermia)

(Historically, the chances of survival were estimated at 85% within 15 minutes, 50% within 30 minutes, 20% within one hour).

Consequently it is vital that everyone surviving an avalanche is used in an immediate search and rescue operation, rather than waiting for help to arrive. Additional help can be called once it can be determined if anyone is seriously injured or still remains unaccountable after the immediate search (i.e., after at least 30 minutes of searching). Even in a well equipped country such as France, it typically takes 45 minutes for a helicopter rescue team to arrive, by which time most of the victims are likely to have died.

In some cases avalanche victims are not located until spring thaw melts the snow, or even years later when objects emerge from a glacier.

Search and Rescue Equipment

Chances of a buried victim being found alive and rescued are increased when everyone in a group is carrying and using standard avalanche equipment, and have trained in how to use it. A beacon, shovel and probe is considered the minimum equipment to carry for companion rescue. Organized rescue involves ski patrols and mountain rescue teams who are often equipped with other technologies to search for buried victims. Rescue equipment can make a difference, and in 2010 the French National Association for the Study of Snow and Avalanches (ANENA) recommended that all off-piste skiers should carry beacons, probes, shovels, and Recco reflectors.

Avalanche Cords

The use of avalanche cords goes back just over 100 years to a Bavarian mountaineer named Eugen Oertel. In the United States the concept was recommended as early as 1908 in the Colorado newspaper - the Ouray Herald (November 13) - when the editor repeated the suggestion that miners in the San Juans Mounains adopt "snowslide ribbons" to safeguard their travels to and from the mines. The principle is simple. An approximately 15 meter long red cord (similar to parachute cord) is attached to the person in question's belt. While skiing, snowboarding, or walking the cord is dragged along behind the person. The assumption is that if the person gets buried in an avalanche, the light cord stays on top of the snow. Due to the color the cord would be easily visible for companions. Commercial avalanche cords have metal markings every one to three meters indicating the direction and length to the victim.

Avalanche cords were popular before beacons became available, and while cords were thought to be effective markers there was never any proof of their effectiveness. In the 1970s Melchoir Schild of the Swiss Federal Institute for Snow and Avalanche Research (SLF) reviewed 30 years of Swiss avalanche accidents and rescues from 1944/45 to 1973/74. Of the 2042 avalanche victims he found only seven cases where avalanche cords were used (not including the 2 mentioned above). In five cases part of the cord was visible on the surface but so too were part of the victims. In the sixth case the victim was completely buried, but part of the cord was visible. Sadly, this victim died of trauma. In the seventh case the completely buried avalanche cord was located by an avalanche rescue dog, however, the cord had become detached from the victim. Her body was found much later. In Knox Williams' and Betsy Armstrong's 1986 book The Avalanche Book they cite an early 1970s study where avalanche cords were tested on sandbag dummies. The dummies were placed onto steep slopes where explosives were used to trigger avalanches. Trials showed a portion of the cord remained on the surface only 40% of the time. The other 60% of the time the cord was completely buried along with the dummy. Typically the cord had spooled around the dummy. 1975, at a symposium of avalanche rescue experts hosted by the International Foundation Vanni Eigenmann, Schild concluded, "On the basis of these results the avalanche cord can no longer be considered reliable."

In the United States there have been two accidents with five buried victims, all wearing avalanche cords. In one accident, an avalanche cord remained on the surface. In the second accident five ski mountaineers with cords deployed triggered an avalanche. One skier was partly buried, but his four friends and cords were completely buried. Moderate snow and the loss of the survivor's eyeglasses only worsened the situation. The search was called off a few days later. The four were eventually found many months later after their bodies with attached cords melted out of the snow. On one victim the cord was wrapped tightly around the body. An avalanche cord should not be used as safety equipment under any circumstances whatsoever.

Beacons

Beacons — known as "beepers", peeps (pieps), ARVAs (Appareil de Recherche de Victimes en Avalanche, in French), LVS (Lawinen-Verschütteten-Suchgerät, Swiss German), avalanche transceivers, or various other trade names, are important for every member of the party. They emit a "beep" via 457 kHz radio signal in normal use, but may be switched to receive mode to locate a buried victim up to 80 meters away. Analog receivers provide audible beeps that rescuers interpret to estimate distance to a victim. To use the receiver effectively requires regular practice. Some older models of beepers operated on a different frequency (2.275 kHz) and a group leader should ensure these are no longer in use.

Since about 2000 nearly all avalanche rescue transceivers use digital displays to give visual indications of direction and distance to victims. Most users find these beacons easier to use, but to be effective still requires considerable practice by the user. Beacons are the primary rescue tool for companion rescue and are considered active devices because the user must learn to use and care for their device.

Probes

Portable (collapsible) probes can be extended to probe into the snow to locate the exact location of a victim at several yards / metres in depth. When multiple victims are buried, probes should be used to decide the order of rescue, with the shallowest being dug out first since they have the greatest chance of survival.

Probing can be a very time-consuming process if a thorough search is undertaken for a victim without a beacon. In the U.S., 86% of the 140 victims found (since 1950) by probing were already dead. Survival/rescue more than 2 m deep is rare (about 4%). Probes should be used immediately after a visual search for surface clues, in coordination with the beacon search.

Shovels

Even when the snowpack consists of loose powder, avalanche debris is hard and dense. The energy of the avalanche causes the snow to melt, and the debris refreezes immediately after it stops.

Shovels are essential for digging through the snow to the victim, as the snow is often too dense to dig with hands or skis. A large strong scoop and sturdy handle are important. Plastic shovels often break, whereas metal ones are less prone to failure.

As excavation of the avalanche victim is extremely time-consuming and many buried victims suffocate before they can be reached, shovelling technique is an essential element of rescue.

Shovels are also useful for digging snow pits as part of evaluating the snowpack for hidden hazards, such as weak layers supporting large loads.

Recco rescue system

The Recco system is used by organized rescue services around the world. The Recco system is a two-part system where the rescue team uses a small hand-held detector. The detector receives a directional signal that is reflected back from a small, passive, transponder called a reflector that is included into outerwear, boots, helmets, and body protection. Recco reflectors are not a substitute for avalanche beacons. The Recco signal does not interfere with beacons. In fact, the current Recco detector also has an avalanche beacon receiver (457 kHz) so one rescuer can search for a Recco signal and a beacon signal at the same time.

Avalung

Recently, a device called an Avalung has been introduced for use in avalanche terrain. The device consists of a mouth piece, a flap valve, an exhaust pipe, and an air collector. Several models of Avalung either mount on one's chest or integrate in a proprietary backpack.

During an avalanche burial, victims not killed by trauma usually suffer from asphyxiation as the snow around them melts from the heat of the victim's breath and then refreezes, disallowing oxygen flow to the victim and allowing toxic levels of CO2 to accumulate. The Avalung ameliorates this situation by drawing breath over a large surface area in front and pushing the warm exhaled carbon dioxide behind. This buys additional time for rescuers to dig the victim out.

Avalanche airbags

Avalanche airbags help a person avoid burial by making the user an even larger object relative to the moving snow, which forces the person toward the surface. Avalanche airbags work on the principle of inverse segregation. Avalanches, like mixed nuts and breakfast cereal are considered granular materials and behave fluid-like (but are not liquids) where smaller particles settle to the bottom of the flow and larger particles rise to the top. Provided the airbag is properly deployed, the chances of a complete burial are significantly reduced.

Other devices

More backcountry adventurers are also carrying Satellite Electronic Notification Devices (SEND) to quickly alert rescuers to a problem. These devices include the SPOT Messenger, Emergency Position-Indicating Radio

Beacon (EPIRB) or Personal Locating Beacons (PLBs) containing the Global Positioning System (GPS). This device can quickly notify search and rescue of an emergency and the general location (within 100 yards), but only if the person with the EPIRB has survived the avalanche and can activate the device. Survivors should also try to use a mobile phone to notify emergency personnel. Unlike the other devices mentioned above, the mobile phone (or satellite phone) provides two-way communications with rescuers.

On-site rescuers (usually companions) are in the best position to save a buried victim. However, organized rescue teams can sometimes respond very quickly to assist in the search for a buried victim. The sooner organized rescue can be notified the sooner they can respond, and this difference can mean the difference in living or dying for a critically injured patient. The International Commission for Alpine Rescue recommends, "early notification is essential, e.g., by mobile phone, satellite phone, or radio, wherever possible"

Other rescue devices are proposed, developed and used, such as avalanche balls, vests and airbags, based on statistics indicating that decreasing the depth of burial increases the chances of survival.

Although inefficient, some rescue equipment can be improvised by unprepared parties: ski poles can become short probes, skis or snowboards can be used as shovels. A first aid kit and equipment is useful for assisting survivors who may have cuts, broken bones, or other injuries, in addition to hypothermia.

Self-rescue

Victims caught in an avalanche are advised to try to escape to side of the avalanche. If not possible, they're instructed to grab onto a tree, brush or rock (each second one hangs on lets snow pass by that cannot end up burying the victim). If knocked off one's feet, victims should jettison any equipment (if possible) and fight for their life. Rolling like a log may help one escape to the side. Conventional wisdom says to make swimming motions to stay on the surface. Anecdotal stories tell successes; however, analysis of avalanche motion and physics dispute swimming as a successful tactic. Avalanches stop quickly and if under the snow it is critical to get a hand in front of the face to create an airspace before the snow stops. If one is near the surface they may try to thrust an arm, leg or object above the surface. If possible, victims should try to break free once the snow stops. If unable to move one should not struggle except to enlarge the air space.

"You can't dig yourself out. If you could dig yourself out, few people would die in avalanches. Avalanche debris instantly entombs you in place, as if you were frozen in concrete, and most of the time you can't even move your fingers. Sometimes, if it's a small avalanche with soft debris, and they have a hand near the surface, people have been able to dig themselves out, but the vast majority of the time there are only two ways to get out of the snow-to be dug out or to melt out."

Companion Rescue

Survival time is short, if a victim is buried. The search for victims must start immediately; many people have died because the surviving companions or witnesses failed to do even the simplest search.

Witnesses to an avalanche that engulfs people are frequently limited to those in the party involved in the avalanche. Those not caught should try to note the locations where the avalanched person or persons were last seen. In fact, anyone planning to enter an avalanche area should discuss this step as part of their preparation. Once the avalanche has stopped and the danger of secondary slides has passed, witnesses should mark these points with objects for reference. Then, survivors should take a headcount to determine who may be lost. If the area is safe to enter, the searchers should visually scan along a downslope trajectory from the marked points last seen. Victims who are partially or shallowly buried can often be located quickly by visually scanning the avalanche debris and pulling out clothing or equipment that may be attached to someone buried.

Because survival rates plummet as time passes, do not send a searcher for help until you feel you can do no more. However, do use your mobile phone or radio to call for help as soon as you suspect a burial. Generally, the telephone connection will be better from the top of a slope than from the bottom. Go to and mark the Last Seen Area, switch transceivers to receive mode, and check them. Select likely burial areas and search them, listening for beeps (or voices), expanding to other areas of the avalanche, always looking and listening for other clues (movement, equipment, body parts). Probe randomly in probable burial areas. Mark any points where signal was received or equipment found. Continue scanning and probing near marked clues and other likely burial areas. After 30 to 60 minutes, consider sending a searcher to get more help, because at this point, the remaining victims have probably not survived.

Line probes are arranged in most likely burial areas and marked as searched. Continue searching and probing the area until it is no longer feasible or reasonable to continue. Avoid contaminating the scent of the avalanche area with urine, food, spit, blood, etc., in case search dogs arrive.

Buried victims are most likely to be found—

— Below the marked point last seen
— Along the line of flow of the avalanche
— Around trees and rocks or other obstacles
— Near the bottom runout of the debris
— Along edges of the avalanche track
— In low spots where the snow may collect (gullies, crevasses, creeks, ditches along roads, etc.)
— Although less likely, check other areas if initial searches are not fruitful.

Once buried victims are found and their heads and chests are freed, perform first aid (airway, breathing, circulation/pulse, arterial bleeding, spinal injuries, fractures, shock, hypothermia, internal injuries, etc.), according to local law and custom.

Organized Rescue

Professional and volunteer rescue teams respond when a victim needs more help than their companions can provide. Traditionally, organized rescue responded after companion rescue efforts failed. However, today, thanks to mobile telephones, helicopters and snow-machines, the distinction between organized and companion rescue sometimes blur together as organized rescue can respond quickly to assist companions. In a some cases in recent years, organized rescue has even replaced companion rescue and saved lives when organized rescue teams reached the debris before the victim's companions.

There are four primary goals of any rescue operation and in organized rescue the goals can be initiated simultaneously.

— *Immediate search*: get rescuers to the site; find and uncover buried victims.
— *Medical*: care for victims and companions
— *Transport/evacuation*: transport rescuers in quickly and safely; get victims out and to advanced medical care; return rescuers safely

— *Support/Logistics*: care for rescuers in the field (food, shelter, rest and replacement)

Immediate search

The first teams travel fast and light to locate and uncover buried victims. These teams carry basic rescue equipment, including rescue dogs and RECCO detectors, and emergency-care gear. These rescuers are generally not equipped for prolonged operations.

Medical

While the immediate search teams carry some basic medical equipment, a special team that can provide advanced life-support follows quickly. This team usually includes paramedic, trauma nurse, or physician, and may also transport in a rescue toboggan and other equipment needed to revive, stabilize, protect and transport their patient.

Transport/evacuation

Upon the first alert of an avalanche incident the rescue leader will appoint a team to arrange transportation for both rescuers and patients.

Support/logistics

Rescue leaders will assess the complexity of the search and rescue operation to determine and anticipate the needs for support. Every incident is different depending upon the number of victims, avalanche danger, weather conditions, terrain, access, availability of rescuers, etc. Support includes getting appropriate resources of people and equipment, transporting the resources, caring for and replacing rescuers.

References

Daffern, Tony. (1999). *Avalanche Safety for Skiers, Climbers and Snowboarders*, Rocky Mountain Books.

Billman, John. (2007). "Mike Elggren on Surviving an Avalanche". *Skiing* magazine Feb 2007: 26.

McClung, David and Shaerer, Peter: (2006). *The Avalanche Handbook*, The Mountaineers.

Tremper, Bruce: (2001). *Staying Alive in Avalanche Terrain*, The Mountaineers.

3

Cyclone Risk Mitigation

Cyclones are huge revolving storms caused by winds blowing around a central area of lowatmospheric pressure. In the northern hemisphere, cyclones are called hurricanes or typhoons and their winds blow in an anti-clockwise circle. In the southern hemisphere, these tropical storms are known as cyclones, whose winds blow in a clockwise circle.

Cyclones develop over warm seas near the Equator. Air heated by the sun rises very swiftly, which creates areas of very low pressure. As the warm air rises, it becomes loaded with moisture which condenses into massive thunderclouds. Cool air rushes in to fill the void that is left, but because of the constant turning of the Earth on its axis, the air is bent inwards and then spirals upwards with great force. The swirling winds rotate faster and faster, forming a huge circle which can be up to 2,000 km across. At the centre of the storm is a calm, cloudless area called the eye, where there is no rain, and the winds are fairly light.

As the cyclone builds up it begins to move. It is sustained by a steady flow of warm, moist air. The strongest winds and heaviest rains are found in the towering clouds which merge into a wall about 20-30 km from the storm's centre. Winds around the eye can reach speeds of up to 200 km/h, and a fully developed cyclone pumps out about two million tonnes of air per second. This results in more rain being released in a day than falls in a year in a city like London.

Cyclones begin in tropical regions, such as northern Australia, South-East Asia and many Pacific islands. They sometimes drift into the temperate coastal areas, threatening more heavily populated regions to the South. Northern Australia has about four or five tropical cyclones every year during the summertime wet season. For a cyclone to develop, the sea surface must have a temperature of at least 26°C.

When warm air rises from the seas and condenses into clouds, massive amounts of heat are released. The result of this mixture of heat and moisture is often a collection of thunderstorms, from which a tropical storm can develop.

The trigger for most Atlantic hurricanes is an easterly wave, a band of low pressure moving westwards, which may have begun as an African thunderstorm. Vigorous thunderstorms and high winds combine to create a cluster of thunderstorms which can become the seedling for a tropical storm.

Typhoons in the Far East and Cyclones in the Indian Ocean often develop from a thunderstorm in the equatorial trough. During the hurricane season, the Coriolis effect of the Earth's rotation starts the winds in the thunderstorm spinning in a circular motion.

Cyclones create several dangers for people living around tropical areas. The most destructive force of a cyclone comes from the fierce winds. These winds are strong enough to easily topple fences, sheds, trees, power poles and caravans, while hurling helpless people through the air. Many people are killed when the cyclone's winds cause buildings to collapse and houses to completely blow away.

A cyclone typically churns up the sea, causing giant waves and surges of water known as storm surges. The water of a storm surge rushes inland with deadly power, flooding low-lying coastal areas. The rains from cyclones are also heavy enough to cause serious flooding, especially along river areas.

Long after a cyclone has passed, road and rail transport can still be blocked by floodwaters. Safe lighting of homes and proper refrigeration of food may be impossible because of failing power supplies. Water often becomes contaminated from dead animals or rotting food, and people are threatened with diseases like gastroenteritis.

Structural Characteristics

There are a number of structural characteristics common to all cyclones.The cyclones have high pressure outside and low pressure inside. A cyclone is a low pressure area. A cyclone's center (often known in a mature tropical cyclone as the eye), is the area of lowest atmospheric pressure in the region. Near the center, the pressure gradient force (from the pressure in the center of the cyclone compared to the pressure outside the cyclone) and the force from the Coriolis effect must be in an approximate balance, or the cyclone would collapse on itself as a result of the difference in pressure.

Because of the Coriolis effect, the wind flow around a large cyclone is counterclockwise in the Northern Hemisphere and clockwise in the Southern Hemisphere. Cyclonic circulation is sometimes referred to as contra solem. In the Northern Hemisphere, the fastest winds relative to the surface of the Earth therefore occur on the eastern side of a northward-moving cyclone and on the northern side of a westward-moving one; the opposite occurs in the Southern Hemisphere. The wind flow around an anticyclone, on the other hand, is clockwise in the northern hemisphere, and counterclockwise in the southern hemisphere.

Cyclogenesis

Cyclogenesis is the development or strengthening of cyclonic circulation in the atmosphere. Cyclogenesis is an umbrella term for several different processes, all of which result in the development of some sort of cyclone. It can occur at various scales, from the microscale to the synoptic scale.

Extratropical cyclones form as waves along weather fronts before occluding later in their life cycle as cold core cyclones.

Tropical cyclones form due to latent heat driven by significant thunderstorm activity, and are warm core.

Mesocyclones form as warm core cyclones over land, and can lead to tornado formation. Waterspouts can also form from mesocyclones, but more often develop from environments of high instability and low vertical wind shear. Cyclogenesis is the opposite of cyclolysis, and has an anticyclonic (high pressure system) equivalent which deals with the formation of high pressure areas—Anticyclogenesis.

The surface low has a variety of ways of forming. Topography can force a surface low when dense low-level high pressure system ridges in east of a north-south mountain barrier. Mesoscale convective systems can spawn surface lows which are initially warm core. The disturbance can grow into a wave-like formation along the front and the low will be positioned at the crest. Around the low, flow will become cyclonic, by definition. This rotational flow will push polar air equator ward west of the low via its trailing cold front, and warmer air with push poleward low via the warm front. Usually the cold front will move at a quicker pace than the warm front and "catch up" with it due to the slow erosion of higher density airmass located out ahead of the cyclone and the higher density airmass sweeping in behind the cyclone, usually resulting in a narrowing warm sector. At this point an occluded front forms where the warm air mass is pushed upwards into a trough of warm air aloft, which is also known as a trowal.

Tropical cyclogenesis is the technical term describing the development and strengthening of atropical cyclone in the atmosphere. The mechanisms through which tropical cyclogenesis occurs are distinctly different from those through which mid-latitude cyclogenesis occurs. Tropical cyclogenesis involves the development of a warm-core cyclone, due to significant convection in a favourable atmospheric environment. There are six main requirements for tropical cyclogenesis: sufficiently warm sea surface temperatures, atmospheric instability, high humidity in the lower to middle levels of the troposphere, enough Coriolis force to develop a low pressure center, a preexisting low level focus or disturbance, and low vertical wind shear. An average of 86 tropical cyclones of tropical storm intensity form annually worldwide, with 47 reaching hurricane/typhoon strength, and 20 becoming intense tropical cyclones.

Types of Cyclones

There are six main types of cyclones: Polar cyclones, Polar lows, Extratropical cyclones, Subtropical cyclones, Tropical cyclones, and Mesocyclones.

Polar Cyclone

Polar cyclones are low-pressure areas which strengthen in the winter and weaken in the summer. A polar cyclone is a low pressure weather system usually spanning 1,000–2,000 kilometers (620–1,240 miles) in which the air is circulating in a counter-clockwise fashion (in the northern hemisphere). The reason for the rotation is the same as any other cyclone, the Coriolis effect. One center lies near Baffin Island and the other over northeast Siberia. In the southern hemisphere, it tends to be located near the edge of the Ross ice shelf near 160 west longitude. When the polar vortex is strong, the Westerlies increase in strength. When the polar cyclone is weak, the general flow pattern across mid-latitudes buckles and significant cold outbreaks occur.

Duration and power

Polar cyclones are climatological features which hover near the poles year-round. They are weaker during summer and strongest during winter. The strength and position of the cyclone shapes the flow pattern across the hemisphere of its influence. An index which is used in then northern hemisphere to gage its magnitude is the Arctic oscillation.

Frequency

Although cyclonic activity is most prevalent in the Eurasian Arctic with approximately 15 cyclones per winter, polar cyclones also occur in Greenland and the Canadian Arctic. Polar cyclones can occur at any time during the year. However, summer cyclones tend to be weaker than winter cyclones. They are not well studied and seldom destructive as they typically take place in sparsely populated areas. The only infrastructure damage that occurs as a direct result of a polar cyclone is to oil and gas rigs present throughout the Antarctic ocean.

Ongoing studies

The Australian and US Federal Governments recently awarded funding for a study into how polar cyclones might influence drought in Australia. Scientists hope that the study will glean valuable insight into why droughts in Southern Australia are getting worse, and whether or not there is a direct link between polar climate activity, and weather patterns elsewhere. "One of the big problems we have in planning for drought has to do with understanding whether the drought that we are in right now is a climate-change signal or part of a natural cycle. If we want to understand that we need to understand where the rain is coming from." The study is expected to be complete by late 2010.

Polar Low

A polar low is a small-scale, long-lived atmospheric low pressure system (depression) that is found over the ocean areas poleward of the main polar front in both the Northern and Southern Hemispheres. The systems usually have a horizontal length scale of less than 1,000 kilometres (620 mi) and exist for no more than a couple of days. They are part of the larger class of mesoscale weather systems. Polar lows can be difficult to detect using conventional weather reports and are a hazard to high-latitude operations, such as shipping and gas and oil platforms. Polar lows have been referred to by many other terms, such as polar mesoscale vortex, Arctic hurricane, Arctic low, and cold air depression. Today the term is usually reserved for the more vigorous systems that have near-surface winds of at least 17 m/s (38 mph).

Polar lows were first identified on the meteorological satellite imagery that became available in the 1960s, which revealed many small-scale cloud vortices at high latitudes. The most active polar lows are found over certain ice-free maritime areas in or near the Arctic during the winter, such as the Norwegian Sea, Barents Sea, Labrador Sea and Gulf of Alaska. Polar lows dissipate rapidly when they make landfall. Antarctic systems tend to be weaker than their northern counterparts since the air-sea temperature differences around the continent are generally smaller. However, vigorous polar lows can be found over the Southern Ocean.

Structure

Polar lows can have a wide range of cloud signatures in satellite imagery, but two broad categories of cloud forms have been identified. The first is the "spiraliform" signature consisting of a number of cloud bands wrapped around the centre of the low. Some polar lows have the appearance in satellite imagery of tropical cyclones, with deep thunderstorm clouds surrounding a cloud-free 'eye', which has given rise to the use of the term "Arctic hurricane" to describe some of the more active lows. These systems are more common deep within the polar air. The second is a "comma-shaped" signature that is found more frequently with systems closer to the polar front.

Formation

Polar lows form for a number of different reasons, and a spectrum of systems is observed on satellite imagery. A number of lows develop on horizontal temperature gradients through baroclinic instability, and these can have the appearance of small frontal depressions. At the other extreme are the polar lows with extensive cumulonimbus clouds, which are often associated with cold pools in the mid- to upper-troposphere. During winter, when cold-core lows with temperatures in the mid-levels of the troposphere reach "45 °C

("49 °F) move over open waters, deep convection forms which allows polar low development to become possible.

Forecasting

Polar lows are very difficult to forecast and a now casting approach is often used, with the systems being advected with the mid-tropospheric flow. Numerical weather prediction models are only just getting the horizontal and vertical resolution to represent these systems.

Extratropical Cyclones

Extratropical cyclones, sometimes called mid-latitude cyclones or wave cyclones, are a group of cyclones defined as synoptic scale low pressure weather systems that occur in the middle latitudes of the Earth (outside the tropics) having neither tropical nor polar characteristics, and are connected with fronts and horizontal gradients in temperature and dew point otherwise known as "baroclinic zones". Extratropical cyclones are the everyday phenomena which, along with anticyclones, drive the weather over much of the Earth, producing anything from cloudiness and mild showers to heavy gales and thunderstorms.

Extratropical cyclones form anywhere within the extratropical regions of the Earth, either through cyclogenesis or extratropical transition. A study of extratropical cyclones in the Southern Hemisphere shows that between the 30th and 70th parallels, there are an average of 37 cyclones in existence during any 6-hour period. A separate study in the Northern Hemisphere suggests that approximately 234 significant extratropical cyclones form each winter.

Surface pressure and wind distribution

The windfield of an extratropical cyclone constricts with distance in relation to surface level pressure, with the lowest pressure being found near the center, and the highest winds typically just on the cold/poleward side of warm fronts, occlusions, and cold fronts, where the pressure gradient force is highest. The area north and west of the cold and warm fronts connected to extratropical cyclones is known as the cold sector, while the area south and east of its associated cold and warm fronts is known as the warm sector.

The wind flow around a large cyclone is counterclockwise in the northern hemisphere, and clockwise in the southern hemisphere, due to the Coriolis effect. Near this center, the pressure gradient force and the Coriolis force must be in an approximate balance for the cyclone to avoid collapsing in on itself as a result of the difference in pressure. The central pressure of the cyclone will lower with increasing maturity, while outside of the cyclone, the sea-level pressure is not very low; its typical value is around 1,013 millibars (29.91 in Hg), which is the average sea level pressure for Earth. In most extratropical cyclones, the part of the cold front ahead of the cyclone will develop into a warm front, giving the frontal zone (as drawn on surface weather maps) a wave-like shape. Due to their appearance on satellite images, extratropical cyclones can also be referred to as frontal waves early in their life cycle. In the United States, an old name for such a system is "warm wave".

Once a cyclone occludes, a trough of warm air aloft, or "trowal" for short, will be caused by strong southerly winds on its eastern periphery rotating aloft around its northeast, and ultimately northwestern, periphery (also known as the warm conveyor belt), forcing a surface trough to continue into the cold sector on a similar curve to the occluded front. The trowal creates the portion of an occluded cyclone known as its comma head, due to the comma-like shape of the mid-tropospheric cloudiness that accompanies the feature. It can also be the focus of locally heavy precipitation, with thunderstorms possible if the atmosphere along the trowal is unstable enough for convection.

Vertical structure

Extratropical cyclones slant back into colder air masses and strengthen with height, sometimes exceeding 30,000 feet (approximately 9 km) in depth. Above the surface of the earth, the air temperature near the center of the cyclone is increasingly colder than the surrounding environment. These characteristics are the direct opposite of those found in their tropical cyclones; thus, they are sometimes called "cold-core lows". Various charts can be examined to check the characteristics of a cold-core system with height, such as the 700 millibars (20.67 inHg) chart, which is at about 10,000 feet (3,048 meters) in height. Cyclone phase diagrams are used to tell whether a cyclone is tropical, subtropical, or extratropical.

Motion

Extratropical cyclones are generally driven, or "steered", by deep westerly winds in a general west to east motion across both the Northern and Southern hemispheres of the Earth. This general motion of atmospheric flow is known as "zonal". Where this general trend is the main steering influence of an extratropical cyclone, it is known as a "zonal flow regime".

When the general flow pattern buckles from a zonal pattern to the meridional pattern, a slower movement in a north or southward direction is more likely. Meridional flow patterns feature strong, amplified troughs and ridges, generally with more northerly and southerly flow.

Changes in direction of this nature are most commonly observed as a result of a cyclone's interaction with other low pressure systems, troughs, ridges, or with anticyclones. A strong and stationary anticyclone can effectively block the path of an extratropical cyclone. Suchblocking patterns are quite normal, and will generally result in a weakening of the cyclone, the weakening of the anticyclone, a diversion of the cyclone towards the anticyclones periphery, or a combination of all three to some extent depending on the precise conditions. It is also common for an extratropical cyclone to strengthen as the blocking anticyclone or ridge weakens in these circumstances.

Where an extratropical cyclone encounters another extratropical cyclone, the two may combine to become a binary cyclone, where the vortices of the two cyclones rotate around each other. This most often results in a merging of the two low pressure systems into a single extratropical cyclone, or can less commonly result in a mere change of direction of either one or both of the cyclones. The precise results of such interactions depend on factors such as the size of the two cyclones, their strength, their distance from each other, and the prevailing atmospheric conditions around them.

Effects

Extratropical cyclones can bring mild weather with a little rain and surface winds of 15–30 km/h (9.3–19 mph), or they can be cold and dangerous with torrential rain and winds exceeding 119 km/h (74 mph). The band of precipitation that is associated with the warm front is often extensive. In mature extratropical cyclones, an area known as the comma head on the northwest periphery of the surface low can be a region of heavy precipitation, frequent thunderstorms, and thunder snows. Cyclones tend to move along a predictable path at a moderate rate of progress. During fall, winter, and spring, the atmosphere over continents can be cold enough through the depth of the troposphere to cause snowfall.

Squall lines, or solid bands of strong thunderstorms, can form ahead of cold fronts and lee troughs due to the presence of significant atmospheric moisture and strong upper level divergence, leading to hail and high winds. When significant directional wind shear exists in the atmosphere ahead of a cold front in the presence of a strong upper level jet stream, tornado formation is possible. Although tornadoes can form anywhere on Earth, the greatest number occur in the Great Plains in the United States, because downsloped winds off the north-south oriented Rocky Mountains, which can form a dryline, aid their development at any strength.

Explosive development of extratropical cyclones can be sudden. The storm known in the UK as the "Great Storm of 1987" deepened to 953 millibars (28.14 inHg) with a highest recorded wind of 220 km/h (140 mph), resulting in the loss of 19 lives, 15 million trees, widespread damage to homes and an estimated economic cost of £1.2 billion (US$2.3 billion).

Although most tropical cyclones that become extratropical quickly dissipate or are absorbed by another weather system, they can still retain winds of hurricane or gale force. In 1954, Hurricane Hazel became extratropical over North Carolina as a strong Category 3 storm. The Columbus Day Storm of 1962, which evolved from the remains of Typhoon Freda, caused heavy damage in Oregon and Washington, with widespread damage equivalent to at least a Category 3. In 2005, Hurricane Wilma began to lose tropical characteristics while still sporting Category 3-force winds.

Subtropical Cyclones

A subtropical cyclone is a weather system that has some characteristics of a tropical and an extratropical cyclone. As early as the 1950s, meteorologists were unclear whether they should be characterized as tropical or extratropical cyclones. They were officially recognized by the National Hurricane Center in 1972. Subtropical cyclones began to receive names from the official tropical cyclone lists in the Atlantic Hurricane Basin and the southwest Indian ocean.

There are two definitions currently used for subtropical cyclones. Across the north Atlantic and southwest Indian ocean, they require central convection fairly near the center and a warming core in the mid-levels of the troposphere. Across the eastern half of the northern Pacific, they require a mid-tropospheric cyclone to cut off from the main belt of the westerlies and only a weak surface circulation. Subtropical cyclones have broad wind patterns with maximum sustained winds located farther from the center than typical tropical cyclones, and have no weather fronts linked into their center.

Since they form from initially extratropical cyclones which have colder temperatures aloft than normally found in the tropics, the sea surface temperatures required for their formation are lower than the tropical cyclone threshold by 3°C (5°F), lying around 23 °C (73 °F). This also means that subtropical cyclones are more likely to form outside the traditional bounds of the hurricane season.

Transition from Extratropical

By gaining tropical characteristics, an extratropical low may transit into a subtropical depression or storm. A subtropical depression/storm may further gain tropical characteristics to become a pure tropical depression or storm, which may eventually develop into a hurricane, and there are at least three cases of tropical storms transforming into a subtropical storm. Generally, a tropical storm or tropical depression is not called subtropical while it is becoming extratropical, after hitting either land or colder waters. This transition normally requires significant instability through the atmosphere, with temperature differences between the underlying ocean and the mid-levels of the troposphere requiring over 40 °C, or 72 °F, of contrast in this roughly 5,900 meters (19,400 ft) layer of the lower atmosphere. The mode of the sea surface temperatures that subtropical cyclones form over is 23 °C.

Characteristics

These storms can have maximum winds extending farther from the center than in a purely tropical cyclone and have no weather fronts linking directly to the center of circulation. The maximum recorded wind speed for a subtropical storm is 33 m/s, also the minimum for a hurricane. In the Atlantic Basin, the United States NOAA classifies subtropical cyclones similarly to their tropical cousins, based on maximum sustained surface winds. Those with winds below 18 m/s, 65 km/h, 35 knots, or 39 mph are called subtropical depressions, while those at or above this speed are referred to as subtropical storms. Subtropical cyclones are also more likely than tropical cyclones to form outside of a region's designated hurricane season. Examples include Subtropical Storm Ana in mid-April of the 2003 hurricane season and Subtropical Storm Andrea in early May and Subtropical Storm Olga in mid-December of the 2007 Atlantic hurricane season. Diagrams which depict a cyclone's phase depict subtropical cyclones with a shallow warm core and as asymmetric systems, similar to tropical cyclones which have begun the transition to an extratropical cyclone.

Types of Extratropical Cyclone

Upper-level low

The most common type of subtropical storm is an upper-level cold low with circulation extending to the surface layer and maximum sustained winds generally occurring at a radius of about 160 kilometers (99 mi) or more from the center. In comparison to tropical cyclones, such systems have a relatively broad zone of maximum winds that is located farther from the center, and typically have a less symmetric wind field and distribution of convection.

Mesoscale low

A second type of subtropical cyclone is a mesoscale low originating in or near a frontolyzing zone of horizontal wind shear, also known as a dying frontal zone, with radius of maximum sustained winds generally less than 50 kilometers (31 mi). The entire circulation may initially have a diameter of less than 160 kilometers (99 mi). These generally short-lived systems may be either cold core or warm core, and in 1972 this type of subtropical cyclone was referred to as a "neutercane".

Kona low

Kona lows are deep cyclones that form during the cool season of the central Pacific ocean. A definition change in the term during the early 1970s makes categorization of the systems more complex, as many kona lows are extratropical cyclones, complete with their own weather fronts. Those across the northeast Pacific ocean consider them subtropical cyclones as long as a weak surface circulation is present. Kona is a Hawaiian term for leeward, which explains the change in wind direction for the Hawaiian Islands from easterly to southerly when this type of cyclone is present.

Tropical Cyclone

A tropical cyclone is a storm system characterized by a low-pressure center and numerous thunderstorms that produce strong winds and heavy rain. Tropical cyclones strengthen when water evaporated from the ocean is released as the saturated air rises, resulting in condensation of water vapour contained in the moist air. They are fuelled by a different heat mechanism than other cyclonic windstorms such as nor' easters, European windstorms, and polar lows. The characteristic that separates tropical cyclones from other cyclonic systems is that at any height in the atmosphere, the center of a tropical cyclone will be warmer than its surroundings; a phenomenon called "warm core" storm systems.

The term "tropical" refers both to the geographical origin of these systems, which usually form in tropical regions of the globe, and to their formation in maritime tropical air masses. The term "cyclone" refers to such storms' cyclonic nature, with counter clockwise wind flow in the Northern Hemisphere and clockwise wind flow in the Southern Hemisphere. The opposite direction of the wind flow is a result of the Coriolis force. Depending on its location and strength, a tropical cyclone is referred to by names such as hurricane, typhoon, tropical storm, cyclonic storm, tropical depression, and simply cyclone.

While tropical cyclones can produce extremely powerful winds and torrential rain, they are also able to produce high waves and damaging storm surge as well as spawning tornadoes. They develop over large bodies of warm water, and lose their strength if they move over land due to increased surface friction and loss of the warm ocean as an energy source. This is why coastal regions can receive significant damage from a tropical cyclone, while inland regions are relatively safe from receiving strong winds. Heavy rains, however, can produce significant flooding inland, and storm surges can produce extensive coastal floodingup to 40 kilometres (25 mi) from the coastline. Although their effects on human populations can be devastating, tropical cyclones can relieve drought conditions. They also carry heat energy away from the tropics and transport it toward temperate latitudes, which makes them an important part of the global atmospheric circulation mechanism. As a result, tropical cyclones help to maintain equilibrium in the Earth's troposphere, and to maintain a relatively stable and warm temperature worldwide.

Many tropical cyclones develop when the atmospheric conditions around a weak disturbance in the atmosphere are favourable. The background environment is modulated by climatological cycles and patterns such as the Madden-Julian oscillation, El Niño-Southern Oscillation, and the Atlantic multidecadal oscillation. Others form when other types of cyclones acquire tropical characteristics. Tropical systems are then moved by steering winds in the troposphere; if the conditions remain favourable, the tropical disturbance intensifies, and can even develop an eye. On the other end of the spectrum, if the conditions around the system deteriorate or the tropical cyclone makes landfall, the system weakens and eventually dissipates. It is not possible to artificially induce the dissipation of these systems with current technology

Physical Structure

All tropical cyclones are areas of low atmospheric pressure in the Earth's atmosphere. The pressures recorded at the centers of tropical cyclones are among the lowest that occur on Earth's surface at sea level. Tropical cyclones are characterized and driven by the release of large amounts of latent heat of condensation, which occurs when moist air is carried upwards and its water vapour condenses. This heat is distributed vertically around the center of the storm. Thus, at any given altitude (except close to the surface, where water temperature dictates air temperature) the environment inside the cyclone is warmer than its outer surroundings.

Eye and center

A strong tropical cyclone will harbour an area of sinking air at the center of circulation. If this area is strong enough, it can develop into a large "eye". Weather in the eye is normally calm and free of clouds, although the sea may be extremely violent. The eye is normally circular in shape, and is typically 30–65 km (19–40 miles) in diameter, though eyes as small as 3 kilometres (1.9 mi) and as large as 370 kilometres (230 mi) have been observed. Intense, mature tropical cyclones can sometimes exhibit an outward curving of the eyewall's top, making it resemble an arena football stadium; this phenomenon is thus sometimes referred to as the stadium effect. It is usually coldest in the center.

There are other features that either surround the eye, or cover it. The central dense overcast is the concentrated area of strong thunderstorm activity near the center of a tropical cyclone; in weaker tropical cyclones, the CDO may cover the center completely. The eyewall is a circle of strong thunderstorms that surrounds the eye; here is where the greatest wind speeds are found, where clouds reach the highest, and precipitation is the heaviest. The heaviest wind damage occurs where a tropical cyclone's eyewall passes over land. Eyewall replacement cycles occur naturally in intense tropical cyclones. When cyclones reach peak intensity they usually have an eyewall and radius of maximum winds that contract to a very small size, around 10 to 25 kilometres (6.2 to 16 mi). Outer rainbands can organize into an outer ring of thunderstorms that slowly moves inward and robs the inner eyewall of its needed moisture and angular momentum. When the inner eyewall weakens, the tropical cyclone weakens. The outer eyewall replaces the inner one completely at the end of the cycle. The storm can be of the same intensity as it was previously or even stronger after the eyewall replacement cycle finishes. The storm may strengthen again as it builds a new outer ring for the next eyewall replacement.

Size

One measure of the size of a tropical cyclone is determined by measuring the distance from its center of circulation to its outermost closed isobar, also known as its ROCI. If the radius is less than two degrees of latitude or 222 kilometres (138 mi), then the cyclone is "very small" or a "midget". A radius between 3 and 6 latitude degrees or 333 to 670 kilometres (207 to 420 mi) are considered "average-sized". "Very large" tropical cyclones have a radius of greater than 8 degrees or 888 kilometres (552 mi). Use of this measure has objectively determined that tropical cyclones in the northwest Pacific Ocean are the largest on earth on average, with Atlantic tropical cyclones roughly half their size. Other methods of determining a tropical cyclone's size include measuring the radius of gale force winds and measuring the radius at which its relative vorticity field decreases to 1×10^{-5} s^{-1} from its center

Major basins and related warning center

There are six Regional Specialized Meteorological Centers (RSMCs) worldwide. These organizations are designated by the World Meteorological Organization and are responsible for tracking and issuing bulletins, warnings, and advisories about tropical cyclones in their designated areas of responsibility. In addition, there are six Tropical Cyclone Warning Centers (TCWCs) that provide information to smaller regions. The RSMCs and TCWCs are not the only organizations that provide information about tropical cyclones to the public. The Joint Typhoon Warning Center (JTWC) issues advisories in all basins except the Northern Atlantic for the purposes of the United States Government. The Philippine Atmospheric, Geophysical and Astronomical Services Administration (PAGASA) issues advisories and names for tropical cyclones that approach the Philippines in the Northwestern Pacific to protect the life and property of its citizens. The Canadian Hurricane

Center (CHC) issues advisories on hurricanes and their remnants for Canadian citizens when they affect Canada.

On 26 March 2004, Cyclone Catarina became the first recorded South Atlantic cyclone and subsequently struck southern Brazil with winds equivalent to Category 2 on the Saffir-Simpson Hurricane Scale. As the cyclone formed outside the authority of another warning center, Brazilian meteorologists initially treated the system as an extratropical cyclone, although subsequently classified it as tropical.

Formation

Worldwide, tropical cyclone activity peaks in late summer, when the difference between temperatures aloft and sea surface temperatures is the greatest. However, each particular basin has its own seasonal patterns. On a worldwide scale, May is the least active month, while September is the most active while November is the only month with all the tropical cyclone basins active.

Times

In the Northern Atlantic Ocean, a distinct cyclone season occurs from June 1 to November 30, sharply peaking from late August through September. The statistical peak of the Atlantic hurricane season is 10 September. The Northeast Pacific Ocean has a broader period of activity, but in a similar time frame to the Atlantic. The Northwest Pacific sees tropical cyclones year-round, with a minimum in February and March and a peak in early September. In the North Indian basin, storms are most common from April to December, with peaks in May and November. In the Southern Hemisphere, the tropical cyclone year begins on July 1 and runs all year-round and encompasses the tropical cyclone seasons, which run from November 1 until the end of April, with peaks in mid-February to early March.

Factors

The formation of tropical cyclones is the topic of extensive ongoing research and is still not fully understood. While six factors appear to be generally necessary, tropical cyclones may occasionally form without meeting all of the following conditions. In most situations, water temperatures of at least 26.5 °C (79.7 °F) are needed down to a depth of at least 50 m (160 ft); waters of this temperature cause the overlying atmosphere to be unstable enough to sustain convection and thunderstorms. Another factor is rapid cooling with height, which allows the release of the heat of condensation that powers a tropical cyclone. High humidity is needed, especially in the lower-to-mid troposphere; when there is a great deal of moisture in the atmosphere, conditions are more favourable for disturbances to develop. Low amounts of wind shear are needed, as high shear is disruptive to the storm's circulation. Tropical cyclones generally need to form more than 555 km (345 mi) or 5 degrees of latitude away from the equator, allowing the Coriolis effect to deflect winds blowing towards the low pressure center and creating a circulation. Lastly, a formative tropical cyclone needs a pre-existing system of disturbed weather, although without a circulation no cyclonic development will take place. Low-latitude and low-level westerly wind bursts associated with the Madden-Julian oscillation can create favourable conditions for tropical cyclogenesis by initiating tropical disturbances.

Locations

Most tropical cyclones form in a worldwide band of thunderstorm activity called by several names: the Intertropical Front (ITF), the Intertropical Convergence Zone (ITCZ), or the monsoon trough. Another important source of atmospheric instability is found intropical waves, which cause about 85% of intense tropical cyclones in the Atlantic ocean, and become most of the tropical cyclones in the Eastern Pacific basin.

Tropical cyclones move westward when equator ward of the subtropical ridge, intensifying as they move. Most of these systems form between 10 and 30 degrees away of the equator, and 87% form no farther away than 20 degrees of latitude, north or south. Because the Coriolis effect initiates and maintains tropical cyclone rotation, tropical cyclones rarely form or move within about 5 degrees of the equator, where the Coriolis effect is weakest. However, it is possible for tropical cyclones to form within this boundary as Tropical Storm Vamei did in 2001 and Cyclone Agni in 2004.

Effects

Tropical cyclones out at sea cause large waves, heavy rain, and high winds, disrupting international shipping and, at times, causing shipwrecks. Tropical cyclones stir up water, leaving a cool wake behind them, which causes the region to be less favourable for subsequent tropical cyclones. On land, strong winds can damage or destroy vehicles, buildings, bridges, and other outside objects, turning loose debris into deadly flying projectiles. The storm surge, or the increase in sea level due to the cyclone, is typically the worst effect from landfalling tropical cyclones, historically resulting in 90% of tropical cyclone deaths. The broad rotation of a landfalling tropical cyclone, and vertical wind shear at its periphery, spawns tornadoes. Tornadoes can also be spawned as a result of eyewall mesovortices, which persist until landfall.

Over the past two centuries, tropical cyclones have been responsible for the deaths of about 1.9 million people worldwide. Large areas of standing water caused by flooding lead to infection, as well as contributing to mosquito-borne illnesses. Crowded evacuees in shelters increase the risk of disease propagation. Tropical cyclones significantly interrupt infrastructure, leading to power outages, bridge destruction, and the hampering of reconstruction efforts.

Although cyclones take an enormous toll in lives and personal property, they may be important factors in the precipitation regimes of places they impact, as they may bring much-needed precipitation to otherwise dry regions. Tropical cyclones also help maintain the global heat balance by moving warm, moist tropical air to the middle latitudes and polar regions, and by regulating the thermohaline circulation through upwelling. The storm surge and winds of hurricanes may be destructive to human-made structures, but they also stir up the waters of coastal estuaries, which are typically important fish breeding locales. Tropical cyclone destruction spurs redevelopment, greatly increasing local property values.

Observation

Intense tropical cyclones pose a particular observation challenge, as they are a dangerous oceanic phenomenon, and weather stations, being relatively sparse, are rarely available on the site of the storm itself. In general, surface observations are available only if the storm is passing over an island or a coastal area, or if there is a nearby ship. Real-time measurements are usually taken in the periphery of the cyclone, where conditions are less catastrophic and its true strength cannot be evaluated. For this reason, there are teams of meteorologists that move into the path of tropical cyclones to help evaluate their strength at the point of landfall.

Tropical cyclones far from land are tracked by weather satellites capturing visible and infrared images from space, usually at half-hour to quarter-hour intervals. As a storm approaches land, it can be observed by land-based Doppler radar. Radar plays a crucial role around landfall by showing a storm's location and intensity every several minutes.

In situ measurements, in real-time, can be taken by sending specially equipped reconnaissance flights into the cyclone. In the Atlantic basin, these flights are regularly flown by United States government hurricane hunters. The aircraft used are WC-130 Hercules and WP-3DOrions, both four-engine turboprop cargo aircraft. These aircraft fly directly into the cyclone and take direct and remote-sensing measurements. The aircraft also launch GPS dropsondes inside the cyclone. These sondes measure temperature, humidity, pressure, and especially winds between flight level and the ocean's surface. A new era in hurricane observation began when a remotely piloted Aerosonde, a small drone aircraft, was flown through Tropical Storm Ophelia as it passed Virginia's Eastern Shore during the 2005 hurricane season.

Forecasting

Because of the forces that affect tropical cyclone tracks, accurate track predictions depend on determining the position and strength of high- and low-pressure areas, and predicting how those areas will change during the life of a tropical system. The deep layer mean flow, or average wind through the depth of the troposphere, is considered the best tool in determining track direction and speed. If storms are significantly sheared, use of wind speed measurements at a lower altitude, such as at the 700 hPa pressure surface will produce better predictions. Tropical forecasters also consider smoothing out short-term wobbles of the storm as it allows them to determine a more accurate long-term trajectory. High-speed computers and sophisticated simulation software allow forecasters to produce computer models that predict tropical cyclone tracks based on the future position and strength of high- and low-pressure systems. Combining forecast models with increased understanding of the forces that act on tropical cyclones, as well as with a wealth of data from Earth-orbiting satellites and other sensors, scientists have increased the accuracy of track forecasts over recent decades. However, scientists are not as skilful at predicting the intensity of tropical cyclones. The lack of improvement in intensity forecasting is attributed to the complexity of tropical systems and an incomplete understanding of factors that affect their development.

Mesocyclone

A mesocyclone is a vortex of air, approximately 2 to 10 miles in diameter, within a convective storm. That is, it is air that rises and rotates around a vertical axis, usually in the same direction as low pressure systems in a given hemisphere. They are most often cyclonic, that is, associated with a localized low-pressure region within a severe thunderstorm. Such storms can feature strong surface winds and severe hail.

Mesocyclones often occur together with updrafts in supercells, where tornadoes may form. Mesocyclones are believed to form when strong changes of wind speed and/or direction with height sets parts of the lower part of the atmosphere spinning in invisible tube-like rolls. The convective updraft of a thunderstorm is then thought to draw up this spinning air, tilting the rolls' orientation upward and causing the entire updraft to rotate as a vertical column.

Mesocyclones are normally relatively localized: they lie between the synoptic scale and small scale . Radar imagery is used to identify these features. Mesoscale convective systems (MCS) can develop mesoscale convective vortexes which can spur later development of either another MCS or a tropical cyclone.

Identification

The best way to detect and verify the presence of a mesocyclone is by Doppler weather radar. Nearby high values of opposite sign within velocity data are how they are detected. Thus the word mesocyclone is associated with weather radar terminology. Mesocyclones are most often identified in the right-rear flank of supercell thunderstorms and squall lines, and may be distinguished by a hook echo rotation signature on a weather radar map. Visual cues such as a rotating wall cloud or tornado may also hint at the presence of a mesocyclone. This is why the term has entered into wider usage in connection with rotating features in severe storms.

Formation

Mesocyclones are believed to form when strong changes of wind speed and/or direction with height sets parts of the lower part of the atmosphere spinning in invisible tube-like rolls. The convective updraft of a thunderstorm is then thought to tilt upwards the layer of spinning air and causing the entire updraft to rotate as a vertical column.

As the updraft rotates, it may form a wall cloud, a spinning layer of clouds descending from the mesocyclone. The wall cloud tends to form closer to the center of the mesocyclone. As it descends, a funnel-shaped cloud may form at its center. This is the first stage of tornado formation.

Forecasting and Predicting Tropical Cyclones

Weather Broadcasts and Radiofacsimile

The marine weather broadcast and radiofacsimile weather maps are the most important tools for avoiding tropical cyclones. These broadcasts, covering all tropical areas, provide information about the tropical cyclone's location, maximum winds and seas, and future conditions expected.

The U S. Navy, the National Oceanic and Atmospheric Administration, and the U.S. Air Force have developed a highly effective surveillance system for the tropical cyclone-prone areas of the world. Routine and special weather reports enable accurate detection, location, and tracking of tropical cyclones. International cooperation is effective. These reports originate from land stations, ships at sea, aircraft, weather satellite imagery, and specially instrumented weather reconnaissance aircraft of National Oceanic and Atmospheric Administration and the U.S. Air Force. Data buoys, both moored and drifting, provide another source of information.

The tropical warning services have three principal functions:

1. Collection and analysis of data
2. Preparation of timely and accurate warnings
3. The distribution of advisories

To provide timely and accurate information and warnings regarding tropical cyclones, the oceans have been divided into overlapping geographical areas of responsibility.

Although the areas of forecasting responsibility are fairly well defined for the Department of Defense, the international and domestic civilian system provides many overlaps and is dependent upon qualitative factors.

For example, when a tropical storm or hurricane is traveling westward and crosses 35°W longitude, the continued issuance of forecasts and warnings to the general public, shipping interests, etc., becomes the responsibility of the National Hurricane Center of the National Weather Service at Miami, Florida. When a tropical storm or hurricane crosses 35°W longitude traveling from west to east, the National Hurricane Center ceases to issue formal public advisories, but will issue marine bulletins on any dangerous tropical cyclone in the North Atlantic, if it is of importance or constitutes a threat to shipping and other interests. These advisories are included in National Weather Service Marine Bulletins broadcast to ships over radio station NAM Norfolk, Virginia. Special advisories may be issued at any time. In the Atlantic Ocean, Department of Defense responsibility rests with the Naval Atlantic Meteorology and Oceanography Center in Norfolk, Virginia.

In the eastern Pacific east of longitude 140°W, responsibility for the issuance of tropical storm and hurricane advisories and warnings for the general public, merchant shipping, and other interests rests with the National Weather Service Eastern Pacific Hurricane Center, San Francisco, California. The Department of Defense responsibility rests with the Naval Pacific Meteorology and Oceanography Center, Pearl Harbor, Hawaii. Formal advisories and warnings are issued daily and are included in the marine bulletins broadcast by radio stations KFS, NMC, and NMQ.

In the central Pacific (between the meridian and longitude 140°W), the civilian responsibility rests with the National Weather Service Central Pacific Hurricane Center, Honolulu, Hawaii. Department of Defense responsibility rests with the Naval Pacific Meteorology and Oceanography Center in Pearl Harbor. Formal tropical storm and hurricane advisories and warnings are issued daily and are included in the marine bulletins broadcast by radio station NMO and NRV.

Tropical cyclone messages contain position of the storm, intensity, direction and speed of movement, and a description of the area of strong winds. Included is a forecast of future movement and intensity. When the storm is likely to affect any land area, details on when and where it will be felt, and data on tides, rain, floods, and maximum winds are also included.

The Naval Pacific Meteorology and Oceanography Center Center-West/ Joint Typhoon Warning Center (NP-MOC-W/JTWC) in Guam is responsible for all U.S. tropical storm and typhoon advisories and warnings from the 180th meridian westward to the mainland of Asia. A secondary area of responsibility extends westward to longitude 90°E. Whenever a tropical cyclone is observed in the western North Pacific area, serially numbered warnings, bearing an "immediate" precedence are broadcast from the NPMOC-W/JTWC at 0000, 0600, 1200, and 1800 GMT.

The responsibility for issuing gale and storm warnings for the Indian Ocean, Arabian Sea, Bay of Bengal, Western Pacific, and South Pacific rests with many countries. In general, warnings of approaching tropical cyclones will include the following information: storm type, central pressure given in hPa, wind speed observed within the storm, storm location, speed and direction of movement, the extent of the affected area, visibility, and the state of the sea, as well as any other pertinent information received. All storm warning messages commence with the international call sign “TTT.”

Avoiding Tropical Cyclones

Approach and Passage of a Tropical Cyclone

An early indication of the approach of a tropical cyclone is the presence of a long swell. In the absence of a tropical cyclone, the crests of swell in the deep waters of the Atlantic pass at the rate of perhaps eight per minute. Swell generated by a hurricane is about twice as long, the crests passing at the rate of perhaps four per minute. Swell may be observed several days before arrival of the storm.

When the storm center is 500 to 1,000 miles away, the barometer usually rises a little, and the skies are relatively clear. Cumulus clouds, if present at all, are few in number and their vertical development appears suppressed. The barometer usually appears restless, pumping up and down a few hundredths of an inch.

As the tropical cyclone comes nearer, a cloud sequence begins which resembles that associated with the approach of a warm front in middle latitudes. Snow-white, fibrous “mare’s tails” (cirrus) appear when the storm is about 300 to 600 miles away. Usually these seem to converge, more or less, in the direction from which the storm is approaching. This convergence is particularly apparent at about the time of sunrise and sunset.

Shortly after the cirrus appears, but sometimes before, the barometer starts a long, slow fall. At first the fall is so gradual that it only appears to alter somewhat the normal daily cycle (two maxima and two minima in the Tropics). As the rate of fall increases, the daily pattern is completely lost in the more or less steady fall.

The cirrus becomes more confused and tangled, and then gradually gives way to a continuous veil of cirrostratus. Below this veil, altostratus forms, and then stratocumulus. These clouds gradually become more dense, and as they do so, the weather becomes unsettled. A fine, mist-like rain begins to fall, interrupted from time to time by rain showers. The barometer has fallen perhaps a tenth of an inch.

As the fall becomes more rapid, the wind increases in gustiness, and its speed becomes greater, reaching perhaps 22 to 40 knots (Beaufort 6-8). On the horizon appears a dark wall of heavy cumulonimbus, called the bar of the storm. This is the heavy bank of clouds comprising the main mass of the cyclone. Portions of this heavy cloud become detached from time to time, and drift across the sky, accompanied by rain squalls and wind of increasing speed. Between squalls, the cirrostratus can be seen through breaks in the stratocumulus.

As the bar approaches, the barometer falls more rapidly and wind speed increases. The seas, which have been gradually mounting, become tempestuous. Squall lines, one after the other, sweep past in ever increasing number and intensity.

With the arrival of the bar, the day becomes very dark, squalls become virtually continuous, and the barometer falls precipitously, with a rapid increase in wind speed. The center may still be 100 to 200 miles away in a fully developed tropical cyclone. As the center of the storm comes closer, the ever-stronger wind shrieks through the rigging, and about the superstructure of the vessel.

As the center approaches, rain falls in torrents. The wind fury increases. The seas become mountainous. The tops of huge waves are blown off to mingle with the rain and fill the air with water. Visibility is virtually zero in blinding rain and spray. Even the largest and most seaworthy vessels become virtually unmanageable, and may sustain heavy damage. Less sturdy vessels may not survive. Navigation virtually stops as safety of the vessel becomes the only consideration. The awesome fury of this condition can only be experienced. Words are inadequate to describe it.

If the eye of the storm passes over the vessel, the winds suddenly drop to a breeze as the wall of the eye passes. The rain stops, and the skies clear sufficiently to permit the Sun or stars to shine through holes in the comparatively thin cloud cover. Visibility improves. Mountainous seas approach from all sides in complete confusion. The barometer reaches its lowest point, which may be $1^1/_2$ or 2 inches below normal in fully developed tropical cyclones. As the wall on the opposite side of the eye arrives, the full fury of the wind strikes as suddenly as it ceased, but from the opposite direction. The sequence of conditions that occurred during approach of the storm is reversed, and passes more quickly, as the various parts of the storm are not as wide in the rear of a storm as on its forward side.

Locating the Center of a Tropical Cyclone

If intelligent action is to be taken to avoid the full fury of a tropical cyclone, early determination of its location and direction of travel relative to the vessel is essential. The bulletins and forecasts are an excellent general guide, but they are not infallible, and may be sufficiently in error to induce a mariner in a critical position to alter course so as to unwittingly increase the danger to his vessel. Often it is possible, using only those observations made aboard ship, to obtain a sufficiently close approximation to enable the vessel to maneuver to the best advantage.

The presence of an exceptionally long swell is usually the first visible indication of the existence of a tropical cyclone. In deep water it approaches from the general direction of origin (the position of the storm center when the swell was generated). However, in shoaling water this is a less reliable indication because the direction is changed by refraction, the crests being more nearly parallel to the bottom contours.

When the cirrus clouds appear, their point of convergence provides an indication of the direction of the storm center. If the storm is to pass well to one side of the observer, the point of convergence shifts slowly in the direction of storm movement. If the storm center will pass near the observer, this point remains steady. When the bar becomes visible, it appears to rest upon the horizon for several hours. The darkest part of this cloud is in the direction of the storm center. If the storm is to pass to one side, the bar appears to drift slowly along the horizon. If the storm is heading directly toward the observer, the position of the bar remains fixed. Once within the area of the dense, low clouds, one should observe their direction of movement, which is almost exactly along the isobars, with the center of the storm being 90° from the direction of cloud movement (left of direction of movement in the Northern Hemisphere, and right in the Southern Hemisphere). The winds are probably the best guide to the direction of the center of a tropical cyclone. The circulation is cyclonic, but because of the steep pressure gradient near the center, the winds there blow with greater violence and are more nearly circular than in extratropical cyclones.

According to Buys Ballot's law, an observer whose back is to the wind has the low pressure on his left in the Northern Hemisphere, and on his right in the Southern Hemisphere. If the wind followed circular isobars exactly, the center would be exactly 90° from behind when facing away from the wind.

However, the track of the wind is usually inclined somewhat toward the center, so that the angle from dead astern varies between perhaps 90° to 135°. The inclination varies in different parts of the same storm. It is least in front of the storm, and greatest in the rear, since the actual wind is the vector sum of the pressure gradient and the motion of the storm along the track.

A good average is perhaps 110° in front, and 120-135° in the rear. These values apply when the storm center is still several hundred miles away. Closer to the center, the wind blows more nearly along the isobars, the inclination being reduced by one or two points at the wall of the eye. Since wind direction usually shifts temporarily during a squall, its direction at this time should not be used for determining the position of the center.

When the center is within radar range, it will probably be visible on the scope. However, since the radar return is predominantly from the rain, results can be deceptive, and other indications should not be neglected. If the eye is out of range, the spiral bands may indicate its direction from the vessel. Tracking the eye or upwind portion of the spiral bands enables determining the direction and speed of movement; this should be done for at least 1 hour because the eye tends to oscillate. The tracking of individual cells, which tend to move tangentially around the eye, for 15 minutes or more, either at the end of the band or between bands, will provide an indication of the wind speed in that area of the storm.

Distance from the storm center is more difficult to determine than direction. Radar is perhaps the best guide. However, the rate of fall of the barometer is some indication.

Statistical Analysis of Barometric Pressure

The lowest-sea-level pressure ever recorded was 877 hPa in typhoon Ida, on September 24, 1958. The observation was taken by a reconnaissance aircraft dropsonde, some 750 miles east of Luzon, Philippines. This observation was obtained again in typhoon Nora on October 6, 1973. The lowest barometric reading of record for the United States is 892.3 hPa, obtained during a hurricane at Lower Matecumbe Key, Florida, in September 1935. In hurricane Camille in 1969, a 905 hPa pressure was measured by reconnaissance aircraft. During a 1927 typhoon, the S.S. Sapoeroea recorded a pressure of 886.6 hPa, the lowest sea-level pressure reported from a ship. Pressure has been observed to drop more than 33 hPa per hour, with a pressure gradient amounting to a change of 3.7 hPa per mile.

A method for alerting the mariner to possible tropical cyclone formation involves a statistical comparison of observed weather parameters with the climatology (30 year averaged conditions) for those parameters. Significant fluctuations away from these average conditions could mean the onset of severe weather. One such statistical method involves a comparison of mean surface pressure in the tropics with the standard deviation (s.d.) of surface pressure. Any significant deviation from the norm could indicate proximity to a tropical cyclone. Analysis shows that surface pressure can be expected to be lower than the mean minus 1 s.d. less than 16% of the time, lower than the mean minus 1.5 s.d. less than 7% of the time, and lower than the mean minus 2 s.d. less than 3% of the time. Comparison of the observed pressure with the mean will indicate how unusual the present conditions are.

As an example, assume the mean surface pressure in the South China Sea to be about 1005 mb during August with a s.d. of about 2 mb. Therefore, surface pressure can be expected to fall below 1003 mb about 16% of the time and below 1000 mb about 7% of the time. Ambient pressure any lower than that would alert the mariner to the possible onset of heavy weather. Charts showing the mean surface pressure and the s.d. of surface pressure for various global regions can be found in the U.S. Navy Marine Climatic Atlas of the World.

Maneuvering to Avoid the Storm Center

The safest procedure with respect to tropical cyclones is to avoid them. If action is taken sufficiently early, this is simply a matter of setting a course that will take the vessel well to one side of the probable track of the storm, and then continuing to plot the positions of the storm center as given in the weather bulletins, revising the course as needed.

However, this is not always possible. If the ship is found to be within the storm area, the proper action to take depends in part upon its position relative to the storm center and its direction of travel. It is customary to divide the circular area of the storm into two parts.

In the Northern Hemisphere, that part to the right of the storm track (facing in the direction toward which the storm is moving) is called the dangerous semicircle. It is considered dangerous because (1) the actual wind speed is greater than that due to the pressure gradient alone, since it is augmented by the forward motion of the storm, and (2) the direction of the wind and sea is such as to carry a vessel into the path of the storm (in the forward part of the semicircle).

The part to the left of the storm track is called the less dangerous semicircle, or navigable semicircle. In this part, the wind is decreased by the forward motion of the storm, and the wind blows vessels away from the storm track (in the forward part). Because of the greater wind speed in the dangerous semicircle, the seas are higher than in the less dangerous semicircle. In the Southern Hemisphere, the dangerous semicircle is to the left of the storm track, and the less dangerous semicircle is to the right of the storm track.

A plot of successive positions of the storm center should indicate the semicircle in which a vessel is located. However, if this is based upon weather bulletins, it may not be a reliable guide because of the lag between the observations upon which the bulletin is based and the time of reception of the bulletin, with the ever-present possibility of a change in the direction of the storm. The use of radar eliminates this lag at short range, but the return may not be a true indication of the center. Perhaps the most reliable guide is the wind. Within the cyclonic circulation, a wind shifting to the right in the northern hemisphere and to the left in the southern hemisphere indicates the vessel is probably in the dangerous semicircle. A steady wind shift opposite to this indicates the vessel is probably in the less dangerous semicircle.

However, if a vessel is underway, its own motion should be considered. If it is outrunning the storm or pulling rapidly toward one side (which is not difficult during the early stages of a storm, when its speed is low), the opposite effect occurs. This should usually be accompanied by a rise in atmospheric pressure, but if motion of the vessel is nearly along an isobar, this may not be a reliable indication. If in doubt, the safest action is usually to stop long enough to define the proper semicircle. The loss in time may be more than offset by the minimizing of the possibility of taking the wrong action, increasing the danger to the vessel. If the wind direction remains steady (for a vessel which is stopped), with increasing speed and falling barometer, the vessel is in or near the path of the storm. If it remains steady with decreasing speed and rising barometer, the vessel is near the storm track, behind the center.

The first action to take if the ship is within the cyclonic circulation is to determine the position of his vessel with respect to the storm center. While the vessel can still make considerable way through the water, a course should be selected to take it as far as possible from the center. If the vessel can move faster than the storm, it is a relatively simple matter to outrun the storm if sea room permits. But when the storm is faster, the solution is not as simple. In this case, the vessel, if ahead of the storm, will approach nearer to the center. The problem is to select a course that will produce the greatest possible minimum distance. This is best determined by means of a relative movement plot, as shown in the following example solved on a maneuvering board.

Example: A tropical cyclone is estimated to be moving in direction 320° at 19 knots. Its center bears 170°, at an estimated distance of 200 miles from a vessel which has a maximum speed of 12 knots.

Required:

(1) The course to steer at 12 knots to produce the greatest possible minimum distance between the vessel and the storm center.

(2) The distance to the center at nearest approach.

(3) Elapsed time until nearest approach.

Solution: Consider the vessel remaining at the center of the plot throughout the solution, as on a radar PPI.

(1) To locate the position of the storm center relative to the vessel, plot point C at a distance of 200 miles (scale 20:1) in direction 170° from the center of the diagram. From the center of the diagram, draw RA, the speed vector of the storm center, in direction 320°, speed 19 knots (scale 2:1). From A draw a line tangent to the 12-knot speed circle (labeled 6 at scale 2:1) on the side opposite the storm center. From the center of the diagram, draw a perpendicular to this tangent line, locating point B. The line RB is the required speed vector for the vessel. Its direction, 011°, is the required course.

(2) The path of the storm center relative to the vessel will be along a line from C in the direction BA, if both storm and vessel maintain course and speed. The point of nearest approach will be at D, the foot of a

perpendicular from the center of the diagram. This distance, at scale 20:1, is 187 miles.

(3) The length of the vector BA (14.8 knots) is the speed of the storm with respect to the vessel. Mark this on the lowest scale of the nomogram at the bottom of the diagram. The relative distance CD is 72 miles, by measurement. Mark this (scale 10:1) on the middle scale at the bottom of the diagram. Draw a line between the two points and extend it to intersect the top scale at 29.2 (292 at 10:1 scale). The elapsed time is therefore 292 minutes, or 4 hours 52 minutes.

Answers: (1) C 011°, (2) D 187 mi., (3) 4^h 52^m.

The storm center will be dead astern at its nearest approach.

As a general rule, for a vessel in the Northern Hemisphere, safety lies in placing the wind on the starboard bow in the dangerous semicircle and on the starboard quarter in the less dangerous semicircle. If on the storm track ahead of the storm, the wind should be put about 160° on the starboard quarter until the vessel is well within the less dangerous semicircle, and the rule for that semicircle then followed. In the Southern Hemisphere the same rules

hold, but with respect to the port side. With a faster than average vessel, the wind can be brought a little farther aft in each case. However, as the speed of the storm increases along its track, the wind should be brought farther forward. If land interferes with what would otherwise be the best maneuver, the solution should be altered to fit the circumstances.

If the vessel is faster than the storm, it is possible to overtake it. In this case, the only action usually needed is to slow enough to let the storm pull ahead.

In all cases, one should be alert to changes in the direction of movement of the storm center, particularly in the area where the track normally curves toward the pole. If the storm maintains its direction and speed, the ship's course should be maintained as the wind shifts.

If it becomes necessary for a vessel to heave to, the characteristics of the vessel should be considered. A power vessel is concerned primarily with damage by direct action of the sea. A good general rule is to heave to with head to the sea in the dangerous semicircle, or stern to the sea in the less dangerous semicircle. This will result in greatest amount of headway away from the storm center, and least amount of leeway toward it. If a vessel handles better with the sea astern or on the quarter, it may be placed in this position in the less dangerous semicircle or in the rear half of the dangerous semicircle, but never in the forward half of the dangerous semicircle. It has been reported that when the wind reaches hurricane speed and the seas become confused, some ships ride out the storm best if the engines are stopped, and the vessel is left to seek its own position, or lie ahull. In this way, it is said, the ship rides with the storm instead of fighting against it.

In a sailing vessel attempting to avoid a storm center, one should steer courses as near as possible to those prescribed above for power vessels. However, if it becomes necessary for such a vessel to heave to, the wind is of greater concern than the sea. A good general rule always is to heave to on whichever tack permits the shifting wind to draw aft. In the Northern Hemisphere, this is the starboard tack in the dangerous semicircle, and the port tack in the less dangerous semicircle. In the Southern Hemisphere these are reversed.

While each storm requires its own analysis, and frequent or continual resurvey of the situation, the general rules for a steamer may be summarized as follows:

Northern Hemisphere

Right or dangerous semicircle: Bring the wind on the starboard bow (045° relative), hold course and make as much way as possible. If necessary, heave to with head to the sea.

Left or less dangerous semicircle: Bring the wind on the starboard quarter (135° relative), hold course and make as much way as possible. If necessary, heave to with stern to the sea.

On storm track, ahead of center: Bring the wind 2 points on the starboard quarter (about 160° relative), hold course and make as much way as possible. When well within the less dangerous semicircle, maneuver as indicated above.

On storm track, behind center: Avoid the center by the best practicable course, keeping in mind the tendency of tropical cyclones to curve northward and eastward.

Southern Hemisphere

Left or dangerous semicircle: Bring the wind on the port bow (315° relative), hold course and make as much way as possible. If necessary, heave to with head to the sea.

Right or less dangerous semicircle: Bring the wind on the port quarter (225° relative), hold course and make as much way as possible. If necessary, heave to with stern to the sea.

On storm track, ahead of center: Bring the wind about 200° relative, hold course and make as much way as possible. When well within the less dangerous semicircle, maneuver as indicated above.

On storm track, behind center: Avoid the center by the best practicable course, keeping in mind the tendency of tropical cyclones to curve southward and eastward.

It is possible, particularly in temperate latitudes after the storm has recurved, that the dangerous semicircle is the left one in the Northern Hemisphere (right one in the Southern Hemisphere). This can occur if a large high lies north of the storm and causes a tightening of the pressure gradient in the region.

The Typhoon Havens Handbook for the Western Pacific and Indian Oceans is published by the Naval Oceanographic and Atmospheric Research Lab (NOARL) Monterey, California, as an aid to captains and commanding officers of ships in evaluating a typhoon situation, and to assist them in deciding whether to sortie, to evade, to remain in port, or to head for the shelter of a specific harbor.

Consequences of Cyclones

High Winds and Flooding

The high winds of a tropical cyclone inflict widespread damage when such a storm leaves the ocean and crosses land. Aids to navigation may be blown out of position or destroyed. Craft in harbors, often lifted by the storm surge, break moorings or drag anchor and are blown ashore and against obstructions. Ashore, trees are blown over, houses are damaged, power lines are blown down, etc. The greatest damage usually occurs in the dangerous semicircle a short distance from the center, where the strongest winds occur. As the storm continues on across land, its fury subsides faster than it would if it had remained over water.

Wind instruments are usually incapable of measuring the 175 to 200 knot winds of the more intense hurricanes. Even if the instrument holds up, often the supporting structure is destroyed. Doppler radar may be effective in determining wind speeds, but may also be blown away.

Wind gusts, which are usually 30 to 50 percent higher than sustained winds, add significantly to the destruc-tiveness of the tropical cyclone. Many tropical cyclones that reach hurricane intensity develop winds of more than 90 knots sometime during their lives, but few develop winds of more than 130 knots.

Tropical cyclones have produced some of the world's heaviest rainfalls. While average amounts range from 6 to 10 inches, totals near 100 inches over a 4-day period have been observed. A 24-hour world's record of 73.62 inches fell at Reunion Island during a tropical cyclone in 1952. Forward movement of the storm and land topography have a considerable influence on rainfall totals. Torrential rains can occur when a storm moves against a mountain range; this is common in the Philippines and Japan, where even weak tropical depressions produce considerable rainfall. A 24-hour total of 46 inches was recorded in the Philippines during a typhoon in 1911. As hurricane Camille crossed southern Virginia's Blue Ridge Mountains in August of 1969, there was nearly 30 inches of rain in about 8 hours. This caused some of the most disastrous floods in the state's history.

Flooding is an extremely destructive by-product of the tropical cyclone's torrential rains. Whether an area will be flooded depends on the physical characteristics of the drainage basin, rate and accumulation of precipitation, and river stages at the time the rains begin. When heavy rains fall over flat terrain, the countryside may lie under water for a month or so, and while buildings, furnishings, and underground power lines may be damaged, there are usually few fatalities. In mountainous or hill country, disastrous floods develop rapidly and can cause a great loss of life.

There have been occasional reports in tropical cyclones of waves greater than 40 feet in height, and numerous reports in the 30- to 40-foot category. However, in tropical cyclones, strong winds rarely persist for a sufficiently long time or over a large enough area to permit enormous wave heights to develop. The direction and speed of the wind changes more rapidly in tropical cyclones than in extratropical storms. Thus, the maximum duration and fetch for any wind condition is often less in tropical cyclones than in extratropical storms, and the waves accompanying any given local wind conditions are generally not so high as those expected, with similar local wind conditions, in the high-latitude storms. In hurricane Camille, significant waves of 43 feet were recorded; an extreme wave height reached 72 feet.

Exceptional conditions may arise when waves of certain dimensions travel within the storm at a speed equal to the storm's speed, thus, in effect, extending the duration and fetch of the wave and significantly increasing its height. This occurs most often to the right of the track in the Northern Hemisphere (left of the track in the Southern Hemisphere). Another condition that may give rise to exceptional wave heights is the intersection of waves from two or more distinct directions. This may lead to a zone of confused seas in which the heights of some waves will equal the sums of each individual wave train. This process can occur in any quadrant of the storm, so it should not be assumed that the highest waves will always be encountered to the right of the storm track in the Northern Hemisphere (left of the track in the Southern Hemisphere).

When these waves move beyond the influence of the generating winds, they become known as swell. They are recognized by their smooth, undulating form, in contrast to the steep, ragged crests of wind waves. This swell, particularly that generated by the right side of the storm, can travel a thousand miles or more and may produce tides 3 or 4 feet above normal along several hundred miles of coastline. It may also produce tremendous surf over offshore reefs which normally are calm.

When a tropical cyclone moves close to a coast, wind often causes a rapid rise in water level, and along with the falling pressure may produce a storm surge. This surge is usually confined to the right of the track in the Northern Hemisphere (left of the track in the Southern Hemisphere) and to a relatively small section of the coastline. It most often occurs with the approach of the storm, but in some cases, where a surge moves into a long channel, the effect may be delayed. Occasionally, the greatest rise in water is observed on the opposite side of the track, when northerly winds funnel into a partially landlocked harbor. The surge could be 3 feet or less, or it could be 20 feet or more, depending on the combination of factors involved.

There have been reports of a "hurricane wave," described as a "wall of water," which moves rapidly toward the coastline. Authenticated cases are rare, but some of the world's greatest natural disasters have occurred as a result of this wave, which may be a rapidly rising and abnormally high storm surge. In India, such a disaster occurred in 1876, between Calcutta and Chittagong, and drowned more than 100,000 persons.

Along the coast, greater damage may be inflicted by water than by the wind. There are at least four sources of water damage. First, the unusually high seas generated by the storm winds pound against shore installations and craft in their way. Second, the continued blowing of the wind toward land causes the water level to increase perhaps 3 to 10 feet above its normal level. This storm tide, which may begin when the storm center is 500 miles or even farther from the shore, gradually increases until the storm passes. The highest storm tides are caused by a slow-moving tropical cyclone of large diameter, because both of these effects result in greater duration of wind in the same direction.

The effect is greatest in a partly enclosed body of water, such as the Gulf of Mexico, where the concave coastline does not readily permit the escape of water. It is least on small islands, which present little obstruction to the flow of water. Third, the furious winds which blow around the wall of the eye create a ridge of water called a storm wave, which strikes the coast and often inflicts heavy damage. The effect is similar to that of a seismic sea wave, caused by an earthquake in the ocean floor. Both of these waves are popularly called tidal waves. Storm waves of 20 feet or more have occurred.

About 3 or 4 feet of this wave might be due to the decrease in atmospheric pressure as the sea surface is drawn up into the low pressure area, and the rest to winds. Like the damage caused by wind, damage due to high seas, the storm surge and tide, and the storm wave is greatest in the dangerous semicircle, near the center. The fourth source of water damage is the heavy rain that accompanies a tropical cyclone. This causes floods that add to the damage caused in other ways.

There have been many instances of tornadoes occurring within the circulation of tropical cyclones. Most of these have been associated with tropical cyclones of the North Atlantic Ocean and have occurred in the West Indies and along the gulf and Atlantic coasts of the United States. They are usually observed in the forward semicircle or along the advancing periphery of the storm. These tornadoes are usually short-lived and less intense than those that occur in the midwestern United States.

When proceeding along a shore recently visited by a tropical cyclone, a navigator should remember that time is required to restore aids to navigation which have been blown out of position or destroyed. In some instances the aid may remain but its light, sound apparatus, or radiobeacon may be inoperative. Landmarks may have been damaged or destroyed, and in some instances the coastline and hydrography may be changed.

References

Clark Evans (January 5, 2006). "Favorable trough interactions on tropical cyclones". Flhurricane.com. Retrieved 2006-10-20.

Erik A. Rasmussen and John Turner (2003). *Polar lows: mesoscale weather systems in the polar regions*. Cambridge University Press.

Kerry Emanuel (January 2006). "Anthropogenic Effects on Tropical Cyclone Activity". Massachusetts Institute of Technology. Retrieved 2008-02-25.

Nina A. Zaitseva (2006). "Cyclogenesis". National Snow and Ice Data Center. Retrieved 2006-12-04.

Raymond D. Menard, and J.M. Fritsch (June 1989). "A Mesoscale Convective Complex-Generated Inertially Stable Warm Core Vortex".*Monthly Weather Review* 117 (6): 1237–1261.

Ryan N. Maue (2008). "Chapter 3: Cyclone Paradigms and Extratropical Transition Conceptualizations". Florida State University.

4

Drought Management

A drought is an extended period of months or years when a region notes a deficiency in its water supply whether surface or underground water. Generally, this occurs when a region receives consistently below average precipitation. It can have a substantial impact on the ecosystem and agriculture of the affected region. Although droughts can persist for several years, even a short, intense drought can cause significant damage and harm the local economy. Many plant species, such as cacti, have adaptations such as reduced leaf area and waxy cuticles to enhance their ability to tolerate drought. Some others survive dry periods as buried seeds. Semi-permanent drought produces arid biomes such as deserts and grasslands. Most arid ecosystems have inherently low productivity.

This global phenomenon has a widespread impact on agriculture. Lengthy periods of drought have long been a key trigger for mass migration and played a key role in a number of ongoing migrations and other humanitarian crises in the Horn of Africa and the Sahel.

Periods of drought can have significant environmental, agricultural, health, economic and social consequences. The effect varies according to vulnerability. For example, subsistence farmers are more likely to migrate during drought because they do not have alternative food sources. Areas with populations that depend on as a major food source are more vulnerable to drought-triggered famine. Drought can also reduce water quality, because lower water flows reduce dilution of pollutants and increase contamination of remaining water sources. Common consequences of drought include:

— Diminished crop growth or yield productions and carrying capacity for livestock
— Dust bowls, themselves a sign of erosion, which further erode the landscape
— Dust storms, when drought hits an area suffering from desertification and erosion
— Famine due to lack of water for irrigation
— Habitat damage, affecting both terrestrial and aquatic wildlife
— Malnutrition, dehydration and related diseases
— Mass migration, resulting in internal displacement and international refugees
— Reduced electricity production due to reduced water flow through hydroelectric dams
— Shortages of water for industrial users
— Snake migration and increases in snakebites
— Social unrest
— War over natural resources, including water and food
— Wildfires, such as Australian bushfires, are more common during times of drought.

Drought is a normal, recurring feature of the climate in most parts of the world. It is among the earliest documented climatic events, present in the Epic of Gilgamesh and tied to the biblical story of Joseph's arrival in and the later Exodus from Ancient Egypt. Hunter-gatherer migrations in 9,500 BC Chile have been linked to the phenomenon, as has the exodus of early humans out of Africa and into the rest of the world around 135,000 years ago.

Modern people can effectively mitigate much of the impact of drought through irrigation and crop rotation. Failure to develop adequate drought mitigation strategies carries a grave human cost in the modern era, exacerbated by ever-increasing population densities.

Recurring droughts leading to desertification in the Horn of Africa have created grave ecological catastrophes, prompting massive food shortages, still recurring. To the north-west of the Horn, the Darfur conflict in neighboring Sudan, also affecting Chad, was fueled by decades of drought;

combination of drought, desertification and overpopulation are among the causes of the Darfur conflict, because the Arab Baggara nomads searching for water have to take their livestock further south, to land mainly occupied by non-Arab farming peoples.

Approximately 2.4 billion people live in the drainage basin of the Himalayan rivers. India, China, Pakistan, Bangladesh, Nepal and Myanmar could experience floods followed by droughts in coming decades. Drought in India affecting the Ganges is of particular concern, as it provides drinking water and agricultural irrigation for more than 500 million people. The west coast of North America, which gets much of its water from glaciers in mountain ranges such as the Rocky Mountains and Sierra Nevada, also would be affected.

In 2005, parts of the Amazon basin experienced the worst drought in 100 years. A 23 July 2006 article reported Woods Hole Research Center results showing that the forest in its present form could survive only three years of drought. Scientists at the Brazilian National Institute of Amazonian Research argue in the article that this drought response, coupled with the effects of deforestation on regional climate, are pushing the rainforest towards a "tipping point" where it would irreversibly start to die. It concludes that the rainforest is on the brink of being turned into savanna or desert, with catastrophic consequences for the world's climate. According to the WWF, the combination of climate change and deforestation increases the drying effect of dead trees that fuels forest fires.

By far the largest part of Australia is desert or semi-arid lands commonly known as the outback. A 2005 study by Australian and American researchers investigated the desertification of the interior, and suggested that one explanation was related to human settlers who arrived about 50,000 years ago. Regular burning by these settlers could have prevented monsoons from reaching interior Australia. In June 2008 it became known that an expert panel had warned of long term, maybe irreversible, severe ecological damage for the whole Murray-Darling basin if it does not receive sufficient water by October. Australia could experience more severe droughts and they could become more frequent in the future, a government-commissioned report said on July 6, 2008. Australian environmentalist Tim Flannery, predicted that unless it made drastic changes, Perth in Western Australia could become the world's first ghost metropolis, an abandoned city with no more water to sustain its population.

East Africa currently faces its worst drought in decades, with crops and livestock destroyed. The U.N. World Food Programme recently said that nearly four million Kenyans urgently needed food.

CAUSES

Generally, rainfall is related to the amount and dew point of water vapour carried by regional atmosphere, combined with the upward forcing of the air mass containing that water vapour. If these combined factors do not support precipitation volumes sufficient to reach the surface, the result is a drought. This can be triggered by high levels of reflected sunlight, and above average prevalence of high pressure systems, winds carrying continental, rather than oceanic air masses (i.e. reduced water content), and ridges of high pressure areas form with behaviors which prevent or restrict the developing of thunderstorm activity or rainfall over one certain region. Oceanic and atmospheric weather cycles such as the El Niño-Southern Oscillation (ENSO) make drought a regular recurring feature of the Americas along the Midwest and Australia. Guns, Germs, and Steel author Jared Diamond sees the stark impact of the multi-year ENSO cycles on Australian weather patterns as a key reason that Australian aborigines remained a hunter-gatherer society rather than adopting agriculture. Another climate oscillation known as the North Atlantic Oscillation has been tied to droughts in northeast Spain.

Human activity can directly trigger exacerbating factors such as over farming, excessive irrigation, deforestation, and erosion adversely impact the ability of the land to capture and hold water. While these tend to be relatively isolated in their scope, activities resulting in global climate change are expected to trigger droughts with a substantial impact on agriculture throughout the world, and especially in developing nations. Overall, global warming will result in increased world rainfall. Along with drought in some areas, flooding and erosion will increase in others. Paradoxically, some proposed solutions to global warming that focus on more active techniques, solar radiation management through the use of a space sunshade for one, may also carry with them increased chances of drought.

Causes of Reduced Rainfall

When discussing the causes of drought it is helpful to distinguish between short drought episodes lasting 1-3 years and long dry regimes of predominantly subnormal rainfall spanning about a decade or more and, which may, include several intense drought episodes.

The proximate or immediate cause of a rainfall shortage may be due to one or more factors including an absence of available moisture in the atmosphere; large scale subsidence which suppresses convective activity; and the absence or non-arrival of rain-bearing systems. Changes in such factors involve changes in weather systems on many spatial scales ranging from local to regional to global. While it may be possible to indicate the immediate cause of a meteorological drought occurring in any particular location, it is often not possible to indicate the underlying cause.

Short term episodes can often be linked to global-scale fluctuations in the atmosphere and oceans elsewhere in the world. For example, the El Niño/ Southern Oscillation (ENSO) phenomenon, which involves the periodic invasion of warm surface water into the normally colder waters off the Pacific coast of South America, affects the levels of rainfall in many different parts of the world, including south-eastern Africa. However, knowledge about causes of the invasion of the warmer currents is presently incomplete.

On a larger scale, the link between sea surface temperatures and rainfall has been suggested as a possible cause of long dry regimes. Thus it has been suggested that the fact that the southern Atlantic has been consistently warmer than the northern Atlantic since around 1970 is related to the predominantly dry period in the Sahel since the mid-1960s.

Increasing levels of carbon dioxide and other "greenhouse" gasses have been suggested as causes of rainfall changes in the Sahel and elsewhere. However, as with all the postulated causes there is insufficient understanding of the physical processes involved to state with certainty that the postulations are correct.

Many causes of long dry "regime" have been postulated. Among the local level causes are human-induced changes resulting from vegetation loss due to overgrazing and deforestation either in the general vicinity or "upwind" of the area along the line of the prevailing, moisture carrying winds. Such changes may involve "biogeophysical" feedback mechanisms, i.e. once they start, they feed back on themselves and perpetuate the drought conditions.

However, one of the main problems with the postulations involving human induced change is that of distinguishing human induced change from natural long term fluctuations. For instance, there would seem to be a 50 year fluctuation in rainfall in the western Sahel with the predominantly dry period since the mid-1960s being part of such a cycle. However, reliable rainfall data for the Sahel and many other parts of the world are available only for the last 80-90 years, and this is too short a period to support the assertion that there is such a rainfall cycle in the area. The World Meteorological Office believes that five or six such cycles are necessary to confidently predict trends. Clearly however, land use patterns which result in environmental degradation, desertification, and deforestation are inextricably linked in a causal way to drought.

Types of Drought

As a drought persists, the conditions surrounding it gradually worsen and its impact on the local population gradually increases. People tend to define droughts in three main ways:

1. *Meteorological drought* is brought about when there is a prolonged period with less than average precipitation. Meteorological drought usually precedes the other kinds of drought.
2. *Agricultural droughts* are droughts that affect crop production or the ecology of the range. This condition can also arise independently from any change in precipitation levels when soil conditions and erosion triggered by poorly planned agricultural endeavors cause a shortfall in water available to the crops. However, in a traditional drought, it is caused by an extended period of below average precipitation.
3. *Hydrological drought* is brought about when the water reserves available in sources such as aquifers, lakes and reservoirs fall below the statistical average. Hydrological drought tends to show up more slowly because it involves stored water that is used but not replenished. Like an agricultural drought, this can be triggered by more than just a loss of rainfall. For instance, Kazakhstan was recently awarded a large amount of money by the World Bank to restore water that had been diverted to other nations from the Aral Sea under Soviet rule. Similar circumstances also place their largest lake, Balkhash, at risk of completely drying out.

It is conventional practice to distinguish between three different types of drought, namely meteorological, hydrological and agricultural. Particularly in the case of meteorological and agricultural droughts, these types are frequently, but wrongly, seen as being synonymous. Of the three types of drought, the first two describe the physical event whereas the third describes the particular impact of the first two on agricultural production. It is necessary to carefully distinguish between these types and clarify where and how they overlap.

Water used in support of human activity is derived from either direct rainfall or previous rainfall which is temporarily "stored" in rivers lakes, groundwater aquifers and snowfields/glaciers. In the case of some aquifers and glaciers, such "stores" may contain rain that fell decades or even centuries before. A temporary reduction of either of these two main types of water source may cause a drought.

Meteorological drought describes a situation where there is a reduction in rainfall for a specified period below a specified amount—usually defined as some proportion of the long term average for the specified time period. Its definition involves only precipitation statistics.

Hydrological drought involves a reduction in water resources below a specified level for a given period of time. Its definition involves data on availability and offtake rates in relation to the normal requirements of the system being supplied.

The distinction between the two types can often be blurred as hydrological droughts may be caused by reductions in precipitation anywhere within the catchment area of the river or aquifer system. Thus, irrigated agricultural areas alongside the River Nile in Egypt may experience a hydrological drought as a result of a meteorological drought in the Ethiopian Highlands regardless of the levels of rainfall within Egypt itself.

In the case of rivers fed by snowmelt, irrigated areas downstream may experience reduced water availability as a result of reduced snowmelt caused by below normal temperatures during the summer months. Areas drawing water from underground aquifers through wells and boreholes may experience hydrological drought as a result of geological changes which cut off parts of the aquifer. Overutilization of the aquifer may also result in its exhaustion.

Agricultural drought is the impact of meteorological and/or hydrological droughts on crop yields. Crops have particular temperature, moisture and nutrient requirements during their growth cycle in order to achieve optimum growth. If moisture availability falls below the required amount during the growth cycle then crop growth will be impaired and yields reduced. However, droughts have different impacts on different crops, e.g. sesame often thrives in dry years. Because of the complexity of the relationships involved, agricultural drought is difficult to measure. A fall in yields may be due to insufficient moisture but it may also stem from, or have been exacerbated by, such factors as the unavailability of fertilizers, lack of weeding, the presence of pests and crop diseases, the lack of labour at critical periods in the growth cycle, and unattractive crop prices. Also these factors can interact with each other and exacerbate conditions. For example, in the 1984 drought in Ethiopia, the drought contributed to army worm infestation which substantially increased the amount of crop damage.

Factors Affecting the Severity of Drought

While it is usually true that decreased rainfall results in decreased crop yields, the following factors influence the strength of the relationship.

Proportion of Production which is Irrigated

The correlation between rainfall and yields is weaker in irrigated rather than rainfed areas. The extent to which this is the case however, will be determined by the importance of local rainfall in the irrigated water supply and whether all or only part of the crops' moisture requirements are normally met through irrigation.

Moisture Retention Capacity of the Soil

Different soil types have different capacities to "hold" or retain moisture. For instance the water retention capacity of sandy soils is generally significantly lower than that of clay soils. In areas Where soil moisture retention capacities are high, crop growth may not be affected by prolonged dry periods (as much as 20 days) and some moisture may actually be held over from one wet season to another.In contrast, in areas where retention capacity is low, dry periods of only a week may result in reduced yields and moisture present in the soil at the end of one season will not last to the next. In many arid and semi-arid areas of the tropics the predominant soil types are sandy. To attain optimum crop growth such areas need frequent and evenly spaced rainfall throughout the growing season.National soil surveys are available for most countries, either from the Ministry of Agriculture or the local FAO office. Geography departments at local universities frequently have information on soil types and characteristics.

Timeliness of the Rainfall

Deficiencies in moisture supply at critical stages during the growth cycle (e.g. germination and flowering) can significantly reduce yields. Consequently the distribution or timeliness of the rainfall during the growing season is potentially as important as the overall amount of rain.

Because of the importance of timeliness, particularly in semi-arid areas where soil moisture retention capacity is low, rainfall must be described and analysed in appropriately short time periods so that prolonged dry periods are not "hidden" within aggregate monthly figures which may indicate that rainfall has been around or even above the average.

Models for different types of crops indicate the moisture requirements for optimum crop growth. In some countries such "moisture satisfaction" models are used to produce forecasts, at different stages within the normal growing season, of crop yield on the basis of rainfall occurring during the cycle. As part of the FAO's program of strengthening the early warning capacity within countries prone to drought and transitory food insecurity, such agro-meteorological analytical capacity is being developed within Ministries of Agriculture and Meteorological Departments.

In the face of an intermittent start to a wet season, some farmers may respond with repeated replantings of the same crop variety to take account of the rains when, and if, they finally start, while others may replant using other seed varieties. Some farmers may not have seed reserves of their own or be in a position to purchase replacement seeds for the first, failed planting. In this situation some farmers may experience a crop failure while others in the same area are enjoying a satisfactory harvest. Information on farmer behaviour in the face of late or inadequate rains may be available from the Extension Services Departments within Ministries of Agriculture.

While it might appear attractive for all agencies to adopt a standard operational definition of drought, such a definition is likely to prove both elusive and unnecessarily restrictive. To determine, for instance, that "an area should qualify as being drought affected when its rainfall falls below 70% of the average for the previous 20 years" is not particularly useful if most of the area's agriculture is irrigated. Moreover the cut-off chosen is arbitrary and may exclude areas experiencing "classic" drought impacts as a result of average but poorly spaced rainfall. Standardized definitions cannot take account of the wide variations in vulnerability to the effects of drought as a result of wider variations in physical, economic and social conditions between areas and countries.

Impact of Droughts

Of all the natural hazards, droughts are potentially those having the greatest economic impact and affecting the greatest number of people. Earthquakes and cyclones may be of enormous physical intensity but are invariably of short duration and geographically limited. By contrast droughts affect large geographical areas, often covering whole countries or parts of continents and may last for several months and, in some cases, several years.

Of the main natural disasters, droughts are unique in terms of the length of time between the first indications from, for example, rainfall monitoring, that a drought is developing and the point at which it begins to impact significantly upon the population of the affected area. The length of such "warning time" varies significantly between societies.

In many countries the warning time is on the order of several months. In others, for instance those with a high proportion of landless agricultural labourers, the warning time may be much less, perhaps only a few weeks. Whatever the period, a warning time allows for a potential response to mitigate the impacts of the drought before they become significant. In the case of countries where the lead time is on the order of months there is, potentially at least, sufficient time for relief assistance, including food aid, from the international community to be mobilized.

Thus, by virtue of modern meteorological monitoring and telecommunication systems it has become possible to prevent excess mortality resulting from food shortages caused by drought alone. While droughts may continue to be a contributory cause of famines, other factors such as armed conflict and international politics, are now invariably responsible for propelling a situation of economic hardship caused by drought into a famine.

Droughts, almost or virtually always, have a direct and significant impact on food production and the overall economy. The impact on a particular populations is related to the severity and nature of the drought, but equally, and occasionally more importantly, to the nature of the economy and society in the affected area.

First consider an extreme example. Two semi-arid countries experience a 50% reduction in annual rainfall. Country A is a high income economy where agriculture contributes only 10% of the total Gross Domestic Product (GDP) and water for industry, agriculture and domestic use is drawn form reliable underground aquifers. Country B is a low income economy where agriculture is primarily rainfed and contributes 50% of total GDP. Clearly the drought impacts on Country A are likely to be negligible whereas for Country B they are likely to be severe.

The scenario becomes more interesting if the assumption about the reliability of the underground aquifers in Country A is altered so that water is drawn from rivers and reservoirs whose catchment area is affected by the reduction in rainfall—a hydrological drought. Likely impacts include reduced agricultural and industrial production, increased unemployment, domestic water rationing, increased cost of living, increased investment in the exploitation of alternative water resources and so on.

However, by virtue of its grater wealth Country A will still probably be able to cope by purchasing imported food to make up for any domestic production losses and providing compensation to those most seriously affected. Thus, the level and distribution of wealth and how the economy is structured are central to any consideration of the nature and severity of drought impacts.

Social and organizational considerations are also important. Two countries with similarly structured economies and levels of wealth may be affected quite differently by droughts of similar severity as a result of:

1. The extent to which the drought hazard is taken account of in resource allocation decisions by households—planting and consumption/saving decisions
   - *Communities*—construction of dams with reserve capacity, organization of local food stores, and investment in alternative water sources
   - *Governments*—encouragement of research on drought-resistant crop varieties, creation of administrative procedures to respond to drought, and investment in additional transport and storage capacity.
2. The extent to which social and political institutions encourage the recognition of the hazard and a rapid and effective response to it when a drought does occur is also critical. For instance, the existence of a free press, accessible administrative systems, open public debate and

representative political systems are increasingly recognized to be important factors determining the effectiveness of the response to droughts by national governments.

Bearing in mind the variations between economies and societies noted above, the following list of potential economic and social impacts of an agricultural drought may be helpful. The list is neither exhaustive nor comprehensive but is intended to illustrate some of the possible outcomes of drought. Potential information sources on the impacts are noted in brackets.

— Reduced income for farmers and agricultural labourers.

— Reduced spending locally on agricultural inputs and equipment and non-agricultural items and services like travel and non-subsistence foods.

— Decrease in price of livestock as farmers are forced to sell because of increases in the cost of pasture and purchased feeds.

— Increased price of staple foods.

— Inability of certain groups within the population to afford increased food prices results in their:

  — switch to cheaper and sometimes less preferred foods

  — reduction in overall food intake

  — borrowing to maintain food intake

  — selling assets to raise funds

  — engaging in alternative income earning activities locally

  — migrating in search of employment opportunities

  — migration to where relief food is being distributed.

— Reduced food intake leads to deterioration of nutritional status and reduction in ability to resist infection.

— Difficult and scarce availability of water results in a general increase in diarrhoeas and other water/hygiene-related illnesses. Shortage of water and increased mobility of population increase the opportunities for transmission of epidemic diseases such as cholera; dry climatic conditions also facilitate the transmission of mening ococcal meningitis.

— Increased stress and morbidity results form migration journey.

— Drying-up of water sources leads to reduction in water quality, the need to travel further to collect water and possibly migration to better water sources.

— Increased competition for access to remaining water sources may lead to increased incidence of local disputes/conflict.

— Loss of basic services, such as rural area health posts and schools which stop functioning because of lack of water.

Monitoring and Early Warning of Drought

All countries exposed to drought risks should set up a drought monitoring and management system. This system would provide an integrated approach to drought management, covering all the aspects of drought: early warning and forecasting, response, and mitigation. The monitoring and early warning / forecasting system is discussed below. Response and mitigation measures are discussed in subsequent sections. The development of such a system requires coordinated efforts on part of all the affected parties.

As drought is a slow-onset disaster, its monitoring and early warning systems are central to drought management. Drought preparedness and mitigation measures follow these initial steps in drought management. Early warning systems

1. Provide accurate, timely and integrated information on drought conditions at the level of regions, States and districts.
2. Detect drought early; it allows for activation of the drought management plan and evokes both proactive (mitigation) and reactive (emergency) responses.
3. Provide information on all the parameters of drought at the relevant spatial scale to the policy-makers, administrators, NGOs, and citizens. The decision support which the DEWS provides can minimize the economic, social and ecosystem losses associated with drought.
4. Consist of information on a number of variables, such as climate data, soil moisture, stream flow, groundwater, and lake and reservoir levels.
5. Require gathering and integration of existing data as well as seeking new information through State and national networks. It also requires a network of scientific institutions to maintain the physical observing system, collect and analyse the data, and to synthesize the information on drought impacts. For instance, it is necessary to collect and analyse

information on stream flow, lake and reservoir levels, and groundwater status, as drought revolves around the supply of and demand for water.

The early warning system should function at three levels:

1. Receiving forecasts, early warning, and advisories from scientific institutions;
2. Monitoring key drought indices at the National and State levels; and
3. Developing composite index of various drought indicators.

Drogut Monitoring and Early Warning in India

Several institutions in the country provide drought early warning through their long and medium-term forecasts.

Role of India Meteorological Department

The India Meteorological Department (IMD) is the designated agency for providing drought early warning and forecasting. IMD predicted the first scientific monsoon in 1886.

IMD identifies meteorological drought for subdivisions every year based on rainfall analysis. During the past 125 years, IMD has identified meteorological droughts (moderate or severe) over meteorological subdivisions of the country using IMD criteria and also drought years for the country as a whole. And, there have been many refinements in the models and techniques applied by the IMD for weather forecast, from time to time. IMD forecasts drought on the following bases:

— Long-range forecasts of seasonal total rainfall for the entire country, which are done be fore onset and at the beginning of the monsoon. Long-range forecast techniques require further development, for resolution on a smaller spatial and temporal scale.

— Rainfall summaries are compiled weekly giving figures of precipitation at the district level. IMD collects its rainfall data, using a network of 2,800 rain gauge stations distributed across 36 meteorological sub-divisions of the country.

IMD monitors agricultural drought once every two weeks on a real-time basis during the main crop seasons (kharif and rabi) of India. For this, an aridity anomaly index developed on the lines of Thornthwaite's concept is used to monitor the incidence, spread, intensification, and recession of drought.

Aridity anomaly reports are prepared for the country as a whole during the south-west monsoon season and for 6 sub-divisions (Coastal Andhra Pradesh, Rayalaseema, South Interior Karnataka, Tamil Nadu, Pondicherry, and Kerala) during the north-east monsoon season. These anomaly reports are widely circulated to various users, such as Agromet Advisory Services, the agricultural departments of State Governments, agricultural universities, and the National Remote Sensing Centre in Hyderabad.

Agricultural Meteorology Division

The Agricultural Meteorology Division, a specialized division of the IMD, is based in Pune, and has a wide network of agro-meteorological observatories, which generate various kinds of data on agro-meteorological parameters.

The Division, in coordination with the respective State agricultural departments, issues weekly/bi-weekly Agromet Advisory Bulletins from 17 agro-meteorological advisory service units located at State Meteorological Centres (SMCs) / Regional Meteorological Centres (RMCs).

The Division provides timely advice on the actual and expected weather, and its likely impact on the various day-to-day farming operations. Short-range forecasts valid for 12 to 24 hours and then extended to the following 2 to 3 days are used extensively to provide this advice. Secondly, agro-meteorological forecasts extending over a week or 10 days are very important from the users' perspective as well as for planning various agricultural operations and strategies.

Drought Research Unit

The Drought Research Unit, set up at IMD, Pune in 1967, provides Crop Yield Forecasts (CYFs). This unit has developed pre-harvest crop yield forecasting models and issues statewise monthly crop yield and countrywide total production forecasts for the major crops kharif (rice) and rabi (wheat) crops, based on agro-meteorological models.

Pre-harvest CYFs are issued for 15 States comprising 26 meteorological sub-divisions for kharif (rice) and 12 States comprising 16 meteorological subdivisions for rabi (wheat), and also for the total rice / wheat production of the country. The forecasts are supplied to the Directorate of Economics and Statistics, Ministry of Agriculture. The first interim forecast for kharif rice is issued in August and the final forecast is given in November/

December. For wheat, the first interim forecast is issued in January and the final in March/April/May.

National Centre for Medium Range Weather Forecasting

In January 1988, the Government of India approved the establishment of the National Centre for Medium Range Weather Forecasting (NCMRWF) as a constituent unit of the Department of Science and Technology (DST) to help develop suitable numerical weather prediction (NWP) models for medium-range weather forecasts and prepare agro-meteorological advisories for the farming community in 127 agro-climatic zones of India.

The NCMRWF, in collaboration with the IMD, Indian Council of Agricultural Research (ICAR), and State Agricultural Universities (SAUs), provides agro-meteorological advisory service at the scale of agro-climatic zones to the farming community, based on location-specific medium-range weather forecasts.

NCMRWF disseminates weather forecasts to these units for their respective zones and agricultural scientists of the concerned stations prepare advisories for the farmers which are then disseminated to the users through mass media, personal contact, extension personnel, etc. These bulletins are issued twice a week at most of these stations. Agro-meteorological advisory units also provide local agro-meteorological data and farmers' feedback on the advisories.

Central Research Institute for Dryland Agriculture

The Central Research Institute for Dryland Agriculture (CRIDA) in Hyderabad and the All India Coordinated Research Projects on Agri-meteorology and Dryland Agriculture (AICRPAM and AICRPDA), each having 25 centres under SAUs across the country take part in drought studies pertaining to assessment, mitigation, risk transfer, and development of decision support software for drought-prone States.

Central Arid Zone Research Institute

The Central Arid Zone Research Institute (CAZRI), in Jodhpur acts as repository of information on the status of natural resources and desertification processes and their control. It maintains 6 agro-meteorological observatories in their research stations at Jodhpur, Jaisalmer, Chandan, Bikaner, Pali, and Bhopalgarh.

Besides, the CAZRI shares rainfall records of 100 rain gauge stations with the Rajasthan Irrigation Department and also with the IMD network of meteorological stations for assessing agricultural drought situation in 12 arid districts of western Rajasthan. It has developed a crop moisture index to monitor the drought situation. The Institute disseminates bi-weekly crop-weather agro-advisory bulletins to the farmers and other agencies through media and a feedback on the economic impact of these advisories also are obtained from the farmers.

Ministry of Earth Sciences

Ministry of Earth Sciences in collaboration with ICAR has set up 89 centres for short and medium-range monitoring and forecasting of the weather.

National Agricultural Drought Assessment and Monitoring System

The National Agricultural Drought Assessment and Monitoring System (NADAMS) developed by the Department of Space for the Department of Agriculture and Co-operation, primarily monitors the vegetation through National Oceanic and Atmospheric Administration (NOAA) Advanced Very High Resolution Radiometer (AVHHR) data. Drought assessment is based on a comparative evaluation of satellite observed green vegetation cover (both area and greenness) of a district in any specific time period, with that of any similar period in previous years. This comparative evaluation helps in fixing the current season in the scale of historic agricultural situations.

Institutional Mechanism for Drought Monitoring and Early Warning at the National and State Levels

The Central and State Governments should set up institutional mechanisms for drought monitoring and mechanism at the national and State levels. At present, these functions are carried out by inter-departmental agencies and scientific institutions listed above.

Considering the frequency and impact of drought, these mechanisms are not adequate for meeting the demands of drought management. The existing and proposed institutional arrangements for drought management at the national and State levels are described below:

Crop Weather Watch Group

The Government of India acts upon the information, data and early warnings of the IMD through an inter-ministerial mechanism of Crop Weather Watch

Group (CWWG), which works as part of the Ministry of Agriculture. The CWWG meets once a week during the rainy season (June to September) and the frequency of their meetings increases during drought occurrence. The CWWG evaluates information and data furnished by the IMD and other scientific and technical bodies with a view to determine the likely impacts of meteorological events and other environmental parameters on agriculture.

National and state drought monitoring centres

The Central and State Governments should consider setting up a monitoring mechanism at their respective levels in "Drought Monitoring Centres". These centres would consolidate the forecasts, advisories and bulletins emanating from all the scientific institutions at the national level or in the States, as required, analyse these inputs, and disseminate the data and advisories through various media channels (radio, television, internet and newspapers). The centres would serve as the institutional support for drought monitoring and management, and recommend short-term and long-term measures to alleviate drought distress.

These drought monitoring centres would work closely with drought early warning agencies such as the IMD and the Ministries / Departments dealing with relief and disaster management, agriculture, water conservation, water supply, and animal husbandry. It would have the capacity to interpret remote sensing data, use Geographic Information System (GIS) software to prepare maps and maintain a database related to rainfall, agriculture, water level and other related indicators on a continuous basis. It would thus provide regular monitoring support to the Government at the National and State levels.

The centres would be staffed by a multi-disciplinary team of meteorologists, hydrologists and agriculture scientists and could work as autonomous bodies that network with other scientific institutions in the country and assist the Government in dealing with all aspects of drought management (i.e. early warning, response, and mitigation).

Drought Relief Measures

Following drought declaration, planning and implementation of drought relief and response measures is initiated. It is necessary that these measures are undertaken promptly, so that it would mitigate the hardships faced by the people. Though these measures are sector-specific, they require immense inter-departmental coordination. Implementing these measures would require a continuous flow of information from the village-level to the highest level of decision-making in the State and a responsive administrative structure. It would also require careful financial planning so that the implementation of these relief measures could be undertaken on a sustained basis.

Drought relief and response measures need to be planned and implemented as soon as the distress signs of drought are visible. These measures need not be linked to a formal drought declaration, which is necessary only for providing certain tax waivers and exemptions. Also, a Memorandum to the Government of India needs to be submitted only after the declaration of drought. All other measures could, therefore, be planned and implemented before drought declaration.

The State Government should direct all the districts to prepare a contingency plan for drought management as soon a drought situation arises. Such a contingency plan should include all the measures listed in each of the sector-specific responses. The local details may vary in these contingency plans. For example, certain States may prefer setting up fodder depots rather than cattle camps. It is necessary to evolve a consensus at the district level for implementing the contingency plan and seek a wider participation of the civil society.

Contingency Crop Planning

The crop contingency plans should

— be prepared well in advance before the start of kharif and rabi crop seasons. The State Government should prepare the contingency plan in consultation with the Ministry of Agriculture, Government of India and other expert agencies. This would require data inputs from the meteorological, agricultural and hydrological communities.

— be prepared agro-climatic region wise and separate plans laid down for all the three early-, mid- and late-season agricultural droughts.

— be revised every two to three years to take advantage of release of new crop varieties and to utilize the advances made in agricultural production technology.

— be activated based on assessment of type of drought received from early warning and forecasting systems and / or based on reports received from District Collectors.

— promote short duration and less water-intensive crops. Instead of crops like paddy and sugarcane, which consume a lot of water, alternate crops such as maize, pulses, groundnut, sunflower, soyabean, fodder, and vegetables could be grown.

— advocate crop diversification, mixed / inter-cropping of main crop with drought tolerant companion crop, thinning of plant population, weed management, mulching for soil moisture conservation and drip / spray irrigation.

— Prepare agro-advisory bulletins based on crop contingency plans and widely disseminate them among farmers in drought-affected region.

Table 1: Crop Contingency Plan

Crops affected due to inadequate rains	*Alternate crops*
Paddy	Gram, pulses, oilseeds, and fodder
Maize	Pulses and oilseeds
Cotton	Soyabean and pulses
Sugarcane	Pulses, fodder

Crop contingency plan during the kharif season is usually constrained by Uncertainty of climate behaviour during the kharif season; and Lack of lead-time causing logistical problems in organizing delivery of agricultural inputs.

There is a need to utilize spatial and temporal information on the pattern of monsoon variation from the past to improve the efficacy of contingency crop plans to minimize kharif crop losses.

It is necessary that the decision-makers get information on the likely monsoon behaviour even earlier than July to put contingency measures in place. While there are certain risks and uncertainties to respond to anomalous weather conditions in July, the confidence level for crop planning increases during pre-rabi and more certainly during rabi seasons. Better information on the extent of soil moisture and reservoir water levels can help the State Governments in issuing advisories for crop planning.

State Governments need to undertake intensive campaigns through mass media (such as radio, TV, newspapers) for spreading information on the contingency cropping plan. Posters and pamphlets should be published and distributed for educating the farmers about the need to change their crop plan. Water-user associations and self-help groups should be used for disseminating information on mid-season corrections and crop-life saving measures.

Support to Farmers

To undertake alternative cropping, farmers require additional public support (inputs, credit and extension) at higher than existing levels in a timely way, as mentioned below:

When a crop contingency plan is implemented, particularly during the kharif season, the lead time is very little. Farmers, therefore, need to be supported in a number of ways on an urgent basis:

— *Agriculture input support:* Farmers in drought-affected areas need to be provided with input subsidy of seeds and fertilizer for second sowing or planting alternative crops. Farmers can be given cash assistance or agricultural inputs. The assistance needs to be timely, so that farmers could utilize it for their agricultural operations.

— *Energy support:* Farmers need to be provided assured power supply for a minimum of eight hours to irrigate their lands. If drought is declared, the farmers could be given certain concessions in electricity charges through Government support. Inadequate and uncertain power supply would only aggravate the agrarian situation.

— *Extension support:* The State department of agriculture and agricultural universities should provide extension services. These need to be organized extensively, so that farmers can be advised on crop variety, selection of seeds, soil and water conservation measures, contingency crops and cultivation methods.

Relief Employment

Most State Governments have their own food for work programme. The Government of India has started the National Rural Employment Guarantee Scheme (NREGS), providing 100 days of employment to one person per family on demand. The scheme has been extended to the entire country. A large number of public works and watershed programmes could be supported through the NREGS. These programmes together can create substantial employment to tide over the hardship and deprivation caused by drought.

As soon as drought is declared in a State, the State Government must assess the total requirement of employment during the period of drought.

Such planning should be based on the number of households affected by drought and their dependence on agriculture for their livelihoods. The State Government needs to pool resources through different programmes for creating the required level of employment.

The State Relief Commissioner needs to prepare a plan, in consultation with all the departments responsible for labour-intensive works, for providing relief employment to the people at the State level. The Relief Commissioner must prepare a financial plan for meeting the expenditure incurred on relief employment works through different sources.

Relief programmes supported through the Calamity Relief Fund (CRF) or NCCF are generally inadequate to meet the needs of employment. The NREGS also restricts employment to one member per family or / and a specified number of days (100 days in a year in the case of NREGS). It is thus necessary that the State Government combines other development schemes, such as water conservation programmes with relief employment programmes. It would increase the availability of funds for relief and generate employment for a larger workforce or greater number of days. These works can be started under Integrated Watershed Management Programme (IWMP) following programmes:

The departments responsible for the implementation of these programmes need to start works under these programmes in drought-affected areas to maximize the number of people employed. If there is a need to relax certain provisions of these programmes for increasing the workers' attendance under these programmes, the State Government should make such relaxations.

Local Area Development (LAD) programmes for the Members of Parliament and Members of State Legislature can provide resources for relief employment. Further, large-scale employment can be generated through the State irrigation department. Works on canal excavation and minor irrigation projects can be started through which a large number of people can be provided with gainful employment.

The district administration needs to be given all the authority and flexibility within the framework of these guidelines for implementing relief employment programmes.

At the district level, the Collector of a drought-affected district is required to prepare a district plan for relief employment, specifying the types and number of works to be taken in different pockets of the district and the total employment these works would generate.

The district administration must provide employment to people as soon as there is a demand for employment with minimum delay. While planning, it is necessary that people get employment within 1.5–5 kilometers of their residence.

The Collector should direct all technical departments to identify feasible works in all the drought-affected villages and prepare estimates for these works and provide technical sanction to these works. The Collector should prepare such a plan in consultation with all the technical departments and provide administrative and financial approval for all the works included in the plan.

The relief employment plan prepared by the District Collector should be submitted before the District Disaster Management Committee (DDMC) or the District Relief Committee (DRC). The DDMC / DRC should approve the plan and authorize all the technical departments to start these works.

The district administration needs to keep an adequate number of works on a "shelf" so that these works can be started as soon as the demand for employment in a certain area arises. All the line departments need to be in readiness for starting these works. They need to reassign their staff and keep the equipments in readiness for starting these works. Where tools and equipment are not adequate for starting these works, the line departments need to procure them, with a defined responsibility for their safe storage.

The Collectors should be authorized to redeploy technical and administrative staff within the district for implementing and supervising these works in consultation with regional heads of these departments. In such instances, where the relief works have started on a large-scale, the Collectors can request the State Government to post additional officers on a temporary basis. Collectors can be authorized to hire vehicles, provide daily allowance and get administrative support for facilitating the implementation and supervision of relief works. The Collectors need to invoke disciplinary powers for proceeding against officers found to be in dereliction of their duties in accordance with the Disaster Management Act.

In the course of implementing relief employment programmes, priority needs to be given to water conservation, harvesting works (such as check dams, gabion structures, percolation tanks), and minor irrigation works (such as tanks and farm ponds, canal excavation, community wells, nalla bunding, afforestation). These works are useful for enhancing the availability of water and agricultural production. Desilting and cleaning of canals, which is overdue on account of non-availability of resources for many years, is also helpful in supply of water to the tail-end users. Roads and metal breaking works should be taken up only when there is no scope for these productive works. For each State, these priorities may change as per the local situation.

Along with the public works, it would be useful to undertake individual beneficiary works as it creates durable assets, enhancing their sources of income. These include:

— Farm ponds
— New wells / deepening of wells / recharging of wells
— Horticulture / jatropha plantations
— Construction of new water channels / rain harvesting structures
— Sanitation latrines

The State Government should lay down the criteria for the selection of beneficiaries for taking up these individual beneficiary works. While sanctioning these works, technical and financial norms need to be fixed. For the payment of wages, the muster roll must be maintained.

In the tribal and hilly areas, the local conditions may not be conducive for large-scale employment. In such a situation, individual beneficiary works for tribals should be taken up. It should involve land development, plantations and afforestation, water conservation programmes, grass cutting and storage, construction of new farm ponds and wells and rural houses.

It is necessary that spill-over works taken in the previous years as drought relief works be taken up first. Works that can be completed or brought to a safe stage, can be next on the priority list. New works can be taken only where the spill-over plan works are not available. Only after these works are completed, should new works be taken up. A new work can be taken up for execution only after all preliminary steps, such as preparation of plans and estimates and technical sanction and administrative approval of the appropriate authority, are completed.

Collectors must report to the State Government of the number of works, the total attendance of workers, the total wages paid and the distribution of foodgrains on a weekly basis.

In the drought-affected areas, Gram Sabhas need to be convened in all the Gram Panchayats for discussing the drought situation. In the Gram Sabha, water use management, relief employment works, payment of wages, and provision of foodgrains need to be on the agenda for deliberations. Gram Sabhas can become an effective forum for conducting a social audit of drought relief operations and need to be held once a month.

While the district administration must strive to provide employment to all the able-bodied adult, men and women and there cannot be any discrimination in the provision of relief to the people, it must provide special attention to "below poverty line" families, landless labourers, and workers in the Scheduled Caste and Scheduled Tribe categories for their employment in public and individual beneficiary works.

Each worker should be issued a job card, which would help in closely monitoring the attendance on works, payment of wages and amount of foodgrains to each worker. The job card should be available to the Inspecting Officers at work sites. Under the NREGS, all participating families are given job cards. These job cards need to be extended to other relief employment programmes also.

The work hours may vary, depending upon the local conditions, such as climate and distance to work. However, the total number of working hours in a day should not exceed eight, including a lunch break of half an hour. All workers would be allowed one day of rest in a week, either on a Sunday or the local market day.

The State Government needs to lay down the wage policy for relief employment programmes. While all the State Governments are under obligation to pay statutory minimum wages, the payment of these wages need to be linked to the tasks performed by workers. It is necessary to ensure promptness and transparency in the measurement of these works and payment of wages to the workers.

The State Government needs to lay down the cash and foodgrains components of wages at the start. The ratio of cash to foodgrains could differ across programmes, but it is advisable that the same ratio be maintained for all relief employment programmes. The ratio can change, depending upon the availability of foodgrains. The provision of wages in cash and foodgrains need to be made in accordance with their share in the entire wage component.

Wages must be paid to the workers in accordance with the norms laid down for the NREGS. Officials need to make cash payments to the workers on the site. Where the workers have been asked to open bank accounts, particularly under the NREGS, the wages could be transferred to their bank accounts.

In case the State Government decides to distribute foodgrains as part of wages, food coupons may be issued to the workers. Each coupon should specify the quantity of foodgrains to be distributed per coupon. A detailed register should be maintained for the issue of food coupons, with the names of all the workers to whom the coupons have been released. It should be ensured that workers get foodgrains from the nearest available fair price shops under the Public Distribution System. It is necessary to check that the foodgrains are available in these shops before coupons are issued. The issue of coupons and provision of foodgrains through the fair price shops need to be monitored by an officer specially assigned for this purpose for each Taluka.

The district administration should consider setting up labour camps, when there is a large concentration of labourers. The site for such a labour camp should be selected with special regard to sanitation. Provision should be made for the supply of clean drinking water, cheap grain shops, sanitary arrangements, crèches for children, schools for the children of these workers and other amenities. A mobile heath team should visit these relief works on a regular basis. However, labour camps should be organized only when it is not possible to provide them works within a radius of 5 km from their homes.

Engagement of pregnant women and children in relief works should be prohibited, and they should be provided with gratuitous relief. Similarly, sick and infirm people qualify for gratuitous relief and they should not be allowed to participate in these works.

Resource Management

Availability of water depends upon many factors, such as rainfall, the extent of percolation and groundwater recharge, water storage and water use. Areas with high rainfall may also experience severe scarcity of water if the run-off is very high and the level of percolation is poor. Shortage of water is one of the earliest indicators of drought, affecting the entire society, rural and urban. Assessing the demand for water and its total availability in a specific region, therefore, is extremely important for meeting the needs of different user groups.

Provision of Water

The first step involved in the water resource management process is estimating the demand for water. The district administration can undertake such an exercise on the basis of the consumption needs of the total population of the district and the demand for water from industrial, service and agriculture sectors. All the measures aimed at conserving and augmenting water supply could be organized only after estimating the total demand for water in the district.

The following measures need to be taken for managing the water situation in a drought-affected area:

Reservoir management

The Collector undertakes reservoir management with the help and support of the irrigation department. The irrigation department shall provide relevant information to the Collector in respect to storage of water in reservoirs and enforce his instructions regarding its distribution and use.

As deficient or irregular rainfall may not replenish water storage in reservoirs to the full reservoir level (FRL), the Collector must decide the priorities in respect of water use available in reservoirs. The Collector must declare the reservation upon water storage in the reservoir.

The State Government must declare the policy for laying down the priorities for use of reservoir storage. The first priority needs to be given to the provision of drinking water. According to this policy, the Collector must determine the quantity of water that is required to be reserved for drinking water purposes, and intimate the same to the concerned water supply / irrigation authorities. The Collector's order for water reservation for the purpose of drinking should be binding upon the water supply /irrigation authorities.

As per the State policy, the Collector should, after taking into account the availability of water, decide upon other priorities: augmentation for the existing water supply scheme of any town, industrial and commercial use, power plants and irrigation. Water required to be supplied to a village or town for the purpose of drinking water should, as far as possible, be taken from the reservoir and conveyed to the village or town through a pipeline.

Only in exceptional circumstances, such as where the village or town is situated within a short distance from the reservoir, the water could be released in the river.

Repairs and augmentation of existing water supply schemes

The State Government should issue special orders for repairs and augmentation of all the existing water supply schemes. This may include a piped water supply scheme, electrical pumps fitted on bore-wells, hand pumps, dug wells and any other source of drinking water.

In repairs and augmentation of the existing water supply schemes, the Collector shall get assistance from the departments of water supply, public health engineering and rural development as the case may be. These departments will provide necessary information regarding water supply to the Collector and implement his decisions.

The Collector needs to prepare a Taluka-wise list of all the water supply schemes in the district which need repairs. The Collector can accordingly prepare a contingency plan, in consultation with the technical agencies and local bodies, which can provide the details of mechanical supervisors, mechanics and electricians and an inventory of spare parts and accessories. In those cases, where technically qualified people are not available with the Government agencies, they could be employed on a contract basis at the Taluka or village level.

At the village level, it should be the duty of the Sarpanch or Gram Sevak, or any other functionary appointed for this purpose, to promptly report to the Tehsildar and Block Development Officer when any hand pump or power pump goes out of order. The Tehsildar and Block Development Officer, with the assistance of engineers of the relevant departments, should ensure that the hand pump or the electrical pump fitted on a bore-well is immediately repaired. In many cases where the repairs needed are major, a mobile repairs unit can be sent for carrying out the necessary repairs.

When drought is declared, a district-level campaign should be organized for repairing all the hand pumps and electricity pumps fitted on bore-wells. The campaign would be more effective if it is supported by indenting in advance spare parts and accessories that would be required for carrying out necessary repairs to the pumps. For each hand pump and bore-well, a card can be maintained which records the visits of mechanics and electricians and the details of repairs that have been carried out.

The village Panchayat has the overall responsibility for proper maintenance and timely repairs of the piped water supply. A levy and collection of water charges by the village Panchayat would support such repairs and maintenance. However, in a drought situation, village Panchayats can be given suitable grants by the district administration for meeting the expenditure on maintenance and repairs of the water supplies.

The Collector should be provided funds for immediate repairs to water supply schemes, hand pumps, and bore-wells through the Calamity Relief Fund. These funds can be placed with the technical agencies for undertaking necessary repairs to these water supply schemes.

Special measures and schemes for areas with drinking water scarcity

When there is inadequate rainfall, the Collector should direct the Tehsildar and Block Development Officers to visit the affected areas and draw up Taluka-wise lists of villages in which drinking water scarcity has already developed, or likely to arise. Such visits will always be undertaken with the engineers and officials of water supply, public health engineering, or rural development department, as the case may be. Such lists should be developed with maps indicating the location of villages, routes linking these villages and existing sources of water supply in these villages, such as piped water supply, bore-wells, or dug wells.

The Collector would get the list of these problem villages counter checked through the Sub-Divisional Officers and other district officers from the relevant departments. The Collector should also personally visit 5-10% of the villages for verifying the factual position related to availability of drinking water. The Collector should then finalize the list in consultation with the officials dealing with water supply and the State ground water survey and development agency.

On the basis of this information, the Collector should prepare a contingency plan for provision of drinking water in all the villages that are likely to face a water scarcity. The contingency plan should lay down the priority for provision of drinking water as follows:

— Any piped water supply scheme, which is already under execution in any of these villages, should be completed expeditiously;

— Piped water supply, temporary piped water supply, or bore-wells already constructed in any of the villages which are non-functional should be made functional by undertaking necessary repairs or renovation;

- The responsibility for maintaining of hand pumps or electrical pumps fitted on bore-wells in the village should be assigned to the village Panchayats. If an existing bore-well can provide enough water to the village by installation of a power pump, then the district administration should take emergent measures to get the power pump installed;
- The feasibility of a new bore-well in the village should be assessed with the help of State ground water survey and development agency. Where feasible, a programme installing new bore-wells could be taken up. Care should be taken to avoid deep bore-wells as they damage aquifers.
- If any of the above mentioned measures are not feasible, emergent measures such as desilting, deepening, or blasting of existing wells, or construction of open wells in river beds can be undertaken, as suggested in the section on Other Emergency Measures for Supply of Drinking Water.
- If the district administration assesses that these sources of water would not be sufficient to meet the drinking water needs of a village, they can arrange to provide drinking water through tankers or bullock carts, as suggested in the section on Supply of Water through Tankers and Bullock Carts.

Construction of temporary piped water supply

The State Government should decide to construct temporary piped water supply in a village, if the following conditions are fulfilled:

- No source of drinking water supply is available or is likely to be available within a distance of 0.5 kilometre of the village;
- No possibility of constructing a new bore-well at the village or within a distance of one kilometre of the village or to undertake further drilling in the existing bore-well at the village, due to non-availability of groundwater source at the village;
- Where at the source, water supply at the rate of 40 litres per day per head would be available for the projected population of the village;
- Where the supply is based on a private source of water, e.g. a private well, it is ensured that the source is adequate to last until the summer season is over and the drinking water scarcity abates;

— Where, the average per head expenditure of the supply shall not exceed a certain amount to be fixed by each State Government.

The Collector should fix the agency for commissioning temporary water supply in consultation with the department of water supply, public health engineering, or rural development department, as the case may be. It could either be implemented by the agency responsible for water supply in the State or a local body.

Each State Government should assign powers of technical and administrative approval of the temporary water supply schemes to authorities at different levels, within certain financial limits. The level of approvals would go up if the cost increases and when a certain amount is exceeded, new water supply schemes would be approved only by the State Government.

All temporary water supply schemes would be handed over to the village Panchayat for maintenance. Such a scheme can be taken for execution only when the village Panchayat passes a resolution to take over the scheme and maintain it after its completion.

Construction of bore-wells

A bore-well programme can be taken up in a village, which is facing or is likely to face drinking water scarcity, if it is technically feasible to construct bore-wells at such a village. Sites for bore-wells can be selected on the basis of recommendations made by the State ground water survey and development agency.

Bore-wells with a hand pump fitted there on can be set up for a population of 250. If the population exceeds 250, more than one bore-well can be installed to serve the village.

The Collector can request the departments of water supply, public health engineering, or rural development department, as the case may be, to deploy drilling machines for installing bore-wells. Where it is necessary to obtain additional drilling machines, these can be obtained on hire from private owners.

When a village has power supply, for a population of at least 500 one or more bore-wells having high yield power pumps may be installed only on one such bore-well for solving the problem of drinking water in the village.

When a bore-well programme is undertaken in a village, it is necessary to take into account the cattle population of the village. Along with bore-wells, it would be necessary to provide water taps and troughs for the cattle.

Other emergency measures for supply of drinking water

The Collector should undertake emergency measures such as de-silting or deepening of existing public wells to increase the availability of water. Other measures such as in-well drilling, blasting and revitalization can also be attempted for augmenting the capacity of these wells. These measures need to be planned with the support of departments of water supply, public health engineering, or rural development department, as the case may be,

Where no public well is available or is likely to be successful after taking such measures, the Collector may authorize and make available a private well on rent, if the owner of the well agrees to allow public consumption with no discrimination against any caste, creed or religion. In all the cases where a private well is being brought under use, the Collector should fix the rent for drawing drinking water and make the payment to the owner of the well and also make an announcement to this effect so that the owners of private wells come forward to offer their wells for supply of drinking water at a rent fixed by the district administration.

Old wells that have fallen into disuse should be repaired for ensuring drinking water supply to the villagers if the State ground water survey and development agency certifies that after carrying out the necessary repairs the well would provide adequate water supply. Before these old wells are used for drawing drinking water, it should be ensured that water is properly chlorinated, and a certificate obtained from the State health department stating that the water is fit for human consumption.

Where the water in a river or stream gets scarce, holes could be dug in the beds of the stream or river. Where water has been impounded by putting a temporary bund, such holes could preferably be dug on the banks near the impounded water and the water is reserved in those holes for drinking purposes. This would provide practically filtered water to the villagers for the purpose of drinking.

Where the water has sunk much below the bed, it may be necessary to sink concrete pipes in the holes dug in the bed so that water gets collected in the pipes and could then be used for drinking water purposes.

When a certain area faces acute drinking water scarcity, it may become necessary to save and preserve water, particularly from small and shallow tanks, for drinking water purposes by controlling evaporation losses. Certain chemicals can be spread over surfaces of water storages, which would control evaporation. However, such a measure needs to be undertaken in consultation with the State health department. The district administration would be responsible for ensuring that chemicals used for controlling evaporation are safe and would not cause any health hazard to the people consuming such water.

Supply of water through tankers and bullock carts

The Collector should take the decision to supply water through tankers or bullock carts to a village or town in the drought-affected area, where no other source of water supply is available. The Collector should decide after obtaining reports from Taluka / Block-level officials, which are counter checked by Sub-divisional Officers. In such cases too, the Collector should decide to supply water by a tanker or bullock cart, where a permanent or temporary water supply system is under repairs, till the time these repairs are completed.

While making the survey of villages for supply of water through tankers or bullock carts, it shall be obligatory for the departments of water supply, public health engineering or rural development department, as the case may be, to provide necessary technical, administrative and logistical help.

The State Government should issue orders, authorizing the Collector to requisition Government tankers from all the departments for the supply of drinking water. It would be the responsibility of all the departments to provide tankers along with the services of a driver when the Collector makes a demand.

If any of the tankers are in disrepair, it should be the responsibility of the officers of the concerned department to undertake necessary repairs to the tanker before making it available to the Collector.

The Collector would first deploy Government tankers for the supply of drinking water.

Private tankers can be hired only when Government tankers are not available or inadequate for ensuring uninterrupted supply of drinking water to the affected villages. The Collector should hire these vehicles by inviting tenders and fixing the rate for trips involving different distances. The

Collector should issue instructions for the maintenance of logbooks of these vehicles, as payment to the owners of these tankers is to be made on the basis of entries in these logbooks. The operations of these tankers need to be regulated carefully. The Collector should discontinue the deployment of tankers immediately after local sources of water have been recharged or re-developed.

Where water supply is being arranged through tankers or bullock carts, the Government should consider providing big storage tanks in villages or towns with a capacity of more than 5,000 litres, so that water wastage is minimized.

In villages where roads are not motorable, it may be more convenient and economical to engage bullock carts for supplying water. The Collector should hire local bullock carts for supplying water. In all such cases, the Collector should fix the number of trips to be made by bullock carts and pay per trip to the bullock cart owner.In extra ordinary drought situation the drinking water requirement may also be arranged through Railways.

Ensuring Food Security in Drought-affected Areas

The Government of India has started the National Rural Employment Guarantee Scheme (NREGS), which has now been extended to all the districts across the country. This scheme guarantees employment opportunities in the rural areas by providing work that taps labour intensive community assets. It assures manual work to one person per family for a maximum of 100 days in a year.

Provision of Food

Foodgrains are provided through the Public Distribution System (PDS), which is operated under the joint responsibility of the Central and State Governments. PDS with a network of about 4.74 lakh Fair Price Shops (FPS) is one of the largest networks in the world.

In June 1997, a targeted PDS was introduced, which follows a two-tier subsidized pricing for people "Below Poverty Line" (BPL) and "Above Poverty Line" (APL). In the district, the entire FPS network runs under the direct control and supervision of the Collector.

Ensuring food security in the drought-affected areas requires the following actions to be taken with the support of State department of civil supplies:

- The Collector needs to assess the foodgrains requirement in the drought-affected area on the basis of number of households, size of households, the population below poverty line and the local patterns of consumption.
- The Collector should exercise surveillance over prices of essential commodities. If the local prices of foodgrains increase, the Collector should bring it to the notice of the State Government.
- Wherever required, the Collector should take steps to prevent hoarding of essential commodities and prevent manipulation in prices through creation of artificial scarcities.
- The Collector should ensure the availability of foodgrains by starting relief employment works under the NREGS or any other food-for-work programme. Wages can be paid to the workers in the form of foodgrains.
- The Collector should request the State Government to allocate foodgrains for wage payment to the workers. The State Government would fix the ratio of foodgrains to cash for wage payment. The State Government can accordingly make a separate allocation of foodgrains for the wage component.
- The State Government should release foodgrains through the PDS. The Collector should in turn allocate foodgrains to the Fair Price Shop, located close to the work sites. Food coupons could be distributed among the workers, who can redeem them through the nearest Fair Price Shop (FPS).
- The State Government should request the Ministry of Agriculture, Government of India, to allocate foodgrains for the purpose of wage distribution. The Government of India could consider the allocation of foodgrains for this purpose on the basis of total attendance on relief employment works, shortage of agricultural production, and its likely impact on prices.
- If it is not necessary to start relief employment works, the State Government can increase the availability of foodgrains through releasing increased quantities through the PDS. It would mean greater availability of foodgrains per unit.
- Collector should ensure that Fair Price Shops are distributing foodgrains to the people in the drought-affected areas. There should be necessary vigilance against any diversion of foodgrains or its misutilization.

— In those places, where Fair Price Shops are not available, new ones for the distribution of foodgrains can be started through self-help groups or cooperatives or even village Panchayats.

— In remote and difficult to reach areas, mobile Fair Price Shops can be arranged. The schedule of movement of these mobile shops can be fixed and publicized. In the drought-affected area, the State Government should take a decision to distribute foodgrains to the APL families at the same price as BPL families in view of all-pervasive hardship.

— The Collector should monitor the distribution of food coupons, the receipt of foodgrains in Government warehouses and distribution of these foodgrains to the FPS', on a regular basis.

— The Collector should monitor how much foodgrains the households are buying on their ration cards. Monitoring the sale of foodgrains through Fair Price Shops would provide patterns of needs and consumption at the community and household levels. The Collector can accordingly modify the allocation of foodgrains to these shops.

— Inspection of warehouses and Fair Price Shops should be intensified during the drought period. It would ensure the distribution of foodgrains to the people who are genuinely in need of such support.

Relief through Tax Waivers and Concessions

Each State Government may decide on tax waivers and concessions to the people affected by drought, depending on fiscal situation of the State and severity of the drought. The waivers and concessions which can be considered by the State are as follows:

The State Government can decide to grant remission of land revenue as payable under the relevant Land Revenue Code for those farmers in the area affected by drought. Declaration of such a waiver may be linked to annewari / paisewari / girdawari, or any other measure of crop losses, prevalent in the State.

The State Government may decide to postpone the recovery of certain dues from the farmers. It may include Tagai / Taccavi, arrears of water, irrigation and electricity charges, or any other dues related to agriculture. If recovery is not postponed, the State Government can issue instructions for not recovering these dues from the farmers and other agricultural workers by applying coercive measures.

In drought-affected areas, the State Government can consider providing certain concessions for electricity and water charges. It could approve a partial or complete remission of these charges, with a due consideration to its financial implications, in consultation with the concerned State energy / water regulatory authority.

The State Government may consider converting short-term loans and reschedule current instalment of medium-term loans for farmers in the drought-affected areas. The State Government should make necessary provision for restructuring / rescheduling of these loans and pay to the concerned banks.

The State Government may issue instructions to all cooperative banks through the department of cooperation to convert or reschedule kharif loans by the end of March, when assessment of crop losses are available and final annewari / paisewari values are published.

The Collector should furnish details of annewari / paisewari values or any other assessment of crop losses to cooperative banks to facilitate the conversion or re-scheduling of such loans. Tehsildars / Block Development Officer / Circle Officer can issue necessary certificates to the District Registrar of Cooperatives to enable the banks to grant conversion facility to the affected farmers.

The State Government may issue instructions to the cooperative banks not to apply coercive measures for recovering their loans or dues in the drought-affected areas.

The State Government can decide to waive education / examination fees for the students in Government schools located in drought-affected areas.

Cattle Camps and Fodder Supply

Cattle wealth is the mainstay of the rural economy. As small and marginal farmers constitute about 80% of the total community of farmers in the country, their only asset is cattle apart from their small landholdings. Cattle ownership diversifies production and resource management options, increases total farm production and income, provides year-round employment and spreads risk. In all the studies related to vulnerability of farmers, it has been found that the more cattle heads a farmer owns, the less vulnerable the farmer is to fluctuating finances.

During a drought situation, every measure needs to be taken to save useful cattle. When cattle wealth is seriously depleted, the recovery is very slow. While sheep and goats have a potential for rapid growth, perhaps 25% a year or more, the growth of cows, buffaloes, and camels is much slower, rarely more than 1-2% a year in a sustained manner. It is necessary to provide support to farmers for fodder so that they do not engage in distress selling of their cattle. It is also very important that they continue to sell milk and other products so that they have an alternative stream of income.

Public Policy for Drought Management

Drought management will be most effective if it is set in the context of a full understanding of local water supply and demand, which will most likely be addressed in an entity's master water management plan. Water rights management, supply development, and conservation, all discussed below, clearly have both drought and non-drought implications for local water management. In addition, understanding and managing the specific risks and impacts of drought requires integration of long-term and drought-specific planning and policy. Therefore, drought management policy can be effectively developed utilizing risk management analyses and techniques.

Under a risk management focus, drought planning entails impact assessments, economic analyses, and consideration of issues of vulnerability, equity, efficiency, cost and urgency. Understanding the economic, social and physical aspects and impacts of drought allows selection of *drought mitigation* policies, programs, and actions that fit with the overall water management plan and addresses the underlying causes of vulnerability to drought. This will reduce the chances of water supply and demand imbalances in times of drought. Further, the broad perspective afforded by risk management analyses allows entities to develop response plans that minimize economic, social, and other impacts when drought occurs. Development of *mitigation* and *response* plans and related policies should include substantial participation on the part of all affected stakeholders and the general public.

Developing appropriate drought management response plans require that entities have the authority and communication processes in place to take drought response actions, including how and when to declare a drought emergency and determination of when to declare it. The plan should also set out clear objectives and priorities for drought-related actions. Potentially conflicting objectives—which may include reducing economic impacts, minimizing inconvenience to users, avoiding rationing, saving trees and perennial plants, and more— should be addressed and prioritized in the plan, well before an actual drought. A plan should include carefully developed triggers for declaring drought of different levels of intensity (mild, moderate and severe) and the corresponding actions water managers and users should or must take. Specific issues addressed in a drought response plan often include provisions to supply critical uses of water, ways to adjust infrastructure operations to ensure maximum use of available water supplies, water quality monitoring under low flow conditions, water conservation and water use restrictions (and identification of goals for water savings at each level), and identification of state and federal sources of assistance to impacted water users.

Public Education and Relations

Attention to public relations is critical to the overall success of drought management tools. It is important that the local entity is prepared internally with consistent messages for the public and media. Strong media relationships established prior to a drought will help facilitate the exchange and broadcast of information during a drought. Various surveys and studies have investigated what attitudes are often found during drought and what issues should be highlighted to foster success in implementing drought measures. These include conveying the seriousness of drought, highlighting social and moral commitment, establishing perceived efficacy of water restrictions, and managing perceptions of inconvenience, cost, and equity among all members of the community.

In addition, all members of the water community look for guidance and leadership during periods of drought. A strong public education program can help water users better understand issues and limitations that may affect them individually and collectively during a drought. To this point, cooperative agreements and operational flexibility related to water use are facilitated, in part, by good public education and relations programs.

Water Rights Management

Any tools selected to manage drought will need to work within the relevant water laws. In Colorado, the prior appropriation doctrine provides opportunities and limitations for managing water in a drought scenario. One legal tool employed by some municipalities in Colorado is dry-year leasing, a mechanism that allows for temporary water transfer, usually from agriculture to municipalities, during dry years when farming is less feasible or profitable. Local entities may also explore other forms of interruptible supply agreements and inter-system operational coordination that re-allocate water on a temporary basis during times of water need.

Additional mechanisms to obtain drought-time water supplies are under development in Colorado. These include water banking, where surplus water is pooled for rental to other water users, but available during times of drought or other need for increased water supply. Water banking is not yet a well-established concept in Colorado, but a pilot water banking project is being tested in the Arkansas River Basin and its use may be expanded.

Permanent water transfers are of course also possible—for instance, through acquisition of water rights—but often are typically irreversible and limit operational flexibility once water rights are sold.

Supply Augmentation

In addition to water transfers, local entities can secure and augment water supplies through a variety of means. These can include repair and maintenance of existing storage facilities to assure their maximum utility, revision of reservoir operating procedures to increase storage and make more water available, weather modification, ground water use (though effects on surface flows must be considered), and when necessary, establishment of new water storage facilities. Operational and minor infrastructure changes can be very cost-effective, whereas new infrastructure can be costly. Any of these options may require substantial collaboration among several entities.

Monitoring and Evaluation

It is critical to good drought management that information be compiled and maintained on water supply use and infrastructure, and on drought indicators such as precipitation, temperature, evapo-transpiration, meteorological forecasts, soil moisture, stream flow, ground water levels, reservoir and lake levels, and snow pack. Water providers and users can then monitor these data to identify if conditions for drought are developing or persisting. State and federal entities can also collect and monitor these data in support of local drought planning efforts.

In addition, the suite of selected *drought mitigation* and *response* tools should be reviewed periodically to see if they are achieving desired goals related typically to lessening the effects of drought and improving both preparedness and crisis response. Evaluation allows local entities to:

— Assess the effectiveness of *mitigation* efforts in reducing the occurrence and impact of drought-related water supply shortfalls.

— Analyze their drought response needs and gauge the appropriateness of the thresholds they have set for varying degrees of drought severity;

— Generate metrics to determine and justify the level of drought response employed;

— Determine the effectiveness, equity and need for the response actions selected and employed.

Water Conservation and Drought-Time Water Use Restrictions

Water *conservation* is a broad term that can encompass water use efficiency (e.g., low-flush toilets), wise water use (e.g., Xeriscape™), system efficiency (e.g., distribution system leak repair), and supply substitution (e.g., wastewater reclamation). While many people refer to water use *restrictions* during a drought as "water conservation," the objective of long-term water conservation is not to curtail water use. Rather it is to increase the productive use of the water supply in order to satisfy water needs without compromising desired water services. A drought management plan that includes curtailment of water services in response to drought may be appropriate, but curtailment is not a desired long-term result of a conservation program.

Some people believe that conservation "hardens" demand, resulting in less flexibility to respond when drought occurs. On the contrary, water conservation is a highly appropriate *drought mitigation* strategy. Long-term water conservation reduces future demand, resulting in a larger supply margin than would otherwise be the case. Thus, previous water conservation efforts reduce both the likelihood and severity of water supply shortfalls during times of meteorological drought. Without conservation savings "in the bank," a moderate drought event may become a severe one.

It is also important to realize that many water conservation actions require substantial time for implementation. If water conservation actions are not initiated until a "drought hits," it is usually too late to achieve significant gains from toilet change-outs, landscape selection ordinances or incentives, distribution system repair, construction of water reuse infrastructure, and other "technological" measures and programs. On the other hand, "behavioral" *drought response* measures are still available. For instance, consumers can tighten up landscape irrigation schedules, practice extra diligence in fixing in-home leaks and turning off the tap when shaving, and make other choices to use less water. Publicity campaigns and drought surcharges can encourage users to make these short-term adjustments. Finally, if necessary, the same restrictions on lawn watering, car washing, and so on that have conventionally been used to respond to drought are available even if the community has previously achieved substantial long-term conservation savings.

Refeences

American Water Works Association. (2002). *Drought Management Handbook.*

Denver Water, (2002). "Water for Tomorrow, An Integrated Resource Plan/Drought Response Plan." February.

Knutson, C., (1998). Hayes, M., and Phillips, T., "How to Reduce Drought Risk." Prepared for Western Drought Coordination Council. March.

Pinkham, R., (2003). "Technical Assistance to Covered Entities: Review of Conservation Planning Policies and Practices." Prepared for The Colorado Water Conservation Board. May.

Wilhite, D.A., Hayes, M.J., Knutson, C, and Smith K.H., (2003). "The Basics of Drought Planning: A 10-Step Process." National Drought Mitigation Center.

5

Earthquake: Preparedness and Mitigation

An earthquake is the result of a sudden release of energy in the Earth's crust that creates seismic waves. The seismicity, seismism or seismic activity of an area refers to the frequency, type and size of earthquakes experienced over a period of time.

Earthquakes are measured using observations from seismometers. The moment magnitude is the most common scale on which earthquakes larger than approximately 5 are reported for the entire globe. The more numerous earthquakes smaller than magnitude 5 reported by national seismological observatories are measured mostly on the local magnitude scale, also referred to as the Richter scale. These two scales are numerically similar over their range of validity. Magnitude 3 or lower earthquakes are mostly almost imperceptible or weak and magnitude 7 and over potentially cause serious damage over larger areas, depending on their depth. The largest earthquakes in historic times have been of magnitude slightly over 9, although there is no limit to the possible magnitude. The most recent large earthquake of magnitude 9.0 or larger was a 9.0 magnitude earthquake in Japan in 2011 (as of October 2012), and it was the largest Japanese earthquake since records began. Intensity of shaking is measured on the modified Mercalli scale. The shallower an earthquake, the more damage to structures it causes, all else being equal.

At the Earth's surface, earthquakes manifest themselves by shaking and sometimes displacement of the ground. When the epicenter of a large earthquake is located offshore, the seabed may be displaced sufficiently to cause a tsunami. Earthquakes can also trigger landslides, and occasionally volcanic activity.

In its most general sense, the word earthquake is used to describe any seismic event — whether natural or caused by humans — that generates seismic waves. Earthquakes are caused mostly by rupture of geological faults, but also by other events such as volcanic activity, landslides, mine blasts, and nuclear tests. An earthquake's point of initial rupture is called its focus or hypocenter. The epicenter is the point at ground level directly above the hypocenter.

Nature of Earthquakes

Naturally Occurring Earthquakes

Tectonic earthquakes occur anywhere in the earth where there is sufficient stored elastic strain energy to drive fracture propagation along a fault plane. The sides of a fault move past each other smoothly and aseismically only if there are no irregularities or asperities along the fault surface that increase the frictional resistance. Most fault surfaces do have such asperities and this leads to a form of stick-slip behaviour. Once the fault has locked, continued relative motion between the plates leads to increasing stress and therefore, stored strain energy in the volume around the fault surface. This continues until the stress has risen sufficiently to break through the asperity, suddenly allowing sliding over the locked portion of the fault, releasing the stored energy. This energy is released as a combination of radiated elastic strain seismic waves, frictional heating of the fault surface, and cracking of the rock, thus causing an earthquake. This process of gradual build-up of strain and stress punctuated by occasional sudden earthquake failure is referred to as the elastic-rebound theory. It is estimated that only 10 percent or less of an earthquake's total energy is radiated as seismic energy. Most of the earthquake's energy is used to power the earthquake fracture growth or is converted into heat generated by friction. Therefore, earthquakes lower the Earth's available elastic potential energy and raise its temperature, though these changes are negligible compared to the conductive and convective flow of heat out from the Earth's deep interior.

Earthquake Fault Types

There are three main types of fault, all of which may cause an earthquake: normal, reverse (thrust) and strike-slip. Normal and reverse faulting are examples of dip-slip, where the displacement along the fault is in the direction of dip and movement on them involves a vertical component. Normal faults occur mainly in areas where the crust is being extended such as a divergent boundary. Reverse faults occur in areas where the crust is being shortened such as at a convergent boundary. Strike-slip faults are steep structures where the two sides of the fault slip horizontally past each other; transform boundaries are a particular type of strike-slip fault. Many earthquakes are caused by movement on faults that have components of both dip-slip and strike-slip; this is known as oblique slip.

Reverse faults, particularly those along convergent plate boundaries are associated with the most powerful earthquakes, including almost all of those of magnitude 8 or more. Strike-slip faults, particularly continental transforms can produce major earthquakes up to about magnitude 8. Earthquakes associated with normal faults are generally less than magnitude 7.

This is so because the energy released in an earthquake, and thus its magnitude, is proportional to the area of the fault that ruptures and the stress drop. Therefore, the longer the length and the wider the width of the faulted area, the larger the resulting magnitude. The topmost, brittle part of the Earth's crust, and the cool slabs of the tectonic plates that are descending down into the hot mantle, are the only parts of our planet which can store elastic energy and release it in fault ruptures. Rocks hotter than about 300 degrees Celsius flow in response to stress; they do not rupture in earthquakes. The maximum observed lengths of ruptures and mapped faults, which may break in one go are approximately 1000 km. Examples are the earthquakes in Chile, 1960; Alaska, 1957; Sumatra, 2004, all in subduction zones. The longest earthquake ruptures on strike-slip faults, like the San Andreas Fault (1857, 1906), the North Anatolian Fault in Turkey (1939) and the Denali Fault in Alaska (2002), are about half to one third as long as the lengths along subducting plate margins, and those along normal faults are even shorter.

The most important parameter controlling the maximum earthquake magnitude on a fault is however not the maximum available length, but the available width because the latter varies by a factor of 20. Along converging plate margins, the dip angle of the rupture plane is very shallow, typically about 10 degrees. Thus the width of the plane within the top brittle crust of the Earth can become 50 to 100 km, making the most powerful earthquakes possible.

Strike-slip faults tend to be oriented near vertically, resulting in an approximate width of 10 km within the brittle crust, thus earthquakes with magnitudes much larger than 8 are not possible. Maximum magnitudes along many normal faults are even more limited because many of them are located along spreading centers, as in Iceland, where the thickness of the brittle layer is only about 6 km.

In addition, there exists a hierarchy of stress level in the three fault types. Thrust faults are generated by the highest, strike slip by intermediate, and normal faults by the lowest stress levels. This can easily be understood by considering the direction of the greatest principal stress, the direction of the force that 'pushes' the rock mass during the faulting. In the case of normal faults, the rock mass is pushed down in a vertical direction, thus the pushing force (greatest principal stress) equals the weight of the rock mass itself. In the case of thrusting, the rock mass 'escapes' in the direction of the least principal stress, namely upward, lifting the rock mass up, thus the overburden equals the least principal stress. Strike-slip faulting is intermediate between the other two types described above. This difference in stress regime in the three faulting environments can contribute to differences in stress drop during faulting, which contributes to differences in the radiated energy, regardless of fault dimensions.

Earthquakes Away from Plate Boundaries

Where plate boundaries occur within continental lithosphere, deformation is spread out over a much larger area than the plate boundary itself. In the case of the San Andreas fault continental transform, many earthquakes occur away from the plate boundary and are related to strains developed within the broader zone of deformation caused by major irregularities in the fault trace (e.g., the "Big bend" region).

The Northridge earthquake was associated with movement on a blind thrust within such a zone. Another example is the strongly oblique convergent plate boundary between the Arabian and Eurasian plates where it runs through the northwestern part of the Zagros mountains. The deformation associated with this plate boundary is partitioned into nearly pure thrust sense movements perpendicular to the boundary over a wide zone to the southwest and nearly pure strike-slip motion along the Main Recent Fault close to the actual plate boundary itself. This is demonstrated by earthquake focal mechanisms.

All tectonic plates have internal stress fields caused by their interactions with neighbouring plates and sedimentary loading or unloading (e.g. deglaciation). These stresses may be sufficient to cause failure along existing fault planes, giving rise to intraplate earthquakes.

Shallow-focus and Deep-focus Earthquakes

The majority of tectonic earthquakes originate at the ring of fire in depths not exceeding tens of kilometers. Earthquakes occurring at a depth of less than 70 km are classified as 'shallow-focus' earthquakes, while those with a focal-depth between 70 and 300 km are commonly termed 'mid-focus' or 'intermediate-depth' earthquakes. In subduction zones, where older and colder oceanic crust descends beneath another tectonic plate, deep-focus earthquakes may occur at much greater depths (ranging from 300 up to 700 kilometers). These seismically active areas of subduction are known as Wadati-Benioff zones. Deep-focus earthquakes occur at a depth where the subducted lithosphere should no longer be brittle, due to the high temperature and pressure. A possible mechanism for the generation of deep-focus earthquakes is faulting caused by olivine undergoing a phase transition into a spinel structure.

Earthquakes and Volcanic Activity

Earthquakes often occur in volcanic regions and are caused there, both by tectonic faults and the movement of magma in volcanoes. Such earthquakes can serve as an early warning of volcanic eruptions, as during the Mount St. Helens eruption of 1980. Earthquake swarms can serve as markers for the location of the flowing magma throughout the volcanoes. These swarms can be recorded by seismometers and tiltmeters (a device that measures ground slope) and used as sensors to predict imminent or upcoming eruptions.

Rupture Dynamics

A tectonic earthquake begins by an initial rupture at a point on the fault surface, a process known as nucleation. The scale of the nucleation zone is uncertain, with some evidence, such as the rupture dimensions of the smallest earthquakes, suggesting that it is smaller than 100 m while other evidence, such as a slow component revealed by low-frequency spectra of some earthquakes, suggest that it is larger. The possibility that the nucleation involves some sort of preparation process is supported by the observation that about 40% of earthquakes are preceded by foreshocks. Once the rupture has initiated it begins to propagate along the fault surface. The mechanics of this process are poorly understood, partly because it is difficult to recreate the high sliding velocities in a laboratory. Also the effects of strong ground motion make it very difficult to record information close to a nucleation zone.

Rupture propagation is generally modeled using a fracture mechanics approach, likening the rupture to a propagating mixed mode shear crack. The rupture velocity is a function of the fracture energy in the volume around the crack tip, increasing with decreasing fracture energy. The velocity of rupture propagation is orders of magnitude faster than the displacement velocity across the fault. Earthquake ruptures typically propagate at velocities that are in the range 70–90% of the S-wave velocity and this is independent of earthquake size. A small subset of earthquake ruptures appear to have propagated at speeds greater than the S-wave velocity. These supershear earthquakes have all been observed during large strike-slip events. The unusually wide zone of coseismic damage caused by the 2001 Kunlun earthquake has been attributed to the effects of the sonic boom developed in such earthquakes. Some earthquake ruptures travel at unusually low velocities and are referred to as slow earthquakes. A particularly dangerous form of slow earthquake is the tsunami earthquake, observed where the relatively low felt intensities, caused by the slow propagation speed of some great earthquakes, fail to alert the population of the neighbouring coast, as in the 1896 Meiji-Sanriku earthquake.

Tidal Forces

Research work has shown a robust correlation between small tidally induced forces and non-volcanic tremor activity.

Earthquake Clusters

Most earthquakes form part of a sequence, related to each other in terms of location and time. Most earthquake clusters consist of small tremors that cause little to no damage, but there is a theory that earthquakes can recur in a regular pattern.

Aftershocks

An aftershock is an earthquake that occurs after a previous earthquake, the mainshock. An aftershock is in the same region of the main shock but always of a smaller magnitude. If an aftershock is larger than the main shock, the aftershock is redesignated as the main shock and the original main shock is redesignated as a foreshock. Aftershocks are formed as the crust around the displaced fault plane adjusts to the effects of the main shock.

Earthquake Swarms

Earthquake swarms are sequences of earthquakes striking in a specific area within a short period of time. They are different from earthquakes followed by a series of aftershocks by the fact that no single earthquake in the sequence is obviously the main shock, therefore none have notable higher magnitudes than the other. An example of an earthquake swarm is the 2004 activity at Yellowstone National Park. In August 2012, a swarm of earthquakes shook Southern California's Imperial Valley, showing the most recorded activity in the area since the 1970s.

Earthquake Storms

Sometimes a series of earthquakes occur in a sort of earthquake storm, where the earthquakes strike a fault in clusters, each triggered by the shaking or stress redistribution of the previous earthquakes. Similar to aftershocks but on adjacent segments of fault, these storms occur over the course of years, and with some of the later earthquakes as damaging as the early ones. Such a pattern was observed in the sequence of about a dozen earthquakes that struck the North Anatolian Fault in Turkey in the 20th century and has been inferred for older anomalous clusters of large earthquakes in the Middle East.

Size and Frequency of Occurrence

It is estimated that around 500,000 earthquakes occur each year, detectable with current instrumentation. About 100,000 of these can be felt. Minor earthquakes occur nearly constantly around the world in places like California and Alaska in the U.S., as well as in Mexico, Guatemala, Chile, Peru, Indonesia, Iran, Pakistan, the Azores in Portugal, Turkey, New Zealand, Greece, Italy, and Japan, but earthquakes can occur almost anywhere, including New York City, London, and Australia. Larger earthquakes occur less frequently, the relationship being exponential; for example, roughly ten times as many earthquakes larger than magnitude 4 occur in a particular time period than earthquakes larger than magnitude 5.

In the (low seismicity) United Kingdom, for example, it has been calculated that the average recurrences are: an earthquake of 3.7–4.6 every year, an earthquake of 4.7–5.5 every 10 years, and an earthquake of 5.6 or larger every 100 years. This is an example of the Gutenberg-Richter law.

The number of seismic stations has increased from about 350 in 1931 to many thousands today. As a result, many more earthquakes are reported than in the past, but this is because of the vast improvement in instrumentation, rather than an increase in the number of earthquakes. The United States Geological Survey estimates that, since 1900, there have been an average of 18 major earthquakes (magnitude 7.0–7.9) and one great earthquake (magnitude 8.0 or greater) per year, and that this average has been relatively stable. In recent years, the number of major earthquakes per year has decreased, though this is probably a statistical fluctuation rather than a systematic trend. More detailed statistics on the size and frequency of earthquakes is available from the United States Geological Survey (USGS). A recent increase in the number of major earthquakes has been noted, which could be explained by a cyclical pattern of periods of intense tectonic activity, interspersed with longer periods of low-intensity. However, accurate recordings of earthquakes only began in the early 1900s, so it is too early to categorically state that this is the case.

Most of the world's earthquakes (90%, and 81% of the largest) take place in the 40,000 km long, horseshoe-shaped zone called the circum-Pacific seismic belt, known as the Pacific Ring of Fire, which for the most part bounds the Pacific Plate. Massive earthquakes tend to occur along other plate boundaries, too, such as along the Himalayan Mountains.

With the rapid growth of mega-cities such as Mexico City, Tokyo and Tehran, in areas of high seismic risk, some seismologists are warning that a single quake may claim the lives of up to 3 million people.

Induced Seismicity

While most earthquakes are caused by movement of the Earth's tectonic plates, human activity can also produce earthquakes. Four main activities contribute to this phenomenon: storing large amounts of water behind a dam (and possibly building an extremely heavy building), drilling and injecting liquid into wells, and by coal mining and oil drilling. Perhaps the best known example is the 2008 Sichuan earthquake in China's Sichuan Province in May; this tremor resulted in 69,227 fatalities and is the 19th deadliest earthquake of all time. The Zipingpu Dam is believed to have fluctuated the pressure of the fault 1,650 feet (503 m) away; this pressure probably increased the power of the earthquake and accelerated the rate of movement for the fault. The greatest earthquake in Australia's history is also claimed to be induced by humanity, through coal mining. The city of Newcastle was built over a large sector of coal mining areas. The earthquake has been reported to be spawned from a fault that reactivated due to the millions of tonnes of rock removed in the mining process.

Measuring and Locating Earthquakes

Earthquakes can be recorded by seismometers up to great distances, because seismic waves travel through the whole Earth's interior. The absolute magnitude of a quake is conventionally reported by numbers on the Moment magnitude scale (formerly Richter scale, magnitude 7 causing serious damage over large areas), whereas the felt magnitude is reported using the modified Mercalli intensity scale (intensity II–XII).

Every tremor produces different types of seismic waves, which travel through rock with different velocities:

— Longitudinal P-waves (shock- or pressure waves)

— Transverse S-waves (both body waves)

— Surface waves — (Rayleigh and Love waves)

Propagation velocity of the seismic waves ranges from approx. 3 km/s up to 13 km/s, depending on the density and elasticity of the medium. In the Earth's interior the shock- or P waves travel much faster than the S waves (approx. relation 1.7 : 1). The differences in travel time from the epicentre to the observatory are a measure of the distance and can be used to image both sources of quakes and structures within the Earth. Also the depth of the hypocenter can be computed roughly.

In solid rock P-waves travel at about 6 to 7 km per second; the velocity increases within the deep mantle to ~13 km/s. The velocity of S-waves ranges from 2–3 km/s in light sediments and 4–5 km/s in the Earth's crust up to 7 km/s in the deep mantle. As a consequence, the first waves of a distant earthquake arrive at an observatory via the Earth's mantle.

Rule of thumb: On the average, the kilometer distance to the earthquake is the number of seconds between the P and S wave times 8. Slight deviations are caused by inhomogeneities of subsurface structure. By such analyses of seismograms the Earth's core was located in 1913 by Beno Gutenberg. Earthquakes are not only categorized by their magnitude but also by the place where they occur. The world is divided into 754 Flinn-Engdahl regions (F-E regions), which are based on political and geographical boundaries as well as seismic activity. More active zones are divided into smaller F-E regions whereas less active zones belong to larger F-E regions.

Effects of Earthquakes

Depending on its size and location, an earthquake can cause the physical phenomena of ground shaking, surface fault rupture, and ground failure and, in some coastal areas, tsunamis. Smaller earthquakes, aftershocks, may follow the main shock, sometimes several hours, months, or even several years later.

Ground Shaking

Ground shaking or ground motion, a principal cause of the partial or total collapse of structures, is the vibration of the ground caused by seismic waves during an earthquake. Four different types of waves are propagated through and on the surface of the earth at different velocities, arrive at a site at different times, and vibrate a structure in different ways. The first wave to reach the earth's surface the sound wave or P wave and is the first to cause a building to vibrate. The most damaging waves are shear waves, S waves, which travel near the earth's surface and cause the earth to move at right angles to the direction of the wave and structures to vibrate from side to side. Unless a structure is designed and constructed to withstand these vibrations, ground shaking can cause damage. The third and fourth types are slow low-frequency surface waves, usually detected at great distances from the epicenter, which cause buildings to sway and waves to form in bodies of water.

Characteristics (Parameters)

Four principal characteristics which influence the damage that can be caused by an earthquake's ground shaking-size, attenuation, duration, and site response-are discussed here. A fifth parameter, the potential for ground failure (or the propensity of a site to liquefaction or landslides) is dealt with separately later in this section. These factors are also related to the distance of a site from the earthquake's epicenter - the point on the ground above its center.

(1) *Earthquake Severity or Size:* The severity of an earthquake can be measured two ways: its intensity and its magnitude. Intensity is the apparent effect of the earthquake at a specific location. The magnitude is related to the amount of energy released.

Intensity is measured on various scales. The one most commonly used in the Western Hemisphere is the twelve-level Modified Mercalli Index (MMI), on which the intensity is subjectively evaluated by describing the extent of damage.

The Richter Scale, which measures magnitude, is the one most often used by the media to convey to the public the size of an earthquake. Magnitude is easier to determine than intensity, since it is registered on seismic instruments, but it does present some difficulties. While an earthquake can have only one magnitude, it can have many intensities which affect different communities in different ways. Thus, two earthquakes with an identical Richter magnitude may have widely different maximum intensities at different locations.

(2) *Attenuation:* Attenuation is the decrease in the strength of a seismic wave as it travels farther from its source. It is influenced by the type of materials and structures the wave passes through (the transmitting medium) and the magnitude of the earthquake.

(3) *Duration:* Duration refers to the length of time in which ground motion at a site exhibits certain characteristics such as violent shaking, or in which it exceeds a specified level of acceleration measured in percent of gravity (g). Larger earthquakes are of greater duration than smaller ones. This characteristic, as well as stronger shaking, accounts for the greater damage caused by larger earthquakes.

(4) *Site Response:* The site response is the reaction of a specific point on the earth to ground shaking. This also includes the potential for ground failure, which is influenced by the physical properties of the soil and rock underlying a structure and by the structure itself. The depth of the soil layer, its moisture content, and the nature of the underlying geologic formation-unconsolidated material or hard rock-are all relevant factors. Furthermore, if the period of the incoming seismic wave is in resonance with the natural period of structures and/or the subsoil on which they rest, the effect of ground motion may be amplified.

In the 1985 Mexico City earthquake, the period of the seismic wave was close to the natural period of the Mexico City basin, considering the combination of soil type, depth, and shape of the old lake bed. The wave reached bedrock under the city with an acceleration level of about 0.04g. By the time it passed through the clay subsoil and reached the surface, the acceleration level had increased to 0.2g, and the natural vibration period of the buildings with 10 to 20 floors increased the force to 1.2g, 30 times the acceleration in the bedrock. Most buildings would have resisted 0.04g acceleration, and the earthquake-resistant buildings destroyed would have resisted 0.2g, but the waves that were amplified to 1.2g caused all buildings they reached to collapse.

Effects of ground shaking

Buildings, other types of structures, and infrastructure are all subject to damage or collapse from ground shaking. Fire is a common indirect effect of a large earthquake since electrical and gas lines may be ruptured. Furthermore, firefighting efforts may be impeded by blocked transportation routes and broken water mains. Damage to reservoirs and dams may result in flash flooding. In general, structural measures such as earthquake-resistant design, building codes, and retrofitting are effective. Less costly non-structural measures such as land-use zoning and restrictions can also greatly reduce risk.

An important, if little-appreciated, effect of earthquakes is damage to aquifers. The 1985 Mexico City earthquake undermined major aquifers. It not only broke the encasing impermeable layers, allowing the trapped water to escape, but also permitted the infiltration of contaminants.

Surface faulting

Surface faulting is the offset or tearing of the ground surface by differential movement along a fault during an earthquake. This effect is generally associated with Richter magnitudes of 5.5 or greater and is restricted to particularly earthquake-prone areas. Displacements range from a few millimeters to several meters, and the damage usually increases with increasing displacement. Significant damage is usually restricted to a narrow zone ranging up to 300 meters wide along the fault, although subsidiary ruptures may occur three to four kilometers from the main fault. The length of the surface ruptures can range up to several hundred kilometers.

In addition to buildings, linear structures such as roads, railroads, bridges, tunnels, and pipelines are susceptible to damage from surface faulting. Obviously, the most effective way to limit such damage is to avoid construction in the immediate vicinity of active faults. Where this is not possible, some mitigation measures such as installing pipelines above ground or using flexible connections can be considered.

Landslides and Liquefaction

Landslides occur in a wide variety of forms. Not only can earthquakes trigger landslides, they can also cause the soil to liquefy in certain areas. Both of these forms of ground failure are potentially catastrophic.

Induced landslides

Earthquake-induced landslides occur under a broad range of conditions: in steeply sloping to nearly flat land; in bedrock, unconsolidated sediments, fill, and mine dumps; under dry and very wet conditions. The principal criteria for classifying landslides are types of movement and types of material. The types of landslide movement that can occur are falls, slides, spreads, flows, and combinations of these. Materials are classified as bedrock and engineering soils, with the latter subdivided into debris (mixed particle size) and earth (fine particle size).

Moisture content can also be considered a criterion for classification: some earthquake-induced landslides can occur only under very wet conditions. Some types of flow failures, grouped as liquefaction phenomena, occur in unconsolidated materials with virtually no clay content. Other slide and flow failures are caused by slipping on a wet layer or by interstitial clay serving as a lubricant. In addition to earthquake shaking, trigger mechanisms can include volcanic eruptions, heavy rainstorms, rapid snowmelt, rising groundwater, undercutting due to erosion or excavation, human-induced vibrations in the earth, overloading due to construction, and certain chemical phenomena in unconsolidated sediments.

Table 1, which is designed for practical use by planners, contains a simplified classification of earthquake-induced landslides indicating the more damaging and/or more common types.

Rock avalanches, rock falls, mudflows, and rapid earth flows (liquefaction) account for over 90 percent of the deaths due to earthquake-induced landslides.

Table 1. Maximum seismic intensity and conditional probability of occurrence of a large or great earthquake for selected locations in central america

Location	Maximum Likely Seismic Intensity	Conditional Probability [a/]		
		1989-1994(%)	1989-1999(%)	1989-2009(%)
COSTA RICA				
Province				
Alajuela				
West	VIII	9	43	93
Central and East	VIII	£1-3	£1-8	4-25
Guanacaste				
West	VIII	16	31	55
East	VIII	9	43	93
Heredia (West)	VIII	£1	£1	£4
Puntarenas North	VIII	3-9	8-43	25-93
Central	VIII	£1	£1	£4
San José (West)	VIII	£1	£1	£4
EL SALVADOR				
Department				
Ahuachapán	VIII	29	51	79
Cabañas	VII	£1	£1	£1
Cuscatlán	VII	29	51	79
La Libertad	VIII	29	51	79
La Paz				
West	VIII	29	51	79
East	VIII	£1	£1	£1
San Miguel (West)	VIII	£1	£1	£1
San Salvador	VIII	29	51	79
San Vicente	VIII	£1	£1	£1
Santa Ana	VIII	29	51	79
Sonsonate	VIII	29	51	79
Usulatán	VIII	£1	£1	£1
GUATEMALA				
Department				
Alta Verapaz	VIII	(4)	(8)	(15)
Baja Verapaz	VIII	(4)	(8)	(15)
Chimaltenango	VIII	10	23	50
Chiquimula	VIII	29	51	79
El Progreso	VIII	29	51	79
Escuintla	VIII	10	23	50
Guatemala	X	10-29	23-51	50-79
Huehuetenango				
East	X	(4)	(8)	(15)
West	X	5	13	34
Izabal				

East	VIII	£1	£1	£1
West	VIII	(4)	(8)	(15)
Jalapa	VII	29	51	79
Jutiapa	VIII	29	51	79
Quezaltenango	IX	5	13	34
Quiché	VIII	(4)	(8)	(15)
Retalhuleu	VIII	5	13	34
Sacatepéquez	VIII	10	23	50
San Marcos	IX	5	13	34
Santa Rosa	IX	10-29	23-51	50-79
Sololá	VIII	10	23	50
Suchitepéquez	VIII	10	23	50
Totonicapán	VIII	10	23	50
Zacapa	VIII	(4)	(8)	(15)
HONDURAS				
Department				
Comayagua	VIII	?	?	?
Copán				
East	VII	£1	£1	£1
West	VIII	(4)	(8)	(15)
Intibuca	VIII	?	?	?
Lempira	VIII	?	?	?
Ocotepeque				
East	VII	£1	£1	£1
West	VIII	(4)	(8)	(15)
Santa Barbara (West)	VIII	£1	£1	£1
NICARAGUA	VIII	?	?	?

a/Conditional probability refers largely to earthquakes caused by inter-plate movement.
? No information available.
() All values in parentheses represent less reliable estimates.

(1) *Rock Avalanches:* Rock avalanches originate on over-steepened slopes in weak rocks. They are uncommon but can be catastrophic when they occur. The Huascarán, Peru, avalanche which originated as a rock and ice fall caused by the 1970 earthquake was responsible for the death of approximately 20,000 people.

(2) *Rock Falls:* Rock falls occur most commonly in closely jointed or weakly cemented materials on slopes steeper than 40 degrees. While individual rock falls cause relatively few deaths and limited damage, collectively, they rank as a major earthquake-induced hazard because they are so frequent.

(3) *Mud Flows:* Mud flows are rapidly moving wet earth flows that can be initiated by earthquake shaking or a heavy rainstorm. Underwater

landslides, also classified as mud flows, may occur at the margins of large deltas where port facilities are commonly located. Much of the destruction caused by the 1964 Seward, Alaska, earthquake was caused by such a slide. The term "mudflow," in keeping with common practice, is used as a synonym for "lahar," a phenomenon associated with volcanoes.

Liquefaction

Certain types of spreads and flows are designated as liquefaction phenomena. Ground shaking may cause clay-free soil deposits to lose strength temporarily and behave as a viscous liquid rather than as a solid. In the liquefied condition soil deformation may occur with little shear resistance. Deformation large enough to cause damage to constructed works (usually movement of about ten centimeters) is considered ground failure.

The occurrence of liquefaction is restricted to certain geologic and hydrologic environments, primarily in areas with recently deposited sands and silts (usually less than 10,000 years old) with high ground-water levels. It is most common where the water table is at a depth of less than ten meters in Holocene deltas, river channels, areas of floodplain deposits, eolian material, and poorly compacted fills.

Ground failures grouped as liquefaction can be subdivided into several types. The two most important are rapid earth flows and earth lateral spreads.

(1) *Rapid Earth Flows:* Rapid earth flows are the most catastrophic type of liquefaction. Large soil masses can move from tens of meters to several kilometers. These flows usually occur in loose saturated sands or silts on slopes of only a few degrees; yet they can carry boulders weighing hundreds of tons.

(2) *Earth Lateral Spreads:* The movement of surface blocks due to the liquefaction of subsurface layers usually occurs on gentle slopes (up to 3 degrees). Movement is usually a few meters but can also be tens of meters. These ground failures disrupt foundations, break pipelines, and compress or buckle engineered structures. Damage can be serious with displacements on the order of one or two meters.

In areas susceptible to earthquakes, liquefaction may be one of the most critical effects. Flow failure in loess (wind-blown silt) in the 1960 earthquake in China caused 200,000 deaths. Liquefaction was also a major factor in the earthquakes of 1960 in Chile and 1985 in Mexico and in major earthquakes in California, Alaska, India, and Japan.

In general, liquefaction can be prevented by ground-stabilization techniques or accommodated through appropriate engineering design, but both are expensive methods of mitigation. Avoidance is, of course, the best approach, but it is not always practical or possible in areas already developed or with existing transportation routes, pipelines, etc.

Earthquake Prediction

Minimizing or avoiding the risks from earthquakes involves three subject areas. First is the ability to predict their occurrence. While scientists cannot routinely predict earthquakes, this area is of growing interest and may be a key factor in reducing risks in the future. The second area is seismic risk assessment, which enables planners to identify areas at risk of earthquakes and/or their effects. This information is used to address the third area of earthquake risk reduction-mitigation measures. Following a discussion of prediction, assessment, and mitigation, the types and sources of earthquake information are presented.

A report on an erroneous prediction of an earthquake in Lima, Peru, states: Earthquake prediction is still in a research and experimental phase. Although a few successful predictions have been made, reliable and accurate predictions having a long lead time, and useful location and magnitude estimates, are many years in the future.

Some progress is being made in regional, long-term prediction and forecasting. "Seismic gaps" along major plate boundaries have been identified: areas with histories of prior large earthquakes (greater than 7 on the Richter scale-Ms7) and great earthquakes (Ms7.75) which have not had such an event for more than 30 years. Recent studies show that major earthquakes do not recur in the same place along faults until sufficient time has elapsed for stress to build up, usually a matter of several decades. In the main seismic regions, these "quiet" zones present the greatest danger of future earthquakes.

Confirming the seismic gap theory, several gaps that had been identified near the coasts of Alaska, Mexico, and South America experienced large earthquakes during the past decade. Moreover, the behavior of some faults appears to be surprisingly constant: there are areas where earthquakes occur at the same place, but decades apart, and have nearly identical characteristics.

Monitoring these seismic gaps, therefore, is an important component of learning more about earthquakes, predicting them, and preparing for future ones.

On the basis of the seismic gap theory, the U.S. Geological Survey has prepared maps of the coast of Chile and parts of Peru for the U.S. Agency for International Development's Office of Foreign Disaster Assistance (USAID/OFDA), adapted from a study by Stuart Nishenko. These maps give probability estimates and rank earthquake risk for the time period 1986 to 2006. USAID/OFDA has commissioned studies to produce similar information for the remainder of the Latin American Pacific coast.

It can be seen, however, that forecasting of this type only delineates relatively large areas in which an earthquake could potentially occur in a general future period of time. There have been successful earthquake predictions, but these are the exception rather than the rule. Earthquake prediction involves monitoring many aspects of the earth, including slight shifts in the ground, changes in water levels, and emission of gases from the earth, among other things. One successful short-term prediction is the often-mentioned case of Haicheng, China, in February 1975, in which people were evacuated six hours before a Ms7.3 earthquake struck. The worst-hit area was around the epicenter, where about 500,000 people lived, and half the buildings were damaged or destroyed. Among the indicators the Chinese had observed were changes in water level In deep wells, increased levels of radon gas, foreshocks, and unusual behavior of animals. Unfortunately, such successful predictions are offset by failures to predict: one year later in Tangshan, China, a great earthquake reportedly killed between 500,000 and 750,000 people.

Seismic Risk Assessment

A seismic risk assessment is defined as the evaluation of potential economic losses, loss of function, loss of confidence, fatalities, and injuries from earthquake hazards. Given the current state of knowledge of seismic phenomena, little can be done to modify the hazard by controlling tectonic processes, but there are a variety of ways to control the risk or exposure to seismic hazards. There are four steps involved in conducting a seismic risk assessment: (1) an evaluation of earthquake hazards and prepare hazard zonation maps; (2) an inventory of elements at risk, e.g., structures and population; (3) a vulnerability assessment; and (4) determination of levels of acceptable risk.

Evaluating Earthquake Hazards and Hazard Zonation Maps

In an earthquake-prone area, information will undoubtedly exist on past earthquakes and associated seismic hazards. This can be supplemented with existing geologic and geophysical information and field observation, if necessary. Depending on geologic conditions, some combination of ground shaking, surface faulting, landslides, liquefaction, and flooding w may be the most serious potential earthquake-related hazards in an area. Maps should be prepared showing zones of these hazards according to their relative severity. These maps provide the planner with data on such considerations as the spatial application of building codes and the need for local landslide and flood protection. A composite map can be compiled showing the relative severity of all seismic hazards combined.

(1) *Assessing Ground Shaking Potential:* Even though ground shaking may cause the most widespread and destructive earthquake-related damage, it is one of the most difficult seismic hazards to predict and quantify. This is due to the amplification of the shaking effects by the unconsolidated material overlying the bedrock at a site and to the differential resistance of structures. Consequently, the ideal way to express ground shaking is in terms of the likely response of specific types of buildings. These are classified according to whether they are wood frame, single-story masonry, low-rise (3 to 5 stories), moderate-rise (6 to 15 stories), or high-rise. Each of these, in turn, can be translated into occupancy factors and generalized into land-use types.

    Alternative approaches can be used for planning purposes to anticipate where ground shaking would be most severe:

    — The preparation of intensity maps based on damage from past earthquakes rated according to the Modified Mercalli Index.

    — The use of a design earthquake to compute intensity.

    — In the absence of data for such approaches, the use of information on the causative fault, distance from the fault, and depth of soil overlying bedrock to estimate potential damage.

(2) *Assessing Surface Faulting Potential:* This is relatively easy to do, since surface faulting is associated with fault zones. Three factors are important in determining suitable mitigation measures: probability and extent of movement during a given time period, the type of movement

(normal, reverse, or slip faulting), and the distance from the fault trace in which damage is likely to occur.

In areas of active faulting, fault maps should be prepared at scales appropriate for planning purpose and kept updated as new geologic and seismic information becomes available. The extent on the areas in jeopardy along the faults should be determined, and maps should be prepared showin the degree of hazard in each of them. Measures such as land-use zonation and building restrictions should be prescribed for areas in jeopardy.

(3) *Assessing Ground Failure Potential:* This method is applicable to earthquake-induced landslides. Liquefaction potential is determined in four steps: (1) a map of recent sediments is prepared, distinguishing areas that are likely to be subject to liquefaction from those that are unlikely; (2) a map showing depth to groundwater is prepared; (3) these two maps are combined to produce a "liquefaction susceptibility" map; and (4) a "liquefaction opportunity" is prepared by combining the susceptibility map with seismic data to show the distribution of probability that liquefaction will occur in a given time period.

Inventory of elements at risk

The inventory of elements at risk is a determination of the spatial distribution of structures and population exposed to the seismic hazards. It includes the built environment, e.g., buildings, utility transport lines, hydraulic structures, roads, bridges, dams; natural phenomena of value such as aquifers and natural levees; and population distribution and density. Lifelines, facilities for emergency response, and other critical facilities are suitably noted.

Vulnerability assessment

Once an inventory is available, a vulnerability assessment can be made. This will measure the susceptibility of a structure or class of structures to damage. It is difficult, if not impossible, to predict the actual damage that will occur, since this will depend on an earthquake's epicenter, size, duration, etc. The best determination can be made by evaluating the damage caused by a past earthquake with known intensity in the area of interest and relating the results to existing structures.

Assessing risk and its acceptability

It is theoretically possible to combine the hazard evaluation with the determination of the vulnerability of elements at risk to arrive at an assessment of specific risk, a measure of the willingness of the public to incur costs to reduce risk. This is a difficult and expensive process, however, applicable to advanced stages of the development planning process. For any particular situation, planners and hazard experts working together may be able to devise suitable alternative procedures that will identify approximate risk and provide technical guidance to the political decisions as to what levels are acceptable and what would be acceptable costs to reduce the risk.

Earthquake Mitigation Measures

The range of mechanisms includes land-use zoning; engineering approaches such as building codes, strengthening of existing structures, stabilizing unstable ground, redevelopment; the establishment of warning systems; and the distribution of losses. Some of these mitigation measures are applicable to new development, some to existing development, and some to both. Consideration must be given to the administrative and political aspects of applying mitigation techniques such as obtaining community support, mobilizing local interests, and incorporating the seismic aspects into a comprehensive zoning ordinance.

Ground Shaking Mitigation Measures

Once the potential severity and effects of ground shaking are established as explained above, several types of seismic zoning measures can be applied. These include:

- Relating general ground shaking potential to allowable density of building occupancy.
- Relating building design and construction standards to the degree of ground shaking risk.
- Adopting ordinances that require geologic and seismic site investigations before development proposals can be approved.
- In areas already developed, adopting a hazardous building abatement ordinance and an ordinance to require removal of dangerous parapets.

Surface Faulting Mitigation Measures

Since fault zones are relatively easy to delineate, they lend themselves to effective land-use planning. Where assessment of the consequences of surface rupture indicates an unacceptably high possibility of damage, several alternative mitigation measures are available:

— Restricting permissible uses to those compatible with the hazard, i.e., open space and recreation areas, freeways, parking lots, cemeteries, solid-waste disposal sites, etc.
— Establishing an easement that requires a setback distance from active fault traces.
— Prohibiting all uses except utility or transportation facilities in areas of extremely high hazard, and setting tight design and construction standards for utility systems traversing active fault zones.

Ground Failure Mitigation Measures

Land-use measures to reduce potential damage due to landslides or liquefaction are similar to those taken for other geologic hazards: land uses can be restricted, geologic investigations can be required before development is allowed, and grading and foundation design can be regulated. Land-use zoning may not be appropriate in some areas because of the potential for substantial variation within each mapped unit, but even without mandatory use restrictions, stability categories can indicate the precautions appropriate for the use of any parcel of land.

General Land-use Measures

Where development has already taken place in areas prone to earthquake hazards, measures can be adopted to identify unsafe structures and ordain their removal, starting with those that endanger the greatest number of lives. Tax incentives can be established for the removal of hazardous buildings, and urban renewal policies should restrict reconstruction in hazardous areas after earthquake destruction. The political acceptability of zoning measures can be increased by developing policies which combine earthquake hazards with other land-use considerations.

References

Donald Hyndman, David Hyndman (2009). "Chapter 3: Earthquakes and their causes". *Natural Hazards and Disasters* (2nd ed.). Brooks/Cole: Cengage Learning

Jackson, James, "Fatal attraction: living with earthquakes, the growth of villages into megacities, and earthquake vulnerability in the modern world," *Philosophical Transactions of the Royal Society*. Phil. Trans. R. Soc. A 15 August 2006 vol. 364 no. 1845 1911–1925.

Noson, Qamar, and Thorsen (1988). *Washington State Earthquake Hazards: Washington State Department of Natural Resources*. Washington Division of Geology and Earth Resources Information Circular 85.

Schorlemmer, D.; Wiemer, S.; Wyss, M. (2005). "Variations in earthquake-size distribution across different stress regimes". *Nature* 437 (7058): 539–542.

Spence, William; S. A. Sipkin, G. L. Choy (1989). "Measuring the Size of an Earthquake". United States Geological Survey. Retrieved 2006-11-03.

Wyss, M. (1979). "Estimating expectable maximum magnitude of earthquakes from fault dimensions". *Geology* 7 (7): 336–340.

6

Flood Management

A flood is an overflow of water that submerges land. Flooding may result from the volume of water within a body of water, such as a river or lake, which overflows or breaks levees, with the result that some of the water escapes its usual boundaries, or may be due to accumulation of rainwater on saturated ground in an areal flood. While the size of a lake or other body of water will vary with seasonal changes in precipitation and snow melt, it is not a significant flood unless such escapes of water endanger land areas used by man like a village, city or other inhabited area.

Floods can also occur in rivers, when flow exceeds the capacity of the river channel, particularly at bends or meanders. Floods often cause damage to homes and businesses if they are placed in natural flood plains of rivers. While flood damage can be virtually eliminated by moving away from rivers and other bodies of water, since time out of mind, people have lived and worked by the water to seek sustenance and capitalize on the gains of cheap and easy travel and commerce by being near water. That humans continue to inhabit areas threatened by flood damage is evidence that the perceived value of living near the water exceeds the cost of repeated periodic flooding.

Some floods develop slowly, while others such a flash floods, can develop in just a few minutes and without visible signs of rain. Additionally, floods can be local, impacting a neighborhood or community, or very large, affecting entire river basins.

Almost every year floods of varying magnitude affect some parts of the world or the other. Different regions have different climates and rainfall patterns and, therefore, while some parts face devastating floods, other parts may, at the same time, experience drought conditions. The monsoon regime is a regular phenomenon. Year-to-year variations occur with regard to the onset of the monsoon, its progress over the Indian landmass, and the amount of rainfall distribution. In some years the variation is quite significant. Nevertheless, there is a fundamental regularity and dependability about the monsoon that sets the seasonal rhythms of life, although it also causes unfortunate losses across much of this part of the world.

Causes of Floods

Inadequate capacity of the rivers to contain within their banks the high flows brought down from the upper catchment areas following heavy rainfall, leads to flooding. The tendency to occupy the flood plains has been a serious concern over the years. Because of the varying rainfall distribution, many a time, areas which are not traditionally prone to floods also experience severe inundation. Areas with poor drainage facilities get flooded by accumulation of water from heavy rainfall. Excess irrigation water applied to command areas and increase in ground water levels due to seepage from canals and irrigated fields also are factors that accentuate the problem of water-logging. The problem is exacerbated by factors such as silting of the riverbeds, reduction in the carrying capacity of river channels, erosion of beds and banks leading to changes in river courses, obstructions to flow due to landslides, synchronisation of floods in the main and tributary rivers and retardation due to tidal effects.

Flash Floods

Flash floods are characterised by very fast rise and recession of flow of small volume and high discharge, which causes high damages because of suddenness. This occurs in hilly and not too hilly regions and sloping lands where heavy rainfall and thunderstorms or cloudbursts are common. Depression and cyclonic storms in the coastal areas of Orissa, West Bengal, Andhra Pradesh, Karnataka, and Tamil Nadu also cause flash floods. Arunachal Pradesh, Assam, Orissa, Himachal Pradesh, Uttarakhand, the Western Ghats in Maharastra and Kerala are more vulnerable to flash floods caused by cloud bursts. Sudden release of waters from upstream reservoirs, breaches in landslide dams and embankments on the banks of the rivers leads to disastrous floods. Severe floods in Himachal Pradesh in August 2000 and June 2005, and in Arunachal Pradesh in 2000 are a few examples of flash floods caused by breaches in landslide dams. Floods in Assam, Bihar, Uttar Pradesh, Orissa and Andhra Pradesh are generally caused by breaches in embankments. Incidents of high intensity rainfall over short durations, which cause flash floods even in the area where rains are rare phenomena, are on the rise and the problem needs to be tackled in a scientific manner.

i) Flash floods forecasting and warning systems using Doppler radars will be installed by the India Meteorological Department (IMD) by September 2009.

ii) As a preventive measure, the inhabitation of low-lying areas along the rivers, nallas and drains will be regulated by the state governments/ State Disaster Management Authorities (SDMAs)/District Disaster Management Authorities (DDMAs).

iii) Landslides and blockages in rivers will be monitored by the Central Water Commission (CWC)/National Remote Sensing Agency (NRSA)/ state governments/SDMAs with the help of satellite imageries and in case of their occurrence, warning systems will be set up to reduce losses. If possible, appropriate structural measures to eliminate the damage in case of sudden collapse of the blockages will also be taken up.

Damages Caused by Floods

Morc than thc loss of life and damage to property, the sense of insecurity and fear in the minds of people living in the flood plains is a cause of great concern. The after effects of floods such as the agony of survivors, spread of epidemics, non availability of drinking water, essential commodities and medicines, loss of the dwellings etc. make floods the most feared among the natural disasters faced by mankind.

An area is said to be waterlogged when the water table rises to an extent that the soil pores in the root zone of a crop become saturated, resulting in restriction of the normal circulation of air, decline in the level of oxygen and increase in the level of carbon dioxide. Drainage congestion and consequent water-logging may be either due to surface flooding or rise in water table, as a result of excess inflow as compared to outflow which may be either on account of excess rain and/ or over-irrigation.

The erosion of banks by the rivers and the consequent loss of life and property are major problems. Rivers tend to erode their beds and banks in the hilly regions resulting in the deepening and widening of rivers. When a river enters the flood plains, it shows a tendency to braid and develop number of channels causing silting of the riverbed, change in course and bank erosion. In the plains, a river shows a meandering tendency with meanders moving downstream causing erosion on the concave and deposition on the convex side and cut offs. This causes large-scale bank erosion. In deltaic reaches near the outfall into sea, the river divides itself into a number of branches resulting in bank erosion. Thus bank erosion and consequent loss of land and properties is a constant phenomenon all along the course of the river. The study of the problem and remedial measures for training of the river into defined channel has gained importance due to increase in population pressure and want of alternative sources of livelihood for the people whose land and properties are lost to rivers.

Historically, civilisations have developed along river courses. Towns have grown faster on account of increase/influx of population. Owing to lack of regulation/control, there has been considerable encroachment of flood plains. Damages become serious as a result of inadequate capacity of storm water drainage system. The problem of urban flooding has become serious as evidenced by the floods in Mumbai, Bangalore, Chennai, Vadodara, Ahmedabad, Surat, Kolkata, Hyderabad, Visakhapatnam and Vijayawada.

The flood problems of deltaic regions are attributed to various causes like flatter slope of drains and back flow due to tides. Littoral drift of sand in the form of sand dunes formation and consequent choking of outfalls of rivers into the sea is one of the causes for flood in deltaic regions. The Biccavole and Tulabhaga drains in the Godavari eastern delta and the Panchanadi, Lower Kowsika, Vasalatippa and Kunavaram drains in Godavari central delta are some of the problem reaches.

Straight cuts into the sea with a view to make the slope steeper in outfall reaches are sometimes considered as an effective measure to overcome the problem. These measures must be taken only after an intensive study on the mathematical and hydraulic models is carried out so as to avoid the risk of increased flooding in case of high tides, cyclonic storms and tsunamis.

FLOODPLAINS

Floodplains are land areas adjacent to rivers and streams that are subject to recurring inundation. Owing to their continually changing nature, floodplains and other flood-prone areas need to be examined in the light of how they might affect or be affected by development. The primary objective of remote sensing methods for mapping flood-prone areas in developing countries is to provide planners and disaster management institutions with a practical and cost-effective way to identify floodplains and other susceptible areas and to assess the extent of disaster impact.

This method has the following characteristics:

- It uses remote sensing data covering single or multiple dates or events.
- It permits digital (by computer) or photo-optical (film positive or negative) analysis.
- It is best used as a complement to other available hydrologic and climatic data.
- It is useful in preliminary assessments during the early stages of a development planning study because of the small-to-intermediate scale of the information produced and the ability to meet cost and time constraints.

Flooding is a natural and recurring event for a river or stream. Statistically, streams will equal or exceed the mean annual flood once every 2.33 years. Flooding is a result of heavy or continuous rainfall exceeding the absorptive capacity of soil and the flow capacity of rivers, streams, and coastal areas. This causes a watercourse to overflow its banks onto adjacent lands. Floodplains are, in general, those lands most subject to recurring floods, situated adjacent to rivers and streams. Floodplains are therefore "flood-prone" and are hazardous to development activities if the vulnerability of those activities exceeds an acceptable level.

Floodplains can be looked at from several different perspectives: 'To define a floodplain depends somewhat on the goals in mind. As a topographic category it is quite flat and lies adjacent to a stream; geomorphologically, it is a landform composed primarily of unconsolidated depositional material derived from sediments being transported by the related stream; hydrologically, it is best defined as a landform subject to periodic flooding by a parent stream. A combination of these [characteristics] perhaps comprises the essential criteria for defining the floodplain". Most simply, a flood-plain is defined as "a strip of relatively smooth land bordering a stream and overflowed [sic] at a time of high water".

Floods are usually described in terms of their statistical frequency. A "100-year flood" or "100-year floodplain" describes an event or an area subject to a 1% probability of a certain size flood occurring in any given year. Since floodplains can be mapped, the boundary of the 100-year flood is commonly used in floodplain mitigation programs to identify areas where the risk of flooding is significant. Any other statistical frequency of a flood event may be chosen depending on the degree of risk that is selected for evaluation, e.g., 5-year, 20-year, 50-year, 500-year floodplain.

Frequency of inundation depends on the climate, the material that makes up the banks of the stream, and the channel slope. Where substantial rainfall occurs in a particular season each year, or where the annual flood is derived principally from snowmelt, the floodplain may be inundated nearly every year, even along large streams with very small channel slopes. In regions without extended periods of below-freezing temperatures, floods usually occur in the season of highest precipitation. Where most floods are the result of snowmelt, often accompanied by rainfall, the flood season is spring or early summer.

Gathering hydrologic data directly from rivers and streams is a valuable but time-consuming effort. If such dynamic data have been collected for many years through stream gauging, models can be used to determine the statistical frequency of given flood events, thus determining their probability. However, without a record of at least twenty years, such assessments are difficult.

In many countries, stream-gauging records are insufficient or absent. As a result, flood hazard assessments based on direct measurements may not be possible, because there is no basis to determine the specific flood levels and recurrence intervals for given events. Hazard assessments based on remote sensing data, damage reports, and field observations can substitute when quantitative data are scarce. They present mapped information defining flood-prone areas which will probably be inundated by a flood of a specified interval.

The following land-surface characteristics related to floods:

— Topography or slope of the land, especially its flatness;

— Geomorphology, type and quality of soils, especially unconsolidated fluvial deposit base material; and

— Hydrology and the extent of recurring flooding.

These characteristics are commonly considered in natural resource evaluation activities.

Changing Nature of Floodplains

Floodplains are neither static nor stable. Composed of unconsolidated sediments, they are rapidly eroded during floods and high flows of water, or they may be the site on which new layers of mud, sand, and silt are deposited. As such, the river may change its course and shift from one side of the floodplain to the other. Figure 1 portrays this dynamic pattern whereby the river channel may change within the broader floodplain and the floodplain may be periodically modified by floods as the channel migrates back and forth across the it.

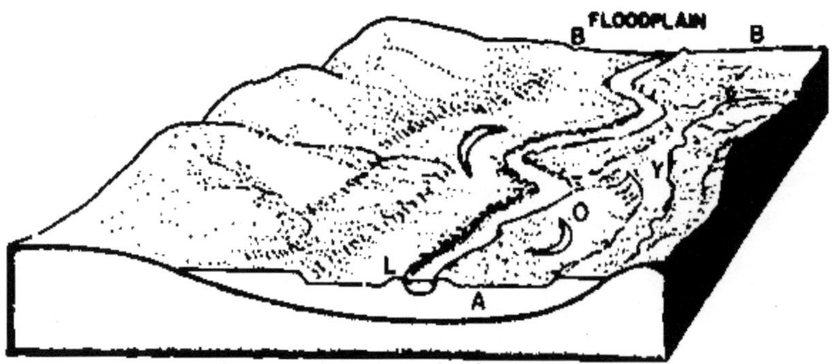

Figure 1. Characteristics of the dynamic pattern of floodplains. Landforms of an alluvial river floodplain with freely developed meanders: A - Alluvium, B - Bluffs, L - Levees, O - Oxbow Lake, Y - Yazoo stream

Floodplain width is a function of the size of the stream, the rates of downcutting, the channel slope, and the hardness of the channel wall. Floodplains are uncommon in headwater channels because the stream is small, the slopes and rate of downcutting are high, and the valley walls are often exposed bedrock.

In moderately small streams the floodplain is commonly found only on the inside of a bend (meander), but the location of the floodplain alternates from side to side as the stream meanders from one side of the valley to the other.

Larger streams, particularly those with low channel slopes, develop broad floodplains. As these plains develop, the sideward migration of the river channel produces oxbow lakes, sloughs, natural levees, and backswamp deposits that are disconnected from the present channel. If a river carries fairly coarse sediment during a flood, it tends to be deposited along the channel bank as a natural levee. This may result in the formation of a perched channel where the channel bottom is continually raised to a point where it may actually be higher than the surrounding topography. This condition can result in surface water elevations contained within the channel being considerably higher than the land surface elevations immediately outside these levees, which results in a flooding potential that is much worse than that in the typical situation where the channel is at the bottom of a U-shaped cross section of the floodplain.

These features change with time. Widening of a river channel and destruction of part of the floodplain by major floods is common and has been observed in semiarid regions. As is the case with these regions having a high erosion potential, the phenomenon of channel migration during flooding events will often cause a large portion of flood waters to be carried in a channel that did not exist prior to the onset of the flooding event. This phenomenon occurs all too frequently in arid regions, where high velocity flood waters make drastic changes in the channel configuration during the flooding event. This can cause the area of inundation to be considerably different than in its original state.

Channel mobility can be an important characteristic when trying to delineate the potential floodplain. While mobility is not much of a problem in areas with dense vegetation and consolidated soil types, in areas where the vegetation is sparse and soil types are coarse and erodible, mapping of the floodplain must include anticipation of the possibility of channel migration in addition to the existing channel configuration.

A major flood in a humid region is less likely to cause channel widening and floodplain destruction, because vegetation inhibits erosion. However, the flood may cut secondary channels through a floodplain and deposit sand and gravel over large areas, particularly those dedicated to agricultural production.

Terraces along a channel may be mistaken for a floodplain. In fact, some terraces may have been floodplain boundaries prior to renewed downcutting or tectonic activity. A terrace can usually be distinguished from an active floodplain by the type of vegetation and the surface material present. Natural events such as landslides, volcanic-ash drop, lahars, and debris slides can increase the amount of sediment available for transport by a stream. Sediments from these events may be deposited both in the channel and on the floodplain. This can result in the channel filling with debris and reducing the capacity of the channel to hold water. The reduction in channel capacity, although it may be temporary, can result in more frequent inundation of the floodplain and contribute to its modification.

Frequency of Flooding

Generally, only annual floods are used in a probability analysis, and the recurrence interval-the reciprocal of probability-is substituted for probability. The annual flood is usually considered the single greatest event each year. The 10-year flood, for example, is the discharge that will exceed a certain volume which has a 10% probability of occurring each year.

The floodplains of some streams, however, are inundated infrequently, at intervals of 10 years or more. Several reasons have been proposed to explain this. In some climates, several years of intense flood activity are followed by many years in which few floods occur. The floodplain may be developed and occupied during the years with the least flood activity. As a result, this development is subject to the risk of flooding as the cycle of flooding returns. Development activity, particularly deforestation and intensive crop production, may drastically change runoff conditions, thereby increasing stream flow during normal rainfall cycles and thus increasing the risk of flooding. More intensive use of the floodplain, even under strict management, almost always results in increased runoff rates. Effects of development practices on the risk of flooding are discussed below.

Length of Inundation

The length of time that a floodplain is inundated depends on the size of the stream, the channel slope, and the climatic characteristics. On small streams, floods induced by rainfall usually last from only a few hours to a few days, but on large rivers flood runoff may exceed channel capacity for a month or more. In 1982-83, the Parana River Basin in Brazil, Paraguay, and Argentina was subject to extensive flooding from late November 1982 through mid-1983. The duration of a flood from tropical storms or snowmelts may inundate a floodplain several times during a single month.

Water on the floodplain usually drains back to the channel as the channel flow recedes. On the wide floodplains of large rivers bordered by natural levees, the water may drain back slowly, causing local inundation or pounding which may last for months. It is eventually disposed of by downstream drainage, water infiltration into the soil, and evapotranspiration. Where channels are perched due to repeated deposition of sediment, flood waters may never drain back to the channel since that channel bottom is higher than the adjacent floodplain.

Vulnerability Analysis

A vulnerability analysis considers the population and structures at risk within the flood-prone area. The analysis evaluates the potential costs of flooding in terms of damages to buildings, crops, roads, bridges and critical infrastructure, such as utilities. Normally the analysis is carried out for various probabilities of floods, and an elevation-damage curve is developed.

A vulnerability analysis, because it identifies the population at greatest risk, can also be used to identify the emergency responses that may be required, including the need for temporary shelters and evacuation requirements.

The analysis is also valuable for making a decision on the level of flood protection. The decision is based on knowledge of the degree of cost effectiveness of various options. However it should be a public process that establishes the "acceptable level of risk" that leads to the return period appropriate for the delineation of flood-prone areas. The analysis may also generate information useful in determining the benefits of flow forecasting.

Flood Risk Mapping

Mapping defines the area at risk and should be the basis for all flood damage reduction programmes and subsequent actions. The maps often have a legal connotation in terms of zoning and other structural and nonstructural measures undertaken, so they need to be accurate and credible. The mapping is normally based on a frequency of flood event determined by public consultation and reflected in policy, which may be based on a vulnerability analysis that is site specific.

If regional or national flood reduction programmes are in place, there are advantages to a common mapping standard. If the historical flood is used, then some attempt should be made to assign a return period to the event for communication and design purposes. Maps become the common element in terms of identification of flood-prone areas, identifying the risk to individuals and lending institutions, preparation of emergency response plans, and design of flood protection and flood proofing measures. Perhaps their greatest value is as an educational and communications tool, and they should be readily available to the public as well as to emergency response agencies at all levels of government. Through modern computational systems, inundation maps can be generated in realtime and be part of the hydrological forecast system. These can greatly assist in communication to residents in areas of potential risk, and in planning response actions and assistance.

Protecting Flood-prone Lands

Policies and programmes to keep future flood damages from rising are based on the delineation and mapping of flood-prone areas. Generally the resulting programmes will mean some form of control over new development in the flood-prone area combined with measures to reduce damages to existing development. Such programmes are needed to curb the rising social and economic losses that results from floods.

Alternate use of flood-prone land should be considered where possible. It is better to have the land zoned and used for purposes such as parks, nature areas or ecological reserves than to try and ensure that future development is flood proofed. Zoning and flood proofing measures can be used to control development and reduce future flood damages, but the effectiveness of such measures is highly reliant on enforcement and maintenance. Local authorities are subject to developmental pressures and standards have a tendency to "slip" as the memory of a flood event fades.

Climatological Forecasting

Climatological or seasonal forecasting has now advanced to the point of being a useful tool in reducing the risk of flooding. Extreme events are correlated to major changes in atmospheric and ocean circulation patterns, and once such patterns have been identified, the potential for a lesser or greater degree of storm activity can be forecast. This information can then be used to increase the degree of readiness of emergency response and forecasting agencies. In certain cases the climatic forecasts can also be used to increase the availability of storage in reservoirs, to influence water management decisions and to create an awareness of the potential for flooding. All of these measures can reduce the severity of flooding, if it occurs.

When the probability of the extreme flooding event is greater than normal, then activities such as the stockpiling of sandbags, emergency food and water supplies, and the evacuation of high value stored crops or goods from floodprone areas can be undertaken. It is a good time to create awareness in the public as to the potential for flooding, highlight the actions that the public and others should take, and to carry out emergency response exercises to test the degree of readiness. In some cases emergency measures such as temporary raising of flood protection works may be warranted.

Supportive Technologies

A number of tools are available to array and display information for the use of technical experts, to explain programmes of flood damage reduction to the decision-makers, and to communicate real time forecasts and warnings to the public. In general the tools should be interactive in the sense that the information can be easily updated, and flexible enough to develop scenarios, and to provide visual and quantitative information regarding the state of conditions during the forecasted event.

Geographic Information Systems

Geographic Information Systems (GIS) provide a computer-based information and manipulation system useful in support of flow forecasting and emergency response. Information from a variety of sources and scales can be combined as a series of layers, provided that the information can be identified in terms of the common denominator of location. For example, information on vegetative cover can be combined with soils and land slope information to estimate infiltration rates for forecasting purposes. Similarly layers of utility, land use, flood plain delineation, and structures information can help in the development and updating of emergency response plans.

A good representation of the basin topography is an important asset in flood forecasting, emergency action and mitigation. A digital elevation model (DEM) or digital terrain model (DTM) for the basin should be developed as part of any GIS. Technologies exist that enable the construction of a "seamless best available" DEM. In other words the DEM is constructed from whatever topographic information is available. Parts of the basin or certain features may be very accurate while others may be quite basic.

The DEM can be improved with time. The development of inexpensive global position indicators has made GIS information easier to obtain. For example, data network sites, buildings or physical features can now be easily located with precision and at low cost. Land use, vegetative cover or soils information is also easier to assemble.

Mapping

Maps of areas at risk from natural disasters are valuable information and communication tools. They can be used for a wide variety of purposes ranging from flood plain delineation, zoning and land use planning to presentation of information at public meetings.

Zoning maps, however, are static and may require updating with time as changes occur. For static information, such as the delineation of the flood-prone area, frequent updating is not required, and maps are a useful reference tool for a wide variety of users.

Visualisation Techniques

GIS and other computer-based information systems allow for a wide range of presentational material to be easily generated and tailored to the target audience. Threedimensional displays, zoom and scan, and rotational techniques can be combined with other informational material such as pictures, overheads or slides. As an example, a GIS flood inundation map can be generated based on hydraulic model derived information. The map can be conveyed to residents in the flood plain and is useful for depicting the probable impact of the approaching flood.

This tailoring of technical information into displays that are more readily understood is valuable for explaining programmes to decision-makers, informed experts, and the public at large. Highly visual information is particularly valuable for public meetings or open houses, but must be tailored carefully for the audience. In particular, the information must be credible and easily understood. The above techniques, combined with the flood forecast, provide a very effective means of delineating areas at risk and for communicating this to the decision-makers, emergency response teams, and the public.

Flood Plain Management

Management of activities within the floodprone area can significantly reduce flood damages to existing development and prevent the amount of damages from rising in the future. The most desirable approach is to prohibit new development in the flood plain and to flood proof existing structures, or to replace the existing development by alternative usage of the land. However, where the amount of present development is substantial or the flood plain is essential for the production of food or other key economic activities, alternate strategies such as flood proofing and protection can be considered.

Structural Measures

Construction of protective works such as flood storage reservoirs, diversion of water to side channel storage or other watersheds, construction of storm channels to carry water around the area to be protected, and levees along the floodway provide tools to reduce flood damages. Such works can be constructed to various levels of protection, usually based on: 1) minimum standards for flood protection; 2) the optimum level of costs and benefits based on an economic analysis; or 3) to meet established levels of acceptable risk.

Protective works should be considered when major infrastructure has already been developed and costs to protect existing investments are far less than those related to reconstruction, lost economic activity, disaster assistance, or relocation of existing structures and activities. For example, flood protection measures for the city of Winnipeg, Canada, were completed in the late 1960s at a cost of $US 92 million. A rough estimate of damages prevented in five large floods since then is approximately $US 2.0 billion.

Protective works have a tendency to increase the level of development in floodprone areas, as the assumption is made that it is now safe to build and invest in areas that are protected. However, it must be recognised that at some point in the future the design event will likely be exceeded and catastrophic damages will result. Levees and storage dams are particularly dangerous when design thresholds are exceeded in that unexpected failure can result in a rapid rise in water level and make evacuation and emergency protection extremely difficult. Diversions or storm channels are less prone to catastrophic failure and the level of protection can temporarily be increased by emergency measures if the lead-time of the flood warning is sufficient.

Flood control storage may be one component of a multi-purpose reservoir development. Over time the operation of the reservoir could be altered to enhance other beneficial uses of storage to the detriment of flood control. A commitment to "designated flood storage" and to reservoir operation procedures to achieve that storage is needed.

Inspection, Rehabilitation and Maintenance

Structural works require a periodic and systematic inspection, rehabilitation and maintenance programme to ensure that the design capabilities are maintained. For example, levees may be subject to weakening due to erosion during a past flood event, by the actions of burrowing animals, or the construction of utility lines through the levee. Of particular importance is an inspection programme and responsibility assigned for rehabilitation and maintenance. Structures such as dams should be subject to a dam safety programme, usually at the national level, to ensure that the specialised expertise required is available for the inspection of all structures. Dam safety programmes are carried out in many countries and standards or guidelines are readily available.

Flood proofing of new and existing structures Any new construction permitted in the flood plain should be flood proofed to reduce future damages. Building codes can be developed that minimise flood damages by ensuring that beneficial uses of buildings are located above the design flood elevation. For example, buildings can be raised above the design flood level by placement of fill; stilts or piles used to elevate the structure; and building utilities can be located above the flood level. Ground floors can be designed in a way that little flood damage occurs through use of masonry materials and specifying that contents must be removable.

If any new development is allowed within the flood-prone area, then the impact of that development must be taken into account to ensure that flood levels do not rise significantly due to the additional constriction to flow. Hydraulic analyses can be undertaken to ascertain the impacts of potential activities and to keep the rise to within acceptable limits.

Flood proofing of existing structures is difficult and expensive. One successful strategy is to link flood disaster assistance available after a flood event to methods of reconstruction that minimise future flood damages. This approach often requires additional funding over and above a payment for damages, but can be costshared between various levels of government and the owner. This strategy is particularly useful when flooding is frequent and future disaster assistance can be expected as part of disaster policies. Flood proofing of existing structures can include raising of structures to prevent damage, relocation of utilities, changed building use, installation of protective walls and waterproof closures, and use of materials that are not damaged by water and can be easily cleaned after the flood event. Relocation of existing buildings and structures to an area that is not floodprone is also an option.

Buyout and relocation programmes for a particularly vulnerable development should form a component of flood proofing initiatives. In many cases it may be more economical to buy out and relocate the existing use than to protect it. A number of critical services such as water lines, power pylons and telephone services often cross the flood plain. These utilities can be protected against the ravages of flooding at relatively low cost through additional depth of burial, a higher design standard for exposed components, and raising of components above design flood levels.

Water supply and treatment plants are particularly vulnerable. They are often located on the flood plain yet are critical for the protection of human health during and after a flood event. Such structures need to be protected against extreme events and designed to prevent cross-contamination from floodwaters or sewers.

Bridges and Roads

Bridges generally constrict the flow of water, and they can act as artificial dams if debris jams on the structure. In all cases, their hydraulic characteristics must be considered at the design stage to prevent an unacceptable rise of water levels upstream of the structure.

Bridges are important in terms of maintaining access for evacuation and delivery of medical and other emergency services. Key transportation corridors should have high design standards that will withstand extreme flooding events. However not all bridges require a high level of protection, and the design criteria can be to a lesser standard that takes into consideration the possibility of overtopping. Bridges are expensive, and difficult to replace quickly after a flood event. An alternative strategy is to design the approach roads to be the weak link in the chain so that extreme events wash out the road but do not damage the bridge. Approaches can be quickly repaired after a flood event and transportation corridors restored.

Road design, either parallel to the river or leading to bridges, must be given careful consideration. There is a temptation to raise roads that have been overtopped by flood events without giving adequate consideration to the number and size of openings necessary to pass local drainage or tributary inflow. In such cases the road can artificially raise water levels upstream and cause additional flood damage. Roads can also act as levees when they are parallel to the river. This is a two-edged sword: while flood protection is provided, the water level upstream can increase, resulting in additional flood damages there. Hydraulic studies must be undertaken before roads are raised to fully establish the impacts of these activities.

Enforcement of Standards and Codes

The enforcement of standards and codes for flood-prone areas is as important as their initial development. There is a tendency to bend the rules as the memory of a flood event and its catastrophic consequences gradually fade away with time. Enforcement procedures and penalties need to be built into the process, and emergency response drills undertaken to ensure that flood prevention measures such as waterproof closures still work. An audit procedure should be performed by higher orders of government with participation of all interested parties to ensure broad national standards are being met and that codes and rules are being suitably followed and enforced.

Governments should consider introducing requirements such as surveyor certificates to verify that design elevations have been met, or inspector reports that flood-proofing measures have been implemented. Lending and insurance institutions could usefully be involved in this process, as they have a vested interest in ensuring that their investments are protected.

Non-structural Measures

Non-structural measures are particularly applicable to flood-prone areas that are not yet developed. As such, they are a complement to structural approaches in areas where additional development may occur, and they also represent an independent approach where some control over flood plain development can be exercised at low cost. Non-structural approaches do not mean "no use", but rather "wise use".

Land-use Planning

Land-use planning at the local or municipal level can be a useful tool in reducing future flood damages. Consideration should be given to ensuring that there are conforming uses in flood-prone areas as part of master plans. The land along a river is highly desirable for parks and recreational uses, as well as for ecological reserves. Supportive infrastructure such as washrooms, picnic facilities and changing rooms can be flood proofed. Private development of conforming uses such as golf courses can also be considered. The important point here is to integrate the land-use planning for floodprone lands into the broader plans for the urban and surrounding area.

Zoning of Flood-prone Lands

The best way to reduce future flood damages is to prevent development from occurring on flood-prone lands. Zoning of such lands is an effective approach, but generally should be coupled with the broader land-use planning mentioned above so that the land has a defined use.

Zoning can be used to reduce damages from flooding and be flexible enough to recognise that other forms of land use are compatible. An example is agricultural use of lands in flood-prone areas where water velocities are low enough not to cause serious erosion. Flood-prone lands can continue to be used for agricultural purposes, particularly in countries where the amount of agricultural land is limited and self-sufficiency in food supply is a national goal. It is important, however, to ensure that the supporting infrastructure such as buildings and houses are located away from the flood-prone area or are flood proofed. It is also important that livestock, machinery or stored crops can be evacuated quickly from the area in the event of a flood. This underscores the importance of a flood forecast, warning and response system.

Zoning of flood-prone lands as ecological reserves or protected wetlands can often help to meet broader environmental or biodiversity goals. In addition, such lands often play an important role in sustaining the fishery, and they can also act as temporary storage and infiltration areas. Riparian buffer strips also reduce the movement of agricultural chemicals and nutrients into the aquatic system.

Redevelopment of flood-prone areas A major flood disaster is sometimes an opportunity to correct the planning errors of the past. Removal of flood-prone development and conversion of the land to a conforming use is an option to consider. It may be less expensive in the long run to physically relocate flood-prone development, buy it out as part of a disaster assistance programme, or include its purchase in long term planning. The success of the latter approach can be enhanced by measures such as prohibiting improvements not required for health and safety, placing caveats on the land title, and by obtaining rights of first refusal on resale.

Compensation and Incentives

Compensation as part of disaster assistance should always have as a goal the reduction of future flood damages. Rather than simply paying for damages, the funds should be focused on flood proofing, buyout, relocation and public education on the risks and consequences of living on flood-prone lands.

In a similar manner, incentives can be developed that encourage flood proofing or relocation, and these can be financed through cost-shared programmes. Here the cost of flood proofing can be shared in proportion to the benefits to the various levels of government of not having to compensate for future flood damages. Property owners should also be expected to pay a reasonable share in view of the enhanced value of a flood-proofed structure and the reduced inconvenience after a flood. Land exchange programmes can be used as an incentive to relocate from flood-prone lands.

In such cases a public entity makes alternate land available and disaster assistance is generally used to pay for relocation or replacement of structures, depending on the costs and benefits. Incentives can also take the form of penalties. For example, if an individual is aware of the risk of flooding through such programmes as flood plain delineation, or caveats on land titles, and still decides to build on flood-prone land, then that person should bear the consequences of his/her actions and not be eligible for disaster assistance. However this is difficult to enforce and is reliant on strong political will at the time of announcing disaster assistance.

Insurance

Flood disaster insurance forms part of the suite of responses to reducing flood losses in the United States of America. When a prospective homebuyer seeks to purchase a property in a designated flood-prone area with funds obtained through a federallyinsured or regulated institution, the lender is required to notify the borrower of the need for flood insurance. The losses covered by flood insurance are paid from the accumulated premiums of policyholders rather than disaster assistance funds. There are some weaknesses in this approach, as not all homeowners in floodprone areas purchase insurance, and there is the necessity for public funding if losses exceed the accumulated premiums.

Flood insurance schemes have been utilised in other countries, including parts of Germany, with varying degrees of success. For insurance schemes to be successful, there needs to be a clear definition of the risk, as premiums should reflect the degree of risk at a given location. It is also desirable for governments to promote or, when possible, mandate universal insurance coverage and guarantee funding when payouts exceed premiums. Such schemes should be designed to be self-sustaining over the long term. An additional problem concerns the information base, which is seldom sufficient to define the degree of risk adequately. It is also difficult to effectively make insurance mandatory.

Often those most at risk due to flooding are the least able to pay, or they refuse to pay because of high premiums. The United States has an advantage from an insurance perspective in that 20,000 communities are at risk from flooding; with such a large number of flood-prone communities, the financial risk can be spread more easily than in smaller countries. Insurance is an option that needs to be considered, but is probably not feasible in many developing countries at this time.

Development of Policies, Strategies and Plans

The development of policies, strategies and plans to combat the risks associated with natural disasters should be based on a comprehensive risk assessment. This requires an integrated approach whereby a wide range of mitigation measures should be considered. For example, mitigation activities such as hazardous land mapping (i.e., flood plain mapping plus landslideand mudslide-prone areas) should be designed so that considerations of other disaster types lead to sounder overall landuse plans.

In essence, there would be very little purpose in moving people and goods from one risk zone to another, especially if the other hazard is equally or more apt to occur under the prevailing conditions such as torrential rain. Within this overall process, full consideration needs to be given to the social, environmental and economic impacts of policy and programme development.

Basin Wide Planning

Reduction of flood losses must be considered, using the basin as the basic planning unit. It is absolutely essential to have knowledge of water uses, diversions, storage, and management practices in all parts of the basin, as well as the antecedent, present, and forecasted meteorological and hydrological conditions.

Transboundary basins represent a special challenge in that international collaboration is required. In such cases consideration should be given to expanding existing bilateral or regional arrangements for exchange of data and information and to the negotiation of treaties or agreements. Agreements can also include the option of projects of mutual advantage funded by all the countries involved, including construction of flood storage or other flood preventative measures at the most advantageous locations in the basin as a whole.

Multijurisdictional Issues

Basin-wide planning for reduction of flood losses can involve government at the local, provincial/state and national levels. As such it is desirable to have the national government develop strategies and policies that ensure a consistent framework wherever they are applied. This can extend to matters such as installation and maintenance of data networks, design standards for protective works, flood proofing standards, cost sharing arrangements, and incentive and insurance programmes.

In general the national level of government should take the lead in bringing the parties together, but should delegate planning of the details and delivery of the emergency response programmes to the local level. Generally the national and provincial/state governments will play some direct role in operation of forecasting centres, and they will need to provide for emergency response that exceeds the capability of the local level. There should also be a role of higher orders of government in auditing enforcement of policy measures by local levels.

Inter-agency collaboration

Reduction of flood losses will involve a number of government agencies and often the private sector if, for example, reservoirs are operated by energy utilities. Development of common objectives and definition of a clear role for each of the players can be a major challenge. From a land-use planning perspective, land developers must also be directly involved in the solutions.

Normally some form of inter-agency body will need to be established, and the leadership role assigned to the agency with the greatest involvement or to a strong central agency. There is probably no ideal model for such a structure, as circumstances are quite different in every country. An independent agency is an attractive option, but in general it is probably better to try and build on the strengths of existing agencies so that supportive resources can be marshalled quickly in case of extreme events. However, within this diverse model, it is imperative that one agency be given the overall lead, and that that agency be held accountable for the overall process.

International Collaboration

There are a number of United Nations specialised agencies and programmes that can be of assistance to a country establishing a programme aimed at reducing the losses that result from flooding. Some of these are described herein and could be contacted by interested parties.

The UN Department of Economic and Social Affairs (UNDESA) has been actively involved in providing advice to governments on water resource management during extreme hydrological events in a wide range of environmental and climatic settings from the drought-prone upland plateaus of central Africa through large river basins and aquifer systems in Asia to vulnerable groundwater lenses on Pacific atolls. If one principal lesson is to be learnt, it is that managing water resources under conditions of climatic variability and extreme events involves no special approach; it is simply sound water resource management.

To this extent, climate change should involve relatively few surprises, and should not be an excuse for poor management. It is only possible to undertake sound management practices, however, if the appropriate and accurate hydro-meteorological data are available to resource managers on a regular basis. One of the critical issues in this area is the breakdown in hydro-meteorological data collection systems and analysis. As funding for water resource organisations declines, monitoring networks and the capacity to collect, store and analyse data break down. Ironically, it is only in times of drought or severe flooding that the political will to fund these activities is revived, by which time it is often too late.

Water resources assessment is a core issue that the UN system is addressing through its technical cooperation activities and the World Water Assessment Programme. UNDESA's technical cooperation with developing countries and economies in transition uses state of the art technologies and software for the assessment of water resources availability as a basis for shortterm and long-term planning horizons. National capacity has been developed to perform and continue these assessments in countries such as Bahrain, Burkina Faso, Cape Verde, China, Jordan, Madagascar, Mali, Mauritania, Niger, Senegal, and Yemen. This is of particular importance in water-scarce countries, where water has become a limiting factor for economic and social development.

UNDESA has been collaborating with governmental organisations to enhance national capacity to address the problems of water quality assessment and overall water management. Guidelines and recommendations concerning water quality protection and management are also prepared for national and regional organisations, dealing with monitoring and protection of environment.

The United Nations Development Programme (UNDP) has a programme for strengthening national capacities related to flood mitigation, prevention and preparedness in developing countries. UNDP works in flood reduction and recovery through practical application at the regional and country levels. UNDP has devoted special attention to reducing social and economic vulnerability and loss of lives, and to protecting livelihoods and broadbased development gains.

The World Meteorological Organisation (WMO), a specialised agency of the UN, was established in 1950 to facilitate worldwide cooperation in meteorology, hydrology and climatology for the benefit of humanity. WMO promotes the following types of activities: the establishment of the networks of stations for acquiring meteorological, hydrological and related geophysical observations and the standardisation of observational methodologies; establishment and maintenance of systems for processing and exchanging data and information; activities in operational hydrology, such as flood forecast and warning systems; multi-agency and interdisciplinary programmes on water resources, climate change, natural disasters, and other environmental issues; and research and training.

The International Strategy for Disaster Reduction (ISDR) was launched by the General Assembly of the United Nations in January 2000, to provide a global framework for action with the objective of reducing human, social, economic and environmental losses due to natural hazards and related technological and environmental phenomena. The ISDR aims at building disaster-resilient communities by promoting awareness of the importance of disaster reduction as an integral component of sustainable development. The General Assembly established two mechanisms for the implementation of the ISDR: the Inter-Agency Secretariat and the Inter-Agency Task Force on Disaster Reduction (IATF/DR).

The ISDR Secretariat serves as a focal point within the United Nations system for coordination of strategies and programmes for disaster reduction and to ensure synergy between disaster reduction activities and those in the socio-economic and humanitarian fields. The ISDR Secretariat also serves as an international clearinghouse for the management and the dissemination of information, in particular on current knowledge and status of disaster reduction through the publication of its Global Review of Disaster Reduction Initiatives. It develops activities such as advocacy campaigns to promote wider understanding of natural hazards, as well as risk assessment and management to motivate a worldwide commitment to disaster reduction. The ISDR Secretariat has a facilitating role, bringing agencies, organisations and different disciplines together, and providing a common platform and understanding of the scope of disaster risk reduction. In this regard, one main function of the Secretariat is to support the Inter-Agency Task Force for the development of policies on natural disaster.

In particular, the ISDR Secretariat supports activities, such as the development of guidelines, related to reducing the risk from water-related hazards. This requires, on the one hand, support for the development of capacities to monitor the magnitude, duration, timing and location of hazards, such as floods and droughts, as well as landslides, storms, earthquakes, and volcanic eruptions. All of these latter hazards also have impacts on freshwater resources and infrastructure. On the other hand, this also requires promoting the assessment and reduction of the vulnerability to such extremes. This requires decision-making on issues such as development and planning control, legislation and land-use, environmental management and financial tools (e.g., insurance).

The ISDR, with its focus on disaster and risk reduction, draws its relevance from previous practices in the disaster management fields, where traditionally the focus has been on preparedness for response. Political authorities, professionals from many different fields, commercial interests, public organisations, educational institutions and local community leaders are increasingly recognising the essential public value of sustained efforts to reduce the social, economic and environmental costs of disasters. There is now increased emphasis placed on risk, and a growing acceptance that disaster, development and environmental problems are inextricably linked.

Emergency Preparedness and Response

The most critical element in the suite of activities associated with flood-loss reduction is emergency preparedness and response activity. The response to a natural disaster warning must be immediate, comprehensive, and demonstrate very clear lines of command. There must also be a mechanism in place to quickly draw upon external resources available at higher levels of government, or even internationally, when the local level of response will not be sufficient. Many countries have systems in place where a provincial/ state wide or national disaster can be declared to bring in the resources needed. The keys to effective emergency response are advance planning, ability to mobilise sufficient resources quickly, and periodic exercises to identify weaknesses and problems.

Emergency planning and preparedness is first a local responsibility, but one that requires collaboration and coordination with others in a growing circle of like-minded and expert groups that can be drawn upon as events unfold. In particular, there must be strong and reliable communication linkages to storm warning and forecast centers so that the emergency response actions taken are appropriate to the magnitude of the probable event. The network of linkages from the local level upward must be established in advance and, more importantly, key players must periodically meet to exchange information and become comfortable working together. Information sharing should be bidirectional, both upward and downward, between the levels of government. Practice drills are important.

Emergency response must include input from the community and political levels but cannot become a collective responsibility. There must be clear lines of authority, even if the lead agency changes dependent on the magnitude of the event. The community and individuals must have a good understanding of what is expected of them. A good example would be evacuation. Information that defines evacuation routes, identifies emergency shelters, and specifies actions to be taken before leaving, such as removing mobile equipment and removing personal goods and furniture, must be available in advance.

Detailed response plans need to be prepared in advance and reviewed with all of the key agencies and players. There is no one "common" response plan as the linkages will be different in each case. The response to a toxic chemical spill is very different from the response to a major fire or flood. Not only must the plan be in writing and available to those that will be responding, but also it must be continually reviewed and updated. Some of the key pieces of information are: which agency and individuals have the specific responsibility; whom to contact for expert advice; and where to go for information on backup communication systems. This information is constantly changing and needs to be verified periodically and tested in exercises.

Multiple contact points need to be established as the emergency may occur on a weekend, holiday, or after regular business hours. Mechanisms for coordination must be included in the plan, including the structure of response committees, where they will meet and sources of resource information available to them. Often this takes the form of something equivalent to a "war room" where maps, plans, other material and support staff are available immediately.

A key component of any emergency preparedness plan is an inventory of resources that can be accessed. In the case of flooding this could include items such as emergency vehicles, buses and trucks, earthmoving equipment, pumps, plastic, plywood, emergency generators, supplies of gravel and sand, sandbags, and mobile communications equipment. The inventory should also include access to expertise such as surveyors, levee or slope stability experts, forecasting specialists, the media and community leaders. Emergency shelters should be designated in advance, their individual capacity defined and plans made for obtaining sufficient supplies of water, food, medicine and medical/social assistance.

If local resources are not sufficient, then the availability circle must be expanded to include adjacent communities, the provincial/state and national government levels.

Triggering Emergency Action

Advance warning is the key to effective response. It is possible to set up a series of warnings in advance of an actual extreme storm event that can be used as alerts. This could start with long-term climatologic forecasts or more immediate hurricane forecasts that identify potential danger. For specific basins an alert could be issued based on antecedent precipitation and rainfall intensity data in advance of an actual flood forecast. A more detailed forecast would then be issued when all of the data and information required to make a flood forecast became available.

The emergency response to such alerts is very site-specific and should be included in the plan. If, for example, emergency actions such as temporary levees are necessary, then the work could begin based on an alert rather than the specific forecast. The same may hold for emergency evacuation. The response to an extreme flood forecast should be immediate, and with no uncertainty as to what actions and activities should be taken. The public expects governments to act quickly and in a professional manner under such circumstances. Community leaders should be visible, informed and active right from the start.

Training and Response Exercises

Emergency response teams need to be well trained in advance and their skills constantly upgraded. Once the disaster strikes, it is too late to train or try to find missing expertise. Trained staff should know their responsibilities, have immediate access to response plans and other critical information, and already have built a working relationship with colleagues in other organisations. The only meaningful way to test response plans is to carry out periodic emergency exercises. These exercises are meant to simulate real emergency situations and test all aspects of the plan. Costs are significant, but have real payback in an actual emergency. Often critical gaps are identified and appropriate backup strategies developed as part of the exercise.

Advance Preparation

Assuming that there is advance warning of a major storm event, a number of steps can be taken to increase readiness. Such steps include: construction of temporary flood protection works; placing emergency response teams on high alert; distribution of critical materials such as stockpiled sandbags to targeted locations; and preparation of emergency shelters and hospitals prepared for occupation.

The population at risk can be informed of what is expected of them in the actuality of an extreme event. As the event becomes more certain, actions such as evacuation of people, goods and machinery can begin. Even if the event is not as extreme as predicted, these preparations help test emergency response plans and inform the public as to the nature of natural hazards. Media and public information sessions help set the stage as well. The media are key players in the link between public officials and the public. It helps if they are familiar with the terminology used in warnings and forecasts and know whom to contact for more detailed information during an actual flood event.

After the Flood Event

The emergency response does not end with the event, but continues through cleanup and resettlement stages. People will want to know what assistance will be made available, who is responsible, and how to go about seeking that assistance. Senior levels of government should develop clearly defined response policies and programmes in advance. In the absence of such policies, the response is often ad hoc, politically and emotionally motivated, and sets precedents that are not wise in the longer run. Often the response is incomplete in that the obvious and immediate requirements are addressed, but fundamental changes in thinking and sustainable strategies are ignored.

After a major flood it is beneficial to conduct an assessment of the causes and effects of the flood and to make recommendations that would improve preparedness for the next event and reduce future flood losses. Such an assessment can also lead to improvements in flood plain management policies. The long-term economic and social implications of flooding become evident in the post-disaster period. Governments need to demonstrate leadership and sometimes take bold steps to restore employment, address social issues and move the economy in a new direction. In that sense, natural disasters can be a positive motivator for change.

Flood Forecasting and Warning System

Establishing a viable flood forecasting and warning system for communities at risk requires the combination of data, forecast tools, and trained forecasters. A floodforecast system must provide sufficient lead time for communities to respond. Increasing lead time increases the potential to lower the level of damages and loss of life. Forecasts must be sufficiently accurate to promote confidence so that communities will respond when warned. If forecasts are inaccurate, then credibility of the programme will be questioned and no response actions will occur.

Flood-warning systems must be reliable and designed to operate during the most severe floods. The greatest benefits for an effective flood-warning programme occur when flooding is severe, widespread, and/or sudden, and when communities and organisations are prepared to mitigate impacts.

The implementation of an end-to-end flood forecast, warning and response system consists of many components. These components must be linked for successful operation. The interaction of components of the integrated flood forecast system or programme could be represented as a chain composed of many links. Each link must be present and functional if benefits are to be achieved.

The essential links or components of the integrated flood forecasting, warning and response system consist of a Data Source, Communications,

Forecasts, Decision Support, Notification (often referred to as dissemination), Coordination, and Actions (or responses). A flood forecast and warning programme should be designed to mitigate floods, and, as such, it is an asset to overall water management. To achieve this, it is important that all of the components of the system be functional. If any component is dysfunctional, then this weak link could break the chain, resulting in an ineffective warning and response process. For example, if critical rainfall or streamflow data are unavailable or if the data are not relayed to a forecast centre for use in forecasting, then the critical lead time required to make decisions, coordinate activities, warn citizens, and take actions is not possible. If a perfect flood forecast is generated but does not reach the population at risk, then the warning system is useless. Equally, should the population at risk receive the warning but not know what actions should be taken, then the system again would not have accomplished its purpose.

Characteristics of Basin

The physical characteristics of the basin, such as surface area, topography, geology, and land surface cover, will help to determine the nature of potential flooding and the basin's susceptibility to related hazards such as landslides and mudflows. The hydrological response of the basin can be impacted upon by changes in land use associated with urbanisation, forestry, agriculture, drainage, or channel modifications. A record of such changes over time is useful in establishing the dynamic relationship between rainfall and runoff. The following also contribute to an understanding of flood hazards: records of climate norms and trends for parameters, such as precipitation and evapotranspiration; and information on the usual effects of ENSO events and extreme events, from synoptic to mesoscale.

Population centres often are adjacent to rivers, and flood plains can be rich agricultural resources. Identification of populations and economic activities at risk should be carried out early in the process, as this will shape the eventual forecast output.

Flood History

Flood history, also known as paleohydrology, can be inferred from study of sediment deposits, tree ring analysis, and examination of a number of other biological indicators. Such analyses will not lead to a determination of flood volumes, but may help put a recent flood into context. Often, such records are of value in defining the flood history in a river basin, particularly when combined with stream gauge records that exist for contemporary periods. Other more recent historical information can be drawn from newspapers, journals and oral histories.

Usually there is a perception level associated with flooding at a given location; large events are noted, smaller events are not. The flood history will identify the portions of a basin subject to flooding, whether flooding is urban or rural or both, seasonal characteristics of flooding, and the feasible warning time. The type of flooding and associated hazards may be significantly different on tributaries compared to the main stem of the river. Knowledge of the factors contributing to or causing the flooding such as meteorological and antecedent conditions should be established for each flood event.

Lake flooding as well as flooding from ocean surge and tsunamis may pose problems quite different from river flooding. These guidelines are oriented to river flooding, but many principles contained herein are also applicable to varying degrees to other water-related disasters.

Environmental Factors

Floods can induce major changes in river morphology, mobilise nutrients and contaminants in the soil, release other contaminants from storage depots, and discharge effluents to the river. Deforestation, fires and erosion of materials combined with saturated soils can lead to landslides, mudflows and other threats to human settlements. Sometimes floods are accompanied by strong winds that also can pose threats to human life and property. An analysis of potential environmental risks will help determine flood forecasting and warning needs. This can help to shape future approaches to flood plain management and regulation, and can assist in the design and establishment of response actions.

Economic Factors

A flood forecasting, warning and response system comprises an important element of integrated water resources management. The benefits of river forecasts for power generation, navigation or irrigated agriculture make implementation of such a system more cost effective and sustainable. Even then, maintaining a system in a state of readiness between floods may be difficult. An examination of past damages and the potential for future damages will help determine priority areas for flood forecasting, warning and response. Rigorous analysis would call for statistical analysis of flood peaks and the calculation of the present value of costs and benefits of flood forecasting and warning. In most cases, however, the benefits of flood forecasting, warning and response are virtually self-evident. The real questions are the affordability of various options and the desire of society to invoke a more pro-active stance to reducing flood losses.

Communities at Risk

While flood losses in rural districts can be devastating to those areas, the most significant losses are usually in urban communities because of the concentration of people and related socio-economic investments. The basin characteristics and flood history of individual communities, combined with damage estimates from previous floods, will give some indication of the type of flood forecasting and warning system that may be most suitable for effective warnings. Once the system is defined, consideration should be given as to how it could benefit rural areas as well.

System Identification

Depending on the nature of the basin and the type of event causing the flooding, potential warning times could vary from hours to several days to weeks. Communities subject to flash flooding require warnings of meteorological conditions that, when combined with antecedent basin conditions, could lead to flooding. This represents a special case of flood forecasting and warning. The challenge in such cases is rapid depiction of critical flood thresholds and their subsequent communication and emergency response. An analysis of historical rainfall records, including storm transposition and the resulting streamflow would help to identify areas of concern.

When warning times are longer than a few hours, full-fledged forecast systems should be contemplated. The degree of desired automation and sophistication must be considered in light of current needs and capabilities. Automation needs can be considered in sub-systems: data acquisition and transmission; data processing; forecast preparation; and forecast distribution. Different levels of automation may be required as the overall system develops and expands, and as financial resources become available. Systems may vary from those using largely manual observations, graphs and tables to highly automated multi-model systems running on computer workstations.

Benefit-Cost Analysis

An analysis of the cost of floods and the potential benefits may help determine the type of forecast and warning system and response mechanisms that would be most cost effective. Costs resulting from flooding can be estimated for various magnitudes of events for various centres. Damage statistics from previous floods are also valuable in establishing the costs associated with such events. Judgement is needed to estimate the benefit of flood forecasting and warning in reducing damages and loss of life. Governments and financial institutions require such information on costs and benefits to help understand where expenditures will reap the largest rewards. Studies and analyses have shown that damage reduction due to forecast improvements can range from a few percentage points to as much as 35% of average annual flood damages.

A standard set of flood damage categories relevant to the basin should be developed. When loss of life is a threat, this too should be identified, even though it is difficult or impossible to quantify in economic terms. Other damage categories could include residential buildings; commercial, institutional and industrial buildings; agricultural lands; and infrastructure. Additional costs include temporary relocation and flood-fighting costs. Floods can have an effect on the population and economy of an entire country, and business losses should also be included in the analysis. Developing standard damage categories allows damages to be more accurately estimated for various levels of flooding.

A rigorous cost-benefit analysis would require determining a flood frequency distribution so that the present value of future benefits can be determined. In the absence of sufficient data or analysis, a more rudimentary presentation of costs and benefits may be sufficient to determine the size of the investment that is justified for flood forecasting, warning and response.

Evaluating Existing Capabilities

Most countries have basic networks of meteorological and hydrometric stations that are necessary for flood forecasting and warning. It is likely that the operators of the existing networks may be in many different agencies. In many cases, the networks may not have been designed to acquire data during extreme events, or they may not provide data in real-time or to common standards. Also, networks may not provide data for key urban centres where forecasts are required or for areas where the major inputs to the flooding are occurring.

Identifying the existing network, its operators, and the existing approaches and capabilities are necessary steps in the evolution of a flood forecast system. Another important element is an examination of existing communications capability. Given that important data are available at a remote site, how can these data be reliably transmitted to a flood-forecasting centre? Will telephone or radio links - manual or automated - function during a flood emergency? Some agencies may have developed hydrological mathematical rainfall-runoff models and flow routing models for their own purposes. These models may be useful as flood forecasting models. An inventory of existing models will also help define current capability within individual agencies.

Establishment of a successful flood forecasting, warning and response system depends on a thorough analysis of existing capabilities, identification of key users for the system, and a good understanding of the interagency arrangements needed in an effective system. Considering these factors will lead to forecasts that meet user needs and that are more likely to be acted upon during an emergency. The ultimate goal of such a system is to ensure the safety and security of the public and to protect property and the environment. To achieve this result, however, means that the public must receive and understand forecasts, and the myriad of agencies having responsibility for emergency action and response also must receive the forecasts, have response strategies in place, and act upon the forecasts accordingly. Key users typically include: civil agencies at the national, provincial/state, and local level; military organisations; corporations, especially those which operate structures; volunteer emergency response organisations; and the media. A user analysis, and close ties and interaction with these groups should be considered to help establish overall flood forecast needs and response measures.

The role of the media in informing the public cannot be underestimated. It is critical that the media receive timely and authoritative forecasts and warnings. Media communications should encourage the appropriate public response and should not lead to counterproductive speculation. Many of the world's river basins have a transboundary component. In some cases transboundary basins are covered by treaty, international agreements, or other institutional arrangements. Such arrangements may or may not include river or flood forecasting. Shared basins imply a shared responsibility; an analysis of user needs should include users in other countries.

Often the mandate and capabilities of governmental organisations are not entirely clear. An institutional analysis of each agency's mandate, needs, capabilities and legal responsibility during a flood emergency will help shape an emergency preparedness and response plan. Overall, one agency should be assigned the lead responsibility (and accountability) for an end-to-end system, with the system itself potentially being operated by a number of organisations.

In the evaluation of the existing system, agencies that operate data collection networks or models, or that can contribute to a forecast system in other ways, will have been identified. In some cases the potential role of a specific agency in a flood forecast system may be relatively clear, while in other cases that role may have to be identified and negotiated. A fundamental question is that of hydrological and meteorological coordination.

In many countries one or more agencies operate meteorological forecast and climate networks, while hydrological networks may be the responsibility of entirely different agencies or departments. Coordination among these bodies is essential because development of a flood forecasting system may require the addition of new sensors or telemetry equipment funded by one agency being installed at a site operated by another one. A successful forecast system will depend upon cooperation among meteorological and hydrological agencies and could involve financial transactions among them.

Similarly there may be a number of agencies with responsibility for operation of structures for water management and flood control. These could include hydroelectric generation facilities, irrigation headworks, water supply reservoirs, and so forth. Individual structures may have an established operating plan, but an integrated plan for operations during extreme events is needed to provide optimal flood control benefits and to avoid structural failure. Interagency co-ordination and cooperation is required to ensure the integrity of the entire water management system during extreme events. A flood forecasting and warning system provides the information necessary to improve decision support for the operation of structures.

Some agencies may have arrangements for technical support or financial assistance with international organisations or with other countries. These may prove beneficial in developing or improving a forecast system through training and in general strengthening of much needed organisational infrastructure. A logical agency to lead a country's flood forecasting and warning effort may emerge from this analysis. The identified agency will require technical support and leadership from several agencies. More importantly, there is a need for long-term political support for the endeavour.

Flood forecasting and warning will have to compete with other national priorities, and resources and financial support can atrophy, particularly in the absence of flooding. There is a need to establish a floodforecasting centre having a legal mandate to issue authoritative forecasts and warnings on the river basin or at the provincial/state or national level. These forecasts must be understood by agencies having the responsibility for emergency response and by the general public. Such agencies, civil organisations and the general public must be aware of their roles, have response mechanisms in place, and know what actions to take under various circumstances.

Analysis of the basin characteristics, flood history, flood damages, and the existing databases will give some indication of the type of forecast system that is achievable and affordable. It is likely that the system will be based on enhancing existing networks and agency capabilities. Establishing a new system implies phased development from the existing system to the new one. Establishing a long-term plan with specific milestones is critical to future success.

Hydrometeorological Network

The hydrometeorological network is the key requirement for most flood forecasting. In particular, precipitation and streamflow data are needed. If snowmelt is a factor in flooding, then measurements of snow water equivalent, extent of snow cover, and air temperature are also important. In many cases agencies other than the forecast agency have useful data. Rather than duplicate networks, it is preferable to develop cooperative arrangements. In some respects, it is preferable that the network serves many purposes as this may result in its broader financial support.

In most cases data network operational performance is the weakest link within the integrated system. Operational data networks must be examined. Are the rainfall and stream gauge (hydrometric) data networks satisfactory in sampling rainfall (intensity and spatial distribution) and streamflow response for the river basin? Are stream gauges operating properly, and are they providing accurate conditions of water level and streamflow? Are data communicated reliably between the gauge sites and the forecast centre? How often are observations taken, and how long does it take for observations to be transmitted to the forecast centre? Are data available to users who need the information for decision making? Are the data archived for future use? Are the data collected to known standards, is the equipment properly maintained and calibrated, and are the data quality controlled?

Network design

It is not possible to manage water or forecast floods without data. Various types and sources of data are needed to monitor the environment, conduct a water balance or provide input to hydrological models that estimate streamflow from rainfall. Operating a real-time hydrometeorological network is essential, as data provide the foundation for establishing the potential for flooding. Insitu observations of meteorological and hydrological parameters are required as inputs to the hydrological prediction system. An analysis of the existing network should be undertaken. Tables and maps should be available providing details on monitoring locations, parameters, sensors, recorders, telemetry equipment and other related data. In addition, monitoring sites in adjacent basins should be inventoried. In low relief basins, data from those sites could be very useful. Analysis should be performed to identify sub-basins that are hydrologically or meteorologically similar.

Based on forecast needs, the adequacy of networks can be determined and required modifications can be noted. These could include new stream gauges, rain gauges and possibly other sensors in the headwaters, or additional telemetry equipment. In some cases, network sites may not be well suited for obtaining flow measurements or other data under extreme conditions. Costly structural alterations may be needed. Interagency agreements may be needed for maintenance and operation of the network. A key variable to be established is the time step needed to adequately forecast a flood for a given location. If the time step is, say, six hours then data must be collected every three hours or even more frequently. In many cases, supplementing a manual observer network with some automated gauges may provide an adequate operational network.

Data acquisition

Generally the design and operation of data networks have a large influence on forecast system accuracy and in the ability of the system to provide the necessary lead-time to issue warnings so that response actions can be taken. It should be underscored that the design of reliable real-time operational observing networks is critical to the success of a forecast, warning and response programme. In order to be effective during extreme conditions, sensor installations may have to be "hardened" to withstand extremes in wind, rain or flood stage.

The advent of remotely sensed data has significantly improved the ability of operational hydrology to infer watershed conditions in data-sparse regions. The application of radar-derived precipitation estimates serves as the principle tool in forecasting floods and flash floods in many countries. The use of geostationary and polar orbiting satellites to derive large volumes of meteorological and hydrological products is rapidly advancing. Remotely sensed data can now be used to provide estimates of precipitation, snowpack extent, vegetation type, land use, evapotranspiration, soil moisture and flood inundation. This information is becoming increasingly useful in data-sparse regions of the world where water availability and flood forecasts are needed.

Telecommunications System

Telecommunications System (GTS) of the World Meteorological Organisation (WMO) for the transfer of real-time meteorological data. More recently, some hydrological data from a number of projects were added to the system. Even with these advances in remotely sensed data and their use, inadequacy of data remains the biggest weakness in establishing a viable flood forecast programme for a river basin or for a country.

Data communications

For data to be useful to the forecast centre, point data observed at remote locations must be converted to digital formats. This may require changing the sensor itself or simply adding another component to an existing system. The format for the digital data must be specified. Remotely sensed images used in forecasts are usually already in a specified digital format. If the sensor output is film, arrangements must be made to make the conversion to a specified digital format within the required time.

Once data have been observed or collected at sites throughout the river basin or country, the data must be transmitted to locations where they can be stored, accessed, and used. The value of data increases with the speed of transmission and processing, from their initial observation to where they are used. Meteorological and hydrological data are needed almost instantaneously so that the hydrological forecast system can produce up-to-date and reliable forecasts. More importantly, this allows the system to provide the critical warning times needed for users to take actions. This is especially true for issuing warnings of flash flood events and of potentially hazardous mudslide conditions.

There are many types of communication technologies that can be applied to transmit data from sites in remote locations to the forecast centres. The most common form of data communication is by telephone. However, telephone lines frequently fail during severe flood events. More reliable but potentially more expensive forms of data communications are satellite, line of site radio, cellular radio and meteor bursts. These also have their strengths and weaknesses. An evaluation should be performed to establish the most suitable, reliable and cost-effective form of communication for the local situation.

Data may be transmitted by dedicated satellite links, radio links, by commercial telephone links or other shared services. In some cases the data link could simply be a voice telephone communication. The forecast centre may be required to poll sites individually, interrogate a third-party system, or use the Internet to obtain data. Data transmission links must be identified, and their reliability and speed should be determined. If image products are to play a role in the real time forecasts, bandwidth of the transmission system and speed of the processing system should be examined. In many cases, national, provincial/state, local governments and the private sector operate real-time data networks to support their individual needs. In most cases, these data are not shared, and each organisation is limited to its own data. Coordination and data sharing can significantly increase the amount of data available for all organisations. These additional data, possibly complemented with new sites, will help increase forecast accuracy at the least cost.

Meteorological Support

Given the importance of meteorological data and forecasts to the production of flood forecasts, it is very important that there be close collaboration between national meteorological and hydrological services. This collaboration could take several forms and should focus on increasing the accuracy and utility of knowledge of existing conditions and forecasted states. Two important products are optimal quantitative precipitation estimates - where, when and how much precipitation has actually fallen - and quantitative precipitation forecasts - where, when, and how much precipitation will actually fall. Other parameters of interest include wind speed and direction, surface temperature, and relative humidity.

Network Operation

Often times the current operator of a site will not have had a need for, or experience with, real time data acquisition. Intensive staff training may be required to ensure that data are available when needed and are of a suitable quality. Long-term maintenance is a major requirement in operational forecasting. The forecast network may be in operation only seasonally or less frequently. Keeping the network in a state of readiness though necessitates major changes in operating philosophy. The development of water management operational forecasts by the forecast centre, as well as flood forecasts, enhances the usefulness of the data network and communications systems, as well as maintaining a state of readiness.

Funding of alterations to existing networks and for future maintenance presents a major challenge. Negotiations among operating or funding agencies may require abandoning entrenched positions if success is to be achieved.

Quantitative Precipitation Estimation (QPE)

Optimal estimates of existing precipitation conditions provide the hydrologist with the most accurate estimates of what are termed “antecedent conditions”. These are extremely important for hydrological process modelling. Much work has been done to increase the accuracy of the estimates through increasing the density of in-situ stations, implementing ground-based surface radar, in processing of satellite based data, and in merging various sources of data.

Quantitative Precipitation Forecasting (QPF)

The ultimate goal of flood forecasting is to provide accurate forecasts of hydrological conditions. Currently, deterministic quantitative precipitation forecasts and other forecasted meteorological parameters can be applied as input to hydrological models in order to derive hydrological forecasts using numerical modelling methods.

It is typical that the hydrological forecaster receives single “best effort” meteorological products such as QPF, wind speeds and direction, temperature, and pressure. These products are based on numerical weather prediction model output and are modified using expert forecaster judgement. Forecast models are typically run once or twice daily depending on the operational practices of the national meteorological service. The useful forecast horizon of such products is typically about five days, with accuracy decreasing rapidly towards that of long-term climatology. The usefulness of QPF products derived from such modelling is usually constrained to one to two days due to poor performance beyond these limits.

When very short forecast horizons on the order of six hours or less could prove beneficial, extrapolative and trend-based meteorological techniques are used. The use of these techniques is referred to as "nowcasting", resulting in short-range QPF. These shorter time horizons associated with nowcasting are particularly useful for flashflood forecasting. Beyond this horizon, numerical weather prediction models combined with expert judgement provide more accurate estimates of future meteorological conditions such as QPF. Work is currently proceeding on the coupling of mesoscale numerical weather prediction models with high-resolution hydrological process models. Questions still exist on how to best incorporate expert judgement into this process in order to provide a single "best effort" estimate of future hydrological conditions.

One forecast methodology that can be applied to both meteorological and hydrological forecasting is the "Ensemble Technique", wherein multiple forecast scenarios are generated by the execution of several model runs, each with slightly varied initial states. The magnitude and degree of the uncertainty associated with the forecast ensemble provide a probabilistic view of the potential future meteorological and hydrological states. Although more study and further development are needed before this becomes more broadly used in operational practice, the technique holds much promise.

Once a flood forecasting centre has been in operation for a period of time and close collaboration exists with meteorological counterparts, weaknesses in both meteorological and hydrological forecast products may become evident. Sometimes the weaknesses can be overcome by improving the database used for the forecast. In other cases, there will be a need to improve understanding of the underlying hydrological processes involved in the production of hydrological forecasts.

Estimation of other parameters is important for flood forecasting and for assessing antecedent basin conditions. These include antecedent temperature, humidity, and evapotranspiration, all of which are very important in assessing soil moisture conditions and water deficits prior to the onset of precipitation.

Flood Forecast Centre

The flood forecast centre must be identifiable to agencies and to the public as the authoritative source of flood forecasts and warnings. The forecasts produced by the centre must be to the highest achievable technical standard and be released to the public unfiltered by agency or political interests. The long-term stability of the centre is dependent on the credibility and utility of its forecasts. Administratively the centre can be part of one agency or it could be a new entity supported by several agencies. The forecast centre could be self-contained or, more likely, will depend on other agencies for support.

Analysis of existing conditions and needs will determine whether a forecast centre will be established by strengthening an existing facility or by creating a completely new enterprise. The decision should be based on political, administrative and technical leadership of candidate agencies, as well as the ability of the selected agency to work with others.

A project initiation team drawn from several national agencies or consultants, with support from international organisations and working to agreed-upon terms of reference, could examine the issues identified in these Guidelines and make recommendations concerning the development of a Forecast Centre. Their report should identify technical issues, personnel needed, administrative issues, costs, and timelines.

Interagency agreements will be needed for provision of data, operation of structures, weather forecasts, technical and administrative support, and other tasks. Depending on the basin, it is possible that such agreements might already exist. They may include clearly articulated roles and responsibilities, clear specifications of work, performance measures, and provisions for financial arrangements. International agreements for provision of data, use of satellite technology, and other support activities may also be required.

The Centre needs financing over both the short and longer term. Short-term financing will be capital intensive as funding may be necessary for network improvements, construction, the acquisition of computers and software, and many other items. These could best be funded by special national appropriations or international support. There may also be a local market for specialised forecast products, which could be paid for by users.

Long-term financing will be needed to operate the Centre, pay staff, upgrade computer systems, and make improvements in the forecast methodologies. This operation will require on-going national support even where specific improvements are funded internationally. If the mandate of the Centre were expanded to include river forecasts for operational water management purposes, financial support could be made available from agencies using the river forecasts. The possibilities include revenue from sale of water licenses, other water use charges, or fees assessed to discourage development within the flood plain.

To operate effectively the Centre will need key personnel. Aside from technical skills, the Centre will need people capable of working collaboratively with other agencies and who can communicate effectively. A significant training programme will be needed at the onset of the Centre, and the costs of on-going training should be built into the budget. In the early stages, forecast procedures may have to be tailored to the ability of existing staff, and a training and development plan should be established to upgrade skills and techniques to improve the accuracy and utility of the forecast. There will be an early need to gather basic data, calibrate and verify models, and establish working arrangements with other agencies. Visiting experts, or placing key staff in other Forecast Centres for training, could aid this process.

One approach in the early stages of development would be to concentrate efforts on a key basin or one of its sub-basins. Such a pilot project could help verify the suitability of models selected and the capabilities of staff. This would give funding agencies a level of comfort. In the very earliest stages of development, the Centre could simply analyse weather forecasts and provide warnings of potential high flow conditions.

Data Processing

Although data may have been pre-processed elsewhere, the Forecast Centre will require inhouse data processing capability. Although some work could be done manually, computer systems should have uninterruptible power supplies. At the very least, emergency power systems should be available.

If Geographic Information Systems and image products are expected to be used for real-time forecasts, computer memory and speed must be taken into account. Overall computing system architecture and design should be planned for as part of the future development of the Centre. Data processing needs will also depend upon the selected forecast models and their data processing requirements. In the absence of other requirements, data should be digitally available and easily converted to formats used by commercially-available spreadsheet programmes.

Arrangements must also be made to electronically archive data so that they are available for use in subsequent years. Some data will have to be brought forward frequently for use, while other data will only be used on occasion.

It is necessary to establish basic operating procedures and assign staff responsibilities early in the operation of the Centre. Part of this is the assignment of responsibilities for ongoing maintenance of systems. Capable staff are the key to producing good forecasts and maintaining the Centre's credibility. Capable staff will also be attracted to positions elsewhere so some staff turnover can be expected.

A systematic plan for staff training and development and the assignment of challenging work will help reduce turnover rates. Some contingency planning will be needed to ensure that the Centre will continue to operate when key staff members leave. Efforts should be made to develop an operations manual in order to reduce the Centre's vulnerability to loss of staff or other unanticipated events. The manual should cover all aspects of the Centre's operation and maintenance, and it should include lists of key contacts beyond the Centre.

Once the Centre has completed its first significant flood forecast season, an end-to-end review of all aspects of the forecast should be conducted to identify what went well and where improvement might be necessary. The review should include interviews with persons from other agencies and forecast users. The results of such a review should be used to modify procedures. Periodic audits of forecast procedures and Centre operations should be carried out, perhaps involving staff from other Forecast Centres.

Forecast Models

There are a large number of public domain and proprietary models available for use in flood forecasting. Sometimes the model can be simply a statistical rainfall-runoff relation with a routing equation, while other models can be much more complex. Hydrological models can be classified as lumped, semidistributed or distributed, and as being single event or continuous. Probabilistic models that take data uncertainties into account are also available. Model selection will depend on available data, basin characteristics, and the needs of the local user community. A lumped model treats the watershed as a single unit for inputting data and calculating runoff. The calculations are statistically based and relate to the underlying hydrological processes as a spatially averaged process.

Models based on scaling unit hydrographs would fall into this category. Some lumped models allow the watershed to be subdivided or for some parameters to be physically estimated and modelled. When subdivisions of a basin are combined to produce a forecast, this modelling approach is termed semidistributed. Depending on forecast needs and the characteristics of the watershed, a lumped model may be all that is required.

A distributed model simulates the key hydrological processes that occur in a watershed using distributed data inputs and processes. For forecasting purposes these commonly include precipitation, interception, infiltration, interflow, and baseflow. Overland flow and channel routing may be incorporated into the model or calculated in a hydraulic model. Distributed models require much more data and knowledge of watershed processes than lumped models. When the model is first established, precipitation and land cover characteristics may be the only distributed features.

Hydraulic models used in channel routing calculate the travel time of the flood wave and its attenuation. These models use the standard equations of unsteady, non-uniform flow with various simplifications depending on the channel characteristics, available data and accuracy requirements. Storage-flow relations are often incorporated into hydrological models. One-dimensional unsteady flow hydraulic models can be used to route flows through multiple channels or in situations where overland flow is a serious concern.

Probabilistic forecasts are typically derived using hydrological process models wherein statistical distributions are used to describe the uncertainty of input data and basin conditions such as precipitation data, soil moisture and snow pack conditions. A large number of model projections are produced that can be statistically analysed to allow for a better understanding of the uncertainty of the forecasted future water conditions. This approach is rapidly gaining popularity, as it provides the decision-maker with the probability of an extreme event to occur, not just that it might occur.

Simplified probabilistic methodologies that provide a range of possible forecasts have existed for some time. This is achieved by the forecaster making assumptions concerning future precipitation to determine runoff under normal, lower, or upper decile conditions. More modern approaches, which tend to be in the pilot testing stage, attempt to better quantify the uncertainty associated with the forecasted meteorological conditions and to directly link this uncertainty to the uncertainty of the flood estimate.

Essentially, the prevailing geomorphological conditions of the river basin and the interaction of communities at risk with the river system dictate the level of sophistication of the modelling solution. The performance of existing models or forecast procedures should be evaluated. Whether the forecast process involves use of simple graphs or tables or a robust integrated modelling system, evaluation of forecast accuracy versus lead-time should be determined. Does the system perform well when adequate data are available? Are model parameters up-to-date? Do model parameters reflect land use changes that have occurred within the basin?

Can the model or its parameters be easily modified to reflect pending land-use changes within the basin? Does the modelling system reflect flood control structures and their operations within the basin? Are there important hydrological processes occurring in the basin that are not reflected in the existing forecast model? Does the forecast system perform well for flooding but is inadequate to meet routine or low flow forecast requirements? Is there a need to convert hydrological forecasts to water level (stage) using a hydraulic model? In general, is the existing modelling system appropriate and sufficient to meet user requirements?

Highly trained hydrologists produce reliable hydrological forecasts. Forecasters use real-time data, knowledge of hydrology, knowledge of the hydrological modelling system and experience in producing forecasts and warnings. In determining the operational readiness or hydrological forecast capability of a forecast centre, the education, knowledge and skills of the forecasters are as important as the tools they use. Is the number of forecasters available sufficient to handle the flooding situation? Do the forecasters have sufficient education in hydrology and meteorology to appropriately apply the tools? Are they properly trained, and do they understand the limitations of the modelling system being used? Do the forecasters know the users, how to contact them, and what information they require for flood response actions? An assessment of the adequacy of the operational forecaster capability is important in determining how to improve flood forecast operations.

In order to produce a flood forecast for the communities and locations at risk, there must be a hydrological modelling capability that uses meteorological and hydrological data. Hydrological models use real-time precipitation and streamflow data. The models translate observed conditions into future stream conditions. Hydrological models or procedures vary in complexity, accuracy and ease of use. Simple hydrological models consist of tables, graphs or empirically derived relationships. More sophisticated hydrological modelling systems use in-situ data, remotely sensed data, and multiple hydrological models that are integrated to produce very accurate hydrological forecasts. Due to advances in Geographic Information Systems and the availability of geo-referenced data, parameters of some hydrological models can now be estimated without having to rely exclusively on historical hydrological data for model calibration. The evolution of personal computer technology has paved the way for quite complex modelling systems to be run on them. These systems are easier to use, are easier to maintain, and are more affordable.

Current hydrological forecast systems are quite affordable and powerful. The degree of success associated with these systems is dependent on the amount of training received by the hydrologists using them. These systems are capable of producing a broad range of forecasts of stream conditions that will occur in a few hours to seasonal probabilistic outlooks targeted to months in advance for larger rivers. Model system selection depends on the amount of data available, complexity of hydrological processes to be modelled, accuracy and reliability required, lead-time required, type and frequency of floods that occur, and user requirements.

Hydraulic models are often used to translate hydrological model-derived streamflow to water-level conditions. Hydraulic models are also valuable in forecasting the streamflow conditions of large rivers where sufficient lead-time is accorded through translation of upstream water levels to downstream communities at risk. Such models can be interfaced with geographical information systems to provide dynamic water level conditions on maps of communities. These types of forecast products can be invaluable to communities and emergency organisations, as they provide very precise information about areas that will be inundated and when.

Decision Support

Hydrometeorological data and accurate forecasts are of no value if the forecasts do not reach users and if decisions are not made as to the appropriate actions required. Hydrological forecasts and hydraulic conditions must be disseminated so that decisions can be made and actions taken to reduce the impact of the pending event. Decision support refers to everything from forecasts reaching decision makers such as a mayor of a flood-prone community to the operator of a flood-control structure. For decision support to be effective, advanced planning must define prescribed actions linked to forecasted values.

Decision support systems vary from rules or procedures that must be followed under prescribed conditions to mathematical optimisation programmes. Such approaches define actions to be taken based on tradeoffs among various options for water allocation.

Forecast Output

Typically, calculations used in preparing a forecast are based on units of discharge, although some simplified systems correlate upstream with downstream water levels. However, decision makers and the public are most often concerned with water levels and velocities at specific points, usually urban centres. Forecasted flows can be converted to water levels and velocities using stagedischarge and stage-velocity relations, hydraulic models, or other techniques. Decision makers and emergency workers should be consulted on their specific forecast requirements.

In many cases, forecast water levels are given according to a local vertical datum. This may be convenient for some purposes but may introduce potential for confusion. With the advent of global positioning systems, it is possible to provide a geodetic datum at any location and this should be done. The forecast water levels released to the public could be in several formats: tabular, hydrographs, or inundation maps. It is very useful to provide comparisons with the previous year or with previous major floods. Inundation maps linked to databases can provide information on individual properties and can be most useful for public awareness and emergency services.

The forecast should be formally released and made available to key agencies as well as the media. The forecast should also be placed on Internet websites for easy access. The points for which the forecast applies should be communicated very clearly. For example, the name of a city in the basin should be identified, or in the case of very large cities, well-known points within the city should be specified. Uncertainty in the forecast should be represented accurately, but in non-technical language. Phrases such as "if present conditions continue…" are useful as are those that require simple statistical knowledge such as "there is an 80% chance that…"

Forecast and warning dissemination is extremely important. Frequently, the lack of ability to disseminate warnings to the population at risk is the weakest link in the integrated system. Forecasts and warnings must reach users without delay and with sufficient lead-time to permit response actions to take place. Dissemination of forecasts and warnings can be achieved through a variety of communication methods. An inventory of the various communications media used by the forecast system will reveal the competency of the dissemination process. How are warnings transmitted to the public, to the flood control agencies, to the emergency services and civil protection organisations? Are communication systems reliable? What types of communication modes are used (such as satellite, radio, meteor bursts, telephone or internet)? How are communications lines maintained? Are there backup modes of communication? In what format are warnings transmitted? Do users understand the content of the warnings? These are a few of the questions that need to be answered in assessing the performance of dissemination systems.

References

Amanda Ripley. (2006). "Floods, Tornadoes, Hurricanes, Wildfires, Earthquakes... Why We Don't Prepare." *Time.* August 28.

Dyhouse, G. (2003). "*Flood modelling Using HEC-RAS.* Haestad Press, Waterbury, USA.

O'Connor, Jim E. and John E. Costa. (2004). *The World's Largest Floods, Past and Present: Their Causes and Magnitudes.* Washington, D.C.: U.S. Department of the Interior, U.S. Geological Survey.

United States National Institute for Occupational Safety and Health (NIOSH). *NIOSH Warns of Hazards of Flood Cleanup Work.* NIOSH Publication No. 94-123.

WMO/GWP Associated Programme on Flood Management (2007). "Environmental Aspects of Integrated Flood Management." WMO.

7

Tornadoes: Preparedness and Response

A tornado is a violently rotating column of air that is in contact with both the surface of the earth and a cumulonimbus cloud or, in rare cases, the base of a cumulus cloud. They are often referred to as twisters or cyclones, although the word cyclone is used in meteorology, in a wider sense, to name any closed low pressure circulation. Tornadoes come in many shapes and sizes, but they are typically in the form of a visible condensation funnel, whose narrow end touches the earth and is often encircled by a cloud of debris and dust. Most tornadoes have wind speeds less than 110 miles per hour (177 km/h), are about 250 feet (76 m) across, and travel a few miles (several kilometers) before dissipating. The most extreme tornadoes can attain wind speeds of more than 300 miles per hour (483 km/h), stretch more than two miles (3.2 km) across, and stay on the ground for dozens of miles (more than 100 km).

Various types of tornadoes include the landspout, multiple vortex tornado, and waterspout. Waterspouts are characterized by a spiraling funnel-shaped wind current, connecting to a large cumulus or cumulonimbus cloud. They are generally classified as non-supercellular tornadoes that develop over bodies of water, but there is disagreement over whether to classify them as true tornadoes. These spiraling columns of air frequently develop in tropical areas close to the equator, and are less common at high latitudes. Other tornado-like phenomena that exist in nature include the gustnado, dust devil, fire whirls, and steam devil.

Tornadoes have been observed on every continent except Antarctica. However, the vast majority of tornadoes in the world occur in the so-called "Tornado Alley" region of the United States, although they can occur nearly anywhere in North America. They also occasionally occur in south-central and eastern Asia, northern and east-central South America, Southern Africa, northwestern and southeast Europe, western and southeastern Australia, and New Zealand. Tornadoes can be detected before or as they occur through the use of Pulse-Doppler radar by recognizing patterns in velocity and reflectivity data, such as hook echoes, as well as by the efforts of storm spotters.

There are several scales for rating the strength of tornadoes. The Fujita scale rates tornadoes by damage caused and has been replaced in some countries by the updated Enhanced Fujita Scale. An F0 or EF0 tornado, the weakest category, damages trees, but not substantial structures. An F5 or EF5 tornado, the strongest category, rips buildings off their foundations and can deform large skyscrapers. The similar TORRO scale ranges from a T0 for extremely weak tornadoes to T11 for the most powerful known tornadoes. Doppler radar data, photogrammetry, and ground swirl patterns (cycloidal marks) may also be analyzed to determine intensity and assign a rating.

Defining tornado

A tornado is "a violently rotating column of air, in contact with the ground, either pendant from a cumuliform cloud or underneath a cumuliform cloud, and often (but not always) visible as a funnel cloud". For a vortex to be classified as a tornado, it must be in contact with both the ground and the cloud base. Scientists have not yet created a complete definition of the word; for example, there is disagreement as to whether separate touchdowns of the same funnel constitute separate tornadoes. Tornado refers to the vortex of wind, not the condensation cloud.

Tornado is not necessarily visible; however, the intense low pressure caused by the high wind speeds (as described by Bernoulli's principle) and rapid rotation (due to cyclostrophic balance) usually causes water vapor in the air to condense into cloud droplets due to adiabatic cooling. This results in the formation of a visible funnel cloud or condensation funnel.

There is some disagreement over the definition of funnel cloud and condensation funnel. According to the Glossary of Meteorology, a funnel cloud is any rotating cloud pendant from a cumulus or cumulonimbus, and thus most tornadoes are included under this definition. Among many meteorologists, the funnel cloud term is strictly defined as a rotating cloud which is not associated with strong winds at the surface, and condensation funnel is a broad term for any rotating cloud below a cumuliform cloud.

Tornadoes often begin as funnel clouds with no associated strong winds at the surface, and not all funnel clouds evolve into tornadoes. Most tornadoes produce strong winds at the surface while the visible funnel is still above the ground, so it is difficult to discern the difference between a funnel cloud and a tornado from a distance.

Occasionally, a single storm will produce more than one tornado, either simultaneously or in succession. Multiple tornadoes produced by the same storm cell are referred to as a "tornado family". Several tornadoes are sometimes spawned from the same large-scale storm system. If there is no break in activity, this is considered a tornado outbreak (although the term "tornado outbreak" has various definitions). A period of several successive days with tornado outbreaks in the same general area (spawned by multiple weather systems) is a tornado outbreak sequence, occasionally called an extended tornado outbreak.

Characteristics of Tornado

Size and Shape

Most tornadoes take on the appearance of a narrow funnel, a few hundred yards (meters) across, with a small cloud of debris near the ground. Tornadoes may be obscured completely by rain or dust. These tornadoes are especially dangerous, as even experienced meteorologists might not see them. Tornadoes can appear in many shapes and sizes.

Small, relatively weak landspouts may be visible only as a small swirl of dust on the ground. Although the condensation funnel may not extend all the way to the ground, if associated surface winds are greater than 40 mph (64 km/h), the circulation is considered a tornado. A tornado with a nearly cylindrical profile and relative low height is sometimes referred to as a "stovepipe" tornado. Large single-vortex tornadoes can look like large wedges stuck into the ground, and so are known as "wedge tornadoes" or "wedges". The "stovepipe" classification is also used for this type of tornado, if it otherwise fits that profile. A wedge can be so wide that it appears to be a block of dark clouds, wider than the distance from the cloud base to the ground. Even experienced storm observers may not be able to tell the difference between a low-hanging cloud and a wedge tornado from a distance. Many, but not all major tornadoes are wedges.

Tornadoes in the dissipating stage can resemble narrow tubes or ropes, and often curl or twist into complex shapes. These tornadoes are said to be "roping out", or becoming a "rope tornado". When they rope out, the length of their funnel increases, which forces the winds within the funnel to weaken due to conservation of angular momentum. Multiple-vortex tornadoes can appear as a family of swirls circling a common center, or they may be completely obscured by condensation, dust, and debris, appearing to be a single funnel.

In the United States, tornadoes are around 500 feet (150 m) across on average and travel on the ground for 5 miles (8.0 km). However, there is a wide range of tornado sizes. Weak tornadoes, or strong yet dissipating tornadoes, can be exceedingly narrow, sometimes only a few feet or couple meters across. One tornado was reported to have a damage path only 7 feet (2 m) long. On the other end of the spectrum, wedge tornadoes can have a damage path a mile (1.6 km) wide or more. A tornado that affected Hallam, Nebraska on May 22, 2004, was up to 2.5 miles (4.0 km) wide at the ground.

In terms of path length, the Tri-State Tornado, which affected parts of Missouri, Illinois, and Indiana on March 18, 1925, was on the ground continuously for 219 miles (352 km). Many tornadoes which appear to have path lengths of 100 miles (160 km) or longer are composed of a family of tornadoes which have formed in quick succession; however, there is no substantial evidence that this occurred in the case of the Tri-State Tornado. In fact, modern reanalysis of the path suggests that the tornado may have begun 15 miles (24 km) further west than previously thought.

Appearance

Tornadoes can have a wide range of colors, depending on the environment in which they form. Those that form in dry environments can be nearly invisible, marked only by swirling debris at the base of the funnel. Condensation funnels that pick up little or no debris can be gray to white. While traveling over a body of water (as a waterspout), tornadoes can turn very white or even blue. Slow-moving funnels, which ingest a considerable amount of debris and dirt, are usually darker, taking on the color of debris. Tornadoes in the Great Plains can turn red because of the reddish tint of the soil, and tornadoes in mountainous areas can travel over snow-covered ground, turning white.

Lighting conditions are a major factor in the appearance of a tornado. A tornado which is "back-lit" (viewed with the sun behind it) appears very dark. The same tornado, viewed with the sun at the observer's back, may appear gray or brilliant white. Tornadoes which occur near the time of sunset can be many different colors, appearing in hues of yellow, orange, and pink.

Dust kicked up by the winds of the parent thunderstorm, heavy rain and hail, and the darkness of night are all factors which can reduce the visibility of tornadoes. Tornadoes occurring in these conditions are especially dangerous, since only weather radar observations, or possibly the sound of an approaching tornado, serve as any warning to those in the storm's path. Most significant tornadoes form under the storm's updraft base, which is rain-free, making them visible. Also, most tornadoes occur in the late afternoon, when the bright sun can penetrate even the thickest clouds. Night-time tornadoes are often illuminated by frequent lightning.

There is mounting evidence, including Doppler On Wheels mobile radar images and eyewitness accounts, that most tornadoes have a clear, calm center with extremely low pressure, akin to the eye of tropical cyclones. This area would be clear (possibly full of dust), have relatively light winds, and be very dark, since the light would be blocked by swirling debris on the outside of the tornado. Lightning is said to be the source of illumination for those who claim to have seen the interior of a tornado.

Rotation

Tornadoes normally rotate cyclonically (when viewed from above, this is counterclockwise in the northern hemisphere and clockwise in the southern). While large-scale storms always rotate cyclonically due to the Coriolis effect, thunderstorms and tornadoes are so small that the direct influence of the Coriolis effect is unimportant, as indicated by their large Rossby numbers. Supercells and tornadoes rotate cyclonically in numerical simulations even when the Coriolis effect is neglected. Low-level mesocyclones and tornadoes owe their rotation to complex processes within the supercell and ambient environment.

Approximately 1 percent of tornadoes rotate in an anticyclonic direction in the northern hemisphere. Typically, systems as weak as landspouts and gustnadoes can rotate anticyclonically, and usually only those which form on the anticyclonic shear side of the descending rear flank downdraft in a cyclonic supercell. On rare occasions, anticyclonic tornadoes form in association with the mesoanticyclone of an anticyclonic supercell, in the same manner as the typical cyclonic tornado, or as a companion tornado either as a satellite tornado or associated with anticyclonic eddies within a supercell.

Sound and Seismology

Tornadoes emit widely on the acoustics spectrum and the sounds are caused by multiple mechanisms. Various sounds of tornadoes have been reported, mostly related to familiar sounds for the witness and generally some variation of a whooshing roar. Popularly reported sounds include a freight train, rushing rapids or waterfall, a nearby jet engine, or combinations of these. Many tornadoes are not audible from much distance; the nature and propagation distance of the audible sound depends on atmospheric conditions and topography.

The winds of the tornado vortex and of constituent turbulent eddies, as well as airflow interaction with the surface and debris, contribute to the sounds. Funnel clouds also produce sounds. Funnel clouds and small tornadoes are reported as whistling, whining, humming, or the buzzing of innumerable bees or electricity, or more or less harmonic, whereas many tornadoes are reported as a continuous, deep rumbling, or an irregular sound of "noise".

Since many tornadoes are audible only when very near, sound is not reliable warning of a tornado. Tornadoes are also not the only source of such sounds in severe thunderstorms; any strong, damaging wind, a severe hail volley, or continuous thunder in a thunderstorm may produce a roaring sound.Tornadoes also produce identifiable inaudible infrasonic signatures. Unlike audible signatures, tornadic signatures have been isolated; due to the long distance propagation of low-frequency sound, efforts are ongoing to develop tornado prediction and detection devices with additional value in understanding tornado morphology, dynamics, and creation. Tornadoes also produce a detectable seismic signature, and research continues on isolating it and understanding the process.

Electromagnetic, Lightning, and Other Effects

Tornadoes emit on the electromagnetic spectrum, with sferics and E-field effects detected. There are observed correlations between tornadoes and patterns of lightning. Tornadic storms do not contain more lightning than other storms and some tornadic cells never produce lightning. More often than not, overall cloud-to-ground (CG) lightning activity decreases as a tornado reaches the surface and returns to the baseline level when the tornado lifts. In many cases, intense tornadoes and thunderstorms exhibit an increased and anomalous dominance of positive polarity CG discharges. Electromagnetics and lightning have little or nothing to do directly with what drives tornadoes (tornadoes are basically a thermodynamic phenomenon), although there are likely connections with the storm and environment affecting both phenomena.

Luminosity has been reported in the past and is probably due to misidentification of external light sources such as lightning, city lights, and power flashes from broken lines, as internal sources are now uncommonly reported and are not known to ever have been recorded. In addition to winds, tornadoes also exhibit changes in atmospheric variables such as temperature, moisture, and pressure. For example, on June 24, 2003 near Manchester, South Dakota, a probe measured a 100 mbar (hPa) (2.95 inHg) pressure decrease. The pressure dropped gradually as the vortex approached then dropped extremely rapidly to 850 mbar (hPa) (25.10 inHg) in the core of the violent tornado before rising rapidly as the vortex moved away, resulting in a V-shape pressure trace. Temperature tends to decrease and moisture content to increase in the immediate vicinity of a tornado.

Life Cycle

Tornadoes often develop from a class of thunderstorms known as supercells. Supercells contain mesocyclones, an area of organized rotation a few miles up in the atmosphere, usually 1–6 miles (2–10 km) across. Most intense tornadoes (EF3 to EF5 on the Enhanced Fujita Scale) develop from supercells. In addition to tornadoes, very heavy rain, frequent lightning, strong wind gusts, and hail are common in such storms.

Most tornadoes from supercells follow a recognizable life cycle. That begins when increasing rainfall drags with it an area of quickly descending air known as the rear flank downdraft (RFD). This downdraft accelerates as it approaches the ground, and drags the supercell's rotating mesocyclone towards the ground with it.

Formation

As the mesocyclone lowers below the cloud base, it begins to take in cool, moist air from the downdraft region of the storm. This convergence of warm air in the updraft, and this cool air, causes a rotating wall cloud to form. The RFD also focuses the mesocyclone's base, causing it to siphon air from a smaller and smaller area on the ground. As the updraft intensifies, it creates an area of low pressure at the surface. This pulls the focused mesocyclone down, in the form of a visible condensation funnel. As the funnel descends, the RFD also reaches the ground, creating a gust front that can cause severe damage a good distance from the tornado. Usually, the funnel cloud begins causing damage on the ground (becoming a tornado) within a few minutes of the RFD reaching the ground.

Maturity

Initially, the tornado has a good source of warm, moist inflow to power it, so it grows until it reaches the "mature stage". This can last anywhere from a few minutes to more than an hour, and during that time a tornado often causes the most damage, and in rare cases can be more than one mile (1.6 km) across. Meanwhile, the RFD, now an area of cool surface winds, begins to wrap around the tornado, cutting off the inflow of warm air which feeds the tornado.

Dissipation

As the RFD completely wraps around and chokes off the tornado's air supply, the vortex begins to weaken, and become thin and rope-like. This is the "dissipating stage"; often lasting no more than a few minutes, after which the tornado fizzles. During this stage the shape of the tornado becomes highly influenced by the winds of the parent storm, and can be blown into fantastic patterns. Even though the tornado is dissipating, it is still capable of causing damage. The storm is contracting into a rope-like tube and, like the ice skater who pulls her arms in to spin faster, winds can increase at this point.

As the tornado enters the dissipating stage, its associated mesocyclone often weakens as well, as the rear flank downdraft cuts off the inflow powering it. In particular, intense supercells tornadoes can develop cyclically. As the first mesocyclone and associated tornado dissipate, the storm's inflow may be concentrated into a new area closer to the center of the storm. If a new mesocyclone develops, the cycle may start again, producing one or more new tornadoes. Occasionally, the old (occluded) mesocyclone and the new mesocyclone produce a tornado at the same time.

Although this is a widely accepted theory for how most tornadoes form, live, and die, it does not explain the formation of smaller tornadoes, such as landspouts, long-lived tornadoes, or tornadoes with multiple vortices. These each have different mechanisms which influence their development—however, most tornadoes follow a pattern similar to this one.

Types of Tornadoes

Multiple Vortex

A multiple-vortex tornado is a type of tornado in which two or more columns of spinning air rotate around a common center. Multivortex structure can occur in almost any circulation, but is very often observed in intense tornadoes. These vortices often create small areas of heavier damage along the main tornado path. This is a distinct phenomenon from a satellite tornado, which is a weaker tornado which forms very near a large, strong tornado contained within the same mesocyclone. The satellite tornado may appear to "orbit" the larger tornado (hence the name), giving the appearance of one, large multi-vortex tornado. However, a satellite tornado is a distinct circulation, and is much smaller than the main funnel.

Waterspout

A waterspout is defined by the National Weather Service as a tornado over water. However, researchers typically distinguish "fair weather" waterspouts from tornadic waterspouts. Fair weather waterspouts are less severe but far more common, and are similar to dust devils and landspouts. They form at the bases of cumulus congestus clouds over tropical and subtropical waters. They have relatively weak winds, smooth laminar walls, and typically travel very slowly. They occur most commonly in the Florida Keys and in the northern Adriatic Sea. In contrast, tornadic waterspouts are stronger tornadoes over water. They form over water similarly to mesocyclonic tornadoes, or are stronger tornadoes which cross over water. Since they form from severe thunderstorms and can be far more intense, faster, and longer-lived than fair weather waterspouts, they are more dangerous. In official tornado statistics, waterspouts are generally not counted unless they impact land, though some European weather agencies count waterspouts and tornadoes together.

Landspout

A landspout, or dust-tube tornado, is a tornado not associated with a mesocyclone. The name stems from their characterization as a "fair weather waterspout on land". Waterspouts and landspouts share many defining characteristics, including relative weakness, short lifespan, and a small, smooth condensation funnel which often does not reach the surface. Landspouts also create a distinctively laminar cloud of dust when they make contact with the ground, due to their differing mechanics from true mesoform tornadoes. Though usually weaker than classic tornadoes, they can produce strong winds which could cause serious damage.

Similar Circulations

Gustnado

A gustnado, or gust front tornado, is a small, vertical swirl associated with a gust front or downburst. Because they are not connected with a cloud base, there is some debate as to whether or not gustnadoes are tornadoes. They are formed when fast moving cold, dry outflow air from a thunderstorm is blown through a mass of stationary, warm, moist air near the outflow boundary, resulting in a "rolling" effect (often exemplified through a roll cloud). If low level wind shear is strong enough, the rotation can be turned vertically or diagonally and make contact with the ground. The result is a gustnado. They usually cause small areas of heavier rotational wind damage among areas of straight-line wind damage.

Dust devil

A dust devil resembles a tornado in that it is a vertical swirling column of air. However, they form under clear skies and are no stronger than the weakest tornadoes. They form when a strong convective updraft is formed near the ground on a hot day. If there is enough low level wind shear, the column of hot, rising air can develop a small cyclonic motion that can be seen near the ground. They are not considered tornadoes because they form during fair weather and are not associated with any clouds. However, they can, on occasion, result in major damage in arid areas.

Fire whirls and steam devils

Small-scale, tornado-like circulations can occur near any intense surface heat source. Those that occur near intense wildfires are called fire whirls. They are not considered tornadoes, except in the rare case where they connect to a pyrocumulus or other cumuliform cloud above. Fire whirls usually are not as strong as tornadoes associated with thunderstorms. They can, however, produce significant damage. A steam devil is a rotating updraft that involves steam or smoke. Steam devils are very rare. They most often form from smoke issuing from a power plant smokestack. Hot springs and deserts may also be suitable locations for a steam devil to form. The phenomenon can occur over water, when cold arctic air passes over relatively warm water.

Intensity and Damage

The Fujita scale and the Enhanced Fujita Scale rate tornadoes by damage caused. The Enhanced Fujita (EF) Scale was an upgrade to the older Fujita scale, by expert elicitation, using engineered wind estimates and better damage descriptions. The EF Scale was designed so that a tornado rated on the Fujita scale would receive the same numerical rating, and was implemented starting in the United States in 2007. An EF0 tornado will probably damage trees but not substantial structures, whereas an EF5 tornado can rip buildings off their foundations leaving them bare and even deform large skyscrapers. The similar TORRO scale ranges from a T0 for extremely weak tornadoes to T11 for the most powerful known tornadoes. Doppler weather radar data, photogrammetry, and ground swirl patterns (cycloidal marks) may also be analyzed to determine intensity and award a rating. Tornadoes vary in intensity regardless of shape, size, and location, though strong tornadoes are typically larger than weak tornadoes. The association with track length and duration also varies, although longer track tornadoes tend to be stronger. In the case of violent tornadoes, only a small portion of the path is of violent intensity, most of the higher intensity from subvortices.

In the United States, 80% of tornadoes are EF0 and EF1 (T0 through T3) tornadoes. The rate of occurrence drops off quickly with increasing strength—less than 1% are violent tornadoes (EF4, T8 or stronger). Outside Tornado Alley, and North America in general, violent tornadoes are extremely rare. This is apparently mostly due to the lesser number of tornadoes overall, as research shows that tornado intensity distributions are fairly similar worldwide. A few significant tornadoes occur annually in Europe, Asia, southern Africa, and southeastern South America, respectively.

Climatic Effects

The United States has the most tornadoes of any country, nearly four times more than estimated in all of Europe, excluding waterspouts. This is mostly due to the unique geography of the continent. North America is a large continent that extends from the tropics north into arctic areas, and has no major east-west mountain range to block air flow between these two areas. In the middle latitudes, where most tornadoes of the world occur, the Rocky Mountains block moisture and buckle the atmospheric flow, forcing drier air at mid-levels of the troposphere due to downsloped winds, and causing the formation of a low pressure area downwind to the east of the mountains. Increased westerly flow off the Rockies force the formation of a dry line when the flow aloft is strong, while the Gulf of Mexico fuels abundant low-level moisture in the southerly flow to its east. This unique topography allows for frequent collisions of warm and cold air, the conditions that breed strong, long-lived storms throughout the year. A large portion of these tornadoes form in an area of the central United States known as Tornado Alley. This area extends into Canada, particularly Ontario and the Prairie Provinces, although southeast Quebec, the interior of British Columbia, and western New Brunswick are also tornado-prone. Tornadoes also occur across northeastern Mexico.

The United States averages about 1,200 tornadoes per year. The Netherlands has the highest average number of recorded tornadoes per area of any country (more than 20, or 0.0013 per sq mi (0.00048 per km2), annually), followed by the UK (around 33, or 0.00035 per sq mi (0.00013 per km2), per year), but most are small and cause minor damage. In absolute number of events, ignoring area, the UK experiences more tornadoes than any other European country, excluding waterspouts.

Tornadoes kill an average of 179 people per year in Bangladesh, the most in the world This is due to high population density, poor quality of construction and lack of tornado safety knowledge, as well as other factors. Other areas of the world that have frequent tornadoes include South Africa, parts of Argentina, Paraguay, and southern Brazil, as well as portions of Europe, Australia and New Zealand, and far eastern Asia.

Tornadoes are most common in spring and least common in winter, but tornadoes can occur any time of year that favorable conditions occur. Spring and fall experience peaks of activity as those are the seasons when stronger winds, wind shear, and atmospheric instability are present. Tornadoes are focused in the right front quadrant of landfalling tropical cyclones, which tend to occur in the late summer and autumn. Tornadoes can also be spawned as a result of eyewall mesovortices, which persist until landfall.

Tornado occurrence is highly dependent on the time of day, because of solar heating. Worldwide, most tornadoes occur in the late afternoon, between 3 pm and 7 pm local time, with a peak near 5 pm. Destructive tornadoes can occur at any time of day. The Gainesville Tornado of 1936, one of the deadliest tornadoes in history, occurred at 8:30 am local time.

Associations to various climate and environmental trends exist. For example, an increase in the sea surface temperature of a source region (e.g. Gulf of Mexico and Mediterranean Sea) increases atmospheric moisture content. Increased moisture can fuel an increase in severe weather and tornado activity, particularly in the cool season.

Some evidence does suggest that the Southern Oscillation is weakly correlated with changes in tornado activity, which vary by season and region, as well as whether the ENSO phase is that of El Niño or La Niña.

Climatic shifts may affect tornadoes via teleconnections in shifting the jet stream and the larger weather patterns. The climate-tornado link is confounded by the forces affecting larger patterns and by the local, nuanced nature of tornadoes. Although it is reasonable that global warming may affect trends in tornado activity, any such effect is not yet identifiable due to the complexity, local nature of the storms, and database quality issues. Any effect would vary by region.

Detection of Tornadoes

Rigorous attempts to warn of tornadoes began in the United States in the mid-20th century. Before the 1950s, the only method of detecting a tornado was by someone seeing it on the ground. Often, news of a tornado would reach a local weather office after the storm. However, with the advent of weather radar, areas near a local office could get advance warning of severe weather. The first public tornado warnings were issued in 1950 and the first tornado watches and convective outlooks in 1952. In 1953 it was confirmed that hook echoes are associated with tornadoes. By recognizing these radar signatures, meteorologists could detect thunderstorms probably producing tornadoes from dozens of miles away.

Radar

Today, most developed countries have a network of weather radars, which remains the main method of detecting signatures probably associated with tornadoes. In the United States and a few other countries, Doppler weather radar stations are used. These devices measure the velocity and radial direction (towards or away from the radar) of the winds in a storm, and so can spot evidence of rotation in storms from more than a hundred miles (160 km) away. When storms are distant from a radar, only areas high within the storm are observed and the important areas below are not sampled. Data resolution also decreases with distance from the radar. Some meteorological situations leading to tornadogenesis are not readily detectable by radar and on occasion tornado development may occur more quickly than radar can complete a scan and send the batch of data. Also, most populated areas on Earth are now visible from the Geostationary Operational Environmental Satellites (GOES), which aid in the nowcasting of tornadic storms.

Storm Spotting

In the mid-1970s, the U.S. National Weather Service (NWS) increased its efforts to train storm spotters to spot key features of storms which indicate severe hail, damaging winds, and tornadoes, as well as damage itself and flash flooding. The program was called Skywarn, and the spotters were local sheriff's deputies, state troopers, firefighters, ambulance drivers, amateur radio operators, civil defense (now emergency management) spotters, storm chasers, and ordinary citizens. When severe weather is anticipated, local weather service offices request that these spotters look out for severe weather, and report any tornadoes immediately, so that the office can warn of the hazard.

Usually spotters are trained by the NWS on behalf of their respective organizations, and report to them. The organizations activate public warning systems such as sirens and the Emergency Alert System, and forward the report to the NWS. There are more than 230,000 trained Skywarn weather spotters across the United States.

In Canada, a similar network of volunteer weather watchers, called Canwarn, helps spot severe weather, with more than 1,000 volunteers. In Europe, several nations are organizing spotter networks under the auspices of Skywarn Europe and the Tornado and Storm Research Organisation (TORRO) has maintained a network of spotters in the United Kingdom since

1974.Storm spotters are needed because radar systems such as NEXRAD do not detect a tornado; merely signatures which hint at the presence of tornadoes. Radar may give a warning before there is any visual evidence of a tornado or imminent tornado, but ground truth from an observer can either verify the threat or determine that a tornado is not imminent. The spotter's ability to see what radar cannot is especially important as distance from the radar site increases, because the radar beam becomes progressively higher in altitude further away from the radar, chiefly due to curvature of Earth, and the beam also spreads out.

Visual Evidence

torm spotters are trained to discern whether a storm seen from a distance is a supercell. They typically look to its rear, the main region of updraft and inflow. Under the updraft is a rain-free base, and the next step of tornadogenesis is the formation of a rotating wall cloud. The vast majority of intense tornadoes occur with a wall cloud on the backside of a supercell.

Evidence of a supercell comes from the storm's shape and structure, and cloud tower features such as a hard and vigorous updraft tower, a persistent, large overshooting top, a hard anvil (especially when backsheared against strong upper level winds), and a corkscrew look or striations. Under the storm and closer to where most tornadoes are found, evidence of a supercell and likelihood of a tornado includes inflow bands (particularly when curved) such as a "beaver tail", and other clues such as strength of inflow, warmth and moistness of inflow air, how outflow- or inflow-dominant a storm appears, and how far is the front flank precipitation core from the wall cloud. Tornadogenesis is most likely at the interface of the updraft and rear flank downdraft, and requires a balance between the outflow and inflow.

Only wall clouds that rotate spawn tornadoes, and usually precede the tornado by five to thirty minutes. Rotating wall clouds are the visual manifestation of a mesocyclone. Barring a low-level boundary, tornadogenesis is highly unlikely unless a rear flank downdraft occurs, which is usually visibly evidenced by evaporation of cloud adjacent to a corner of a wall cloud. A tornado often occurs as this happens or shortly after; first, a funnel cloud dips and in nearly all cases by the time it reaches halfway down, a surface swirl has already developed, signifying a tornado is on the ground before condensation connects the surface circulation to the storm. Tornadoes may also occur without wall clouds, under flanking lines, and on the leading edge. Spotters watch all areas of a storm, and the cloud base and surface.

Extreme Events

The most record-breaking tornado in recorded history was the Tri-State Tornado, which roared through parts of Missouri, Illinois, and Indiana on March 18, 1925. It was likely an F5, though tornadoes were not ranked on any scale in that era. It holds records for longest path length (219 miles, 352 km), longest duration (about 3.5 hours), and fastest forward speed for a significant tornado (73 mph, 117 km/h) anywhere on Earth. In addition, it is the deadliest single tornado in United States history (695 dead). The tornado was also the second costliest tornado in history at the time, but in the years since has been surpassed by several others if population changes over time are not considered. When costs are normalized for wealth and inflation, it ranks third today.

The deadliest tornado in world history was the Daultipur-Salturia Tornado in Bangladesh on April 26, 1989, which killed approximately 1300 people. Bangladesh has had at least 19 tornadoes in its history kill more than 100 people, almost half of the total in the rest of the world.

The most extensive tornado outbreak on record was the Super Outbreak, which affected a large area of the central United States and extreme southern Ontario in Canada on April 3 and 4, 1974. This outbreak, which saw 148 tornadoes develop in 18 hours, included six of F5 intensity and twenty-four that peaked at F4 strength. Sixteen tornadoes were on the ground at the same time during its peak. More than 300 people, possibly as many as 330, were killed by tornadoes during this outbreak.

While direct measurement of the most violent tornado wind speeds is nearly impossible, since conventional anemometers would be destroyed by the intense winds, some tornadoes have been scanned by mobile Doppler radar units, which can provide a good estimate of the tornado's winds. The highest wind speed ever measured in a tornado, which is also the highest wind speed ever recorded on the planet, is 301 ± 20 mph (484 ± 32 km/h) in the F5 Bridge Creek-Moore, Oklahoma, tornado which killed 36 people. Though the reading was taken about 100 feet (30 m) above the ground, this is a testament to the power of the strongest tornadoes.

Storms that produce tornadoes can feature intense updrafts, sometimes exceeding 150 mph (240 km/h). Debris from a tornado can be lofted into the parent storm and carried a very long distance. A tornado which affected Great Bend, Kansas, in November 1915, was an extreme case, where a "rain of debris" occurred 80 miles (130 km) from the town, a sack of flour was found 110 miles (180 km) away, and a cancelled check from the Great Bend bank was found in a field outside of Palmyra, Nebraska, 305 miles (491 km) to the northeast. Waterspouts and tornadoes have been advanced as an explanation for instances of raining fish and other animals.

Safety Issues

Though tornadoes can strike in an instant, there are precautions and preventative measures that people can take to increase the chances of surviving a tornado. Authorities such as the Storm Prediction Center advise having a pre-determined plan should a tornado warning be issued. When a warning is issued, going to a basement or an interior first-floor room of a sturdy building greatly increases chances of survival. In tornado-prone areas, many buildings have storm cellars on the property. These underground refuges have saved thousands of lives.

Some countries have meteorological agencies which distribute tornado forecasts and increase levels of alert of a possible tornado (such as tornado watches and warnings in the United States and Canada). Weather radios provide an alarm when a severe weather advisory is issued for the local area, though these are mainly available only in the United States. Unless the tornado is far away and highly visible, meteorologists advise that drivers park their vehicles far to the side of the road (so as not to block emergency traffic), and find a sturdy shelter. If no sturdy shelter is nearby, getting low in a ditch is the next best option. Highway overpasses are one of the worst places to take shelter during tornadoes, as the constricted space can be subject to increased wind speed and funneling of debris underneath the overpass.

Preparedness

What to do before a tornado strikes:

— Know the terms used to describe tornado threats:

— A tornado watch means tornadoes, severe thunderstorms, or both, are possible. Stay tuned to radio and television reports in your area. Keep watch on the sky.

— A tornado warning means tornadoes have been sighted. You should take shelter immediately.

— Know the locations of designated shelter areas in public facilities, such as schools, public buildings and shopping centers.

— Have emergency supplies on hand during tornado season.

— Be sure everyone in your household knows in advance where to go and what to do in case of a tornado warning.

— Make an inventory of your household furnishings and other possessions. Supplement the written inventory with photographs. Keep inventories and photos in a safe deposit box or some other safe place away from the premises.

Response

What to do during a tornado

— Whenever severe thunderstorms threaten your area, listen to the radio and television newscasts for the latest information and instructions.

— When a tornado has been sighted, stay away from windows, doors and outside walls. Protect your head from falling objects or flying debris.

Take cover immediately, wherever you are:

— In a house or small building, go to the basement or storm cellar. If there is no basement, go to an interior part of the structure on the lower level (closets, interior hallways). In either case, get under something sturdy (such as a heavy table) and stay there until the danger has passed.

— In a school, nursing home, hospital, factory or shopping center, go to pre-designated shelter areas. Interior hallways on the lowest floor are usually safest. Stay away from windows and open spaces. Cooperate with the staff and authorities - they have had training about how to deal with emergencies.

— In a high-rise building, go to small, interior rooms or hallways on the lowest floor possible.

— In a vehicle, trailer or mobile home, get out immediately and go to a more substantial structure. If there is no shelter nearby, lie flat in the nearest ditch, ravine or culvert with your hands shielding your head.

— Do not attempt to flee from a tornado in a car or other vehicle. They are no match for the swift, erratic movement of these storms.

Recovery

What to do after a tornado:

- Use great caution when entering a building damaged from high winds. When entering or cleaning a tornado-damaged building, be sure that the walls, ceiling and roof are in place and that the structure rests firmly on the foundation.
- Look out for broken glass and downed power lines.

References

Howard B Bluestein (1999). *Tornado Alley: Monster Storms of the Great Plains*. New York, NY: Oxford University Press.

Marlene Bradford (2001). *Scanning the Skies: a History of Tornado Forecasting*. University of Oklahoma Press.

Micheal H Mogil (2007). *Extreme Weather*. New York: Black Dog & Leventhal Publisher.

Seymour, Simon (2001). *Tornadoes*. New York City, New York: HarperCollins

Thomas P Grazulis (January 1997). *Significant Tornadoes Update, 1992–1995*. St. Johnsbury, VT: Environmental Film.

8

Tsunami Risk Management

A tsunami is a series of water waves caused by the displacement of a large volume of a body of water, typically an ocean or a large lake. Earthquakes, volcanic eruptions and other underwater explosions, landslides, glacier calvings, meteorite impacts and other disturbances above or below water all have the potential to generate a tsunami.

Tsunami waves do not resemble normal sea waves, because their wavelength is far longer. Rather than appearing as a breaking wave, a tsunami may instead initially resemble a rapidly rising tide, and for this reason they are often referred to as tidal waves. Tsunamis generally consist of a series of waves with periods ranging from minutes to hours, arriving in a so-called "wave train". Wave heights of tens of metres can be generated by large events. Although the impact of tsunamis is limited to coastal areas, their destructive power can be enormous and they can affect entire ocean basins; the 2004 Indian Ocean tsunami was among the deadliest natural disasters in human history with over 230,000 people killed in 14 countries bordering the Indian Ocean.

The Greek historian Thucydides suggested in 426 BC that tsunamis were related to submarine earthquakes, but the understanding of a tsunami's nature remained slim until the 20th century and much remains unknown Major areas of current research include trying to determine why some large earthquakes do not generate tsunamis while other smaller ones do; trying to accurately forecast the passage of tsunamis across the oceans; and also to forecast how tsunami waves would interact with specific shorelines.

Tsunami are sometimes referred to as tidal waves. In recent years, this term has fallen out of favor, especially in the scientific community, because tsunami actually have nothing to do with tides. The once-popular term derives from their most common appearance, which is that of an extraordinarily high tidal bore. Tsunami and tides both produce waves of water that move inland, but in the case of tsunami the inland movement of water is much greater and lasts for a longer period, giving the impression of an incredibly high tide. Although the meanings of "tidal" include "resembling" or "having the form or character of" the tides, and the term tsunami is no more accurate because tsunami are not limited to harbours, use of the term tidal wave is discouraged by geologists and oceanographers.

There are only a few other languages that have an equivalent native word. In Acehnese language, the words are iĕ beuna or alôn buluĕk (depending on the dialect). In Tamil language, it is aazhi peralai. On Simeulue island, off the western coast of Sumatra in Indonesia, in Devayan language the word is smong, while in Sigulai language it is emong. In Singkil (in Aceh province) and surrounding, the people name tsunami with word gloro.

As early as 426 BC the Greek historian Thucydides inquired in his book History of the Peloponnesian War about the causes of tsunami, and was the first to argue that ocean earthquakes must be the cause.

"The cause, in my opinion, of this phcnomenon must be sought in the earthquake. At the point where its shock has been the most violent the sea is driven back, and suddenly recoiling with redoubled force, causes the inundation. Without an earthquake I do not see how such an accident could happen."

The Roman historian Ammianus Marcellinus (Res Gestae 26.10.15-19) described the typical sequence of a tsunami, including an incipient earthquake, the sudden retreat of the sea and a following gigantic wave, after the 365 AD tsunami devastated Alexandria.

While Japan may have the longest recorded history of tsunamis, the sheer destruction caused by the 2004 Indian Ocean earthquake and tsunami event mark it as the most devastating of its kind in modern times, killing around 230,000 people. The Sumatran region is not unused to tsunamis either, with earthquakes of varying magnitudes regularly occurring off the coast of the island.

Generation Mechanisms

The principal generation mechanism (or cause) of a tsunami is the displacement of a substantial volume of water or perturbation of the sea. This displacement of water is usually attributed to either earthquakes, landslides, volcanic eruptions, glacier calvings or more rarely by meteorites and nuclear tests. The waves formed in this way are then sustained by gravity. Tides do not play any part in the generation of tsunamis.

Tsunami Generated by Seismicity

Tsunami can be generated when the sea floor abruptly deforms and vertically displaces the overlying water. Tectonic earthquakes are a particular kind of earthquake that are associated with the Earth's crustal deformation; when these earthquakes occur beneath the sea, the water above the deformed area is displaced from its equilibrium position. More specifically, a tsunami can be generated when thrust faults associated with convergent or destructive plate boundaries move abruptly, resulting in water displacement, owing to the vertical component of movement involved. Movement on normal faults will also cause displacement of the seabed, but the size of the largest of such events is normally too small to give rise to a significant tsunami.

Tsunamis have a small amplitude (wave height) offshore, and a very long wavelength (often hundreds of kilometers long, whereas normal ocean waves have a wavelength of only 30 or 40 metres), which is why they generally pass unnoticed at sea, forming only a slight swell usually about 300 millimetres (12 in) above the normal sea surface. They grow in height when they reach shallower water, in a wave shoaling process described below. A tsunami can occur in any tidal state and even at low tide can still inundate coastal areas.

On April 1, 1946, a magnitude-7.8 (Richter Scale) earthquake occurred near the Aleutian Islands, Alaska. It generated a tsunami which inundated Hilo on the island of Hawai'i with a 14 metres (46 ft) high surge. The area where the earthquake occurred is where the Pacific Ocean floor is subducting (or being pushed downwards) under Alaska.

Examples of tsunami originating at locations away from convergent boundaries include Storegga about 8,000 years ago, Grand Banks 1929, Papua New Guinea 1998 (Tappin, 2001). The Grand Banks and Papua New Guinea tsunamis came from earthquakes which destabilized sediments, causing them to flow into the ocean and generate a tsunami. They dissipated before traveling transoceanic distances.

The cause of the Storegga sediment failure is unknown. Possibilities include an overloading of the sediments, an earthquake or a release of gas hydrates (methane etc.)

The 1960 Valdivia earthquake (Mw 9.5) (19:11 hrs UTC), 1964 Alaska earthquake (Mw 9.2), 2004 Indian Ocean earthquake (Mw 9.2) (00:58:53 UTC) and 2011 Tohoku earthquake (Mw9.0) are recent examples of powerful megathrust earthquakes that generated tsunamis (known as teletsunamis) that can cross entire oceans. Smaller (Mw 4.2) earthquakes in Japan can trigger tsunamis (called local and regional tsunamis) that can only devastate nearby coasts, but can do so in only a few minutes.

Tsunami Generated by Landslides

In the 1950s, it was discovered that larger tsunamis than had previously been believed possible could be caused by giant landslides. Underwater landslides that generate tsunamis are called sciorrucks. These phenomena rapidly displace large water volumes, as energy from falling debris or expansion transfers to the water at a rate faster than the water can absorb. Their existence was confirmed in 1958, when a giant landslide in Lituya Bay, Alaska, caused the highest wave ever recorded, which had a height of 524 metres (over 1700 feet). The wave didn't travel far, as it struck land almost immediately. Two people fishing in the bay were killed, but another boat amazingly managed to ride the wave. Scientists named these waves megatsunami.

Meteotsunamis

Some meteorological conditions, such as deep depressions that cause tropical cyclones, can generate a storm surge, called a meteotsunami, which can raise tides several metres above normal levels. The displacement comes from low atmospheric pressure within the centre of the depression. As these storm surges reach shore, they may resemble (though are not) tsunamis, inundating vast areas of land.

Characteristics

Tsunamis cause damage by two mechanisms: the smashing force of a wall of water travelling at high speed, and the destructive power of a large volume of water draining off the land and carrying all with it, even if the wave did not look large.

While everyday wind waves have a wavelength (from crest to crest) of about 100 metres (330 ft) and a height of roughly 2 metres (6.6 ft), a tsunami in the deep ocean has a wavelength of about 200 kilometres (120 mi). Such a wave travels at well over 800 kilometres per hour (500 mph), but owing to the enormous wavelength the wave oscillation at any given point takes 20 or 30 minutes to complete a cycle and has an amplitude of only about 1 metre (3.3 ft). This makes tsunamis difficult to detect over deep water, where ships are unable to feel their passage.

The reason for the Japanese name "harbor wave" is that sometimes a village's fishermen would sail out, and encounter no unusual waves while out at sea fishing, and come back to land to find their village devastated by a huge wave.

As the tsunami approaches the coast and the waters become shallow, wave shoaling compresses the wave and its speed decreases below 80 kilometres per hour (50 mph). Its wavelength diminishes to less than 20 kilometres (12 mi) and its amplitude grows enormously. Since the wave still has the same very long period, the tsunami may take minutes to reach full height. Except for the very largest tsunamis, the approaching wave does not break, but rather appears like a fast-moving tidal bore. Open bays and coastlines adjacent to very deep water may shape the tsunami further into a step-like wave with a steep-breaking front.

When the tsunami's wave peak reaches the shore, the resulting temporary rise in sea level is termed run up. Run up is measured in metres above a reference sea level. A large tsunami may feature multiple waves arriving over a period of hours, with significant time between the wave crests. The first wave to reach the shore may not have the highest run up.

About 80% of tsunamis occur in the Pacific Ocean, but they are possible wherever there are large bodies of water, including lakes. They are caused by earthquakes, landslides, volcanic explosions, glacier calvings, and bolides.

Causes of Tsunamis

A tsunami can be generated when the plate boundaries abruptly deform and vertically displace the overlying water. Such large vertical movements of the Earth's crust can occur at plate boundaries. Subduction earthquakes are particularly effective in generating tsunami. Also, one tsunami in the 1940's in Hilo, Hawaii, was actually caused by an earthquake on one of the Aleutian Islands in Alaska. That earthquake was 7.8 on the Richter Scale.

Tsunami take place when a huge earthquake occurs causing the plates below the water to push up causing the water to create a huge wave.

In the 1950s it was discovered that larger tsunami than previously believed possible could be caused by landslides, explosive volcanic action, and impact events when they contact water. These phenomena rapidly displace large volumes of water, as energy from falling debris or expansion is transferred to the water into which the debris falls.

Tsunami caused by these mechanisms, unlike the ocean-wide tsunami caused by some earthquakes, generally dissipate quickly and rarely affect coastlines distant from the source due to the small area of sea affected. These events can give rise to much larger local shock waves (solitons), such as the landslide at the head of Lituya Bay which produced a water wave estimated at 50 – 150 m and reached 524 m up local mountains. However, an extremely large landslide could generate a "megatsunami" that might have ocean-wide impacts. The geological record tells us that there have been massive tsunami in Earth's past.

Signs of an Approaching Tsunami

There is often no advance warning of an approaching tsunami. However, since earthquakes are often a cause of tsunami, an earthquake felt near a body of water may be considered an indication that a tsunami will shortly follow. When the first part of a tsunami to reach land is a trough rather than a crest of the wave, the water along the shoreline may recede dramatically, exposing areas that are normally always submerged. This can serve as an advance warning of the approaching crest of the tsunami, although the warning arrives only a very short time before the crest, which typically arrives seconds to minutes later. In the 2004 tsunami that occurred in the Indian Ocean the sea receding was not reported on the African coast or any other western coasts it hit, when the tsunami approached from the east.

Tsunamis occur most frequently in the Pacific Ocean, but are a global phenomenon; they are possible wherever large bodies of water are found, including inland lakes, where they can be caused by landslides. Very small tsunamis, non-destructive and undetectable without specialised equipment, occur frequently as a result of minor earthquakes and other events.

Meteotsunami

A meteotsunami is a tsunami-like wave phenomenon of meteorological origin. Tsunamis and meteotsunamis propagate in the water in the same way and have the same coastal dynamics. In other words, for an observer on the coast where it strikes the two types would look the same. The difference is in their source only. One definition of a meteotsunami is as an atmospherically generated large amplitude seiche oscillation.

The principal source of these tsunami-like ocean waves are travelling air pressure disturbances, including those associated with atmospheric gravity waves, roll clouds, pressure jumps, frontal passages, and squalls, which normally generate barotropic ocean waves in the open ocean and amplify them near the coast through specific resonance mechanisms. In contrast to 'ordinary' impulse-type tsunami sources, a travelling atmospheric disturbance normally interacts with the ocean over a limited period of time (from several minutes to several hours). These types of waves are common all over the world and are better known by their local names: *Rissaga* (Spain), *Milghuba* (Malta), *Marrubio* (Italy), *Abiki* (Japan).

Megatsunami

Megatsunami (often hyphenated as mega-tsunami, also known as iminami or "wave of purification") is an informal term used mostly by popular media and popular scientific societies to describe a very large tsunami wave beyond the typical size reached by most tsunamis. A megatsunami is associated with waves beyond the norm for tsunamis, ranging from over 40 metres (131 feet) to giants over 100 metres (328 ft) tall. Note that the waves are often much higher when they meet land, as the water often floods upwards from the force of impact.

Megatsunamis are caused by a very large impact or landslide into a body of water when the water cannot disperse in all directions. For this reason, they are usually a highly localised effect, either occurring when the origin of a tsunami is extremely close to the shore, or in deep, narrow inlets, lakes or other water passages. The astounding heights quoted for megatsunami waves are caused by the displacement of a very large volume of water in a limited space in a very short time creating a single powerful surge.Megatsunamis may be caused by landslide and rockfall phenomena, explosive volcanic events, or meteor impacts. Underwater earthquakes do not normally generate such large tsunamis; typically tsunamis caused by earthquakes (such as the 2004 Indian Ocean earthquake) have a height of less than ten metres at the shore (depending on how much water was displaced by the earthquake and on various natural factors such as tree cover and the general shore characteristics) but can affect thousands of kilometres of coastline and reach many kilometres inland.

Discovery and Confirmation

Megatsunamis were first hypothesized by geologists searching for oil in Alaska in 1953. They observed that mature forestation did not extend to the shoreline as it did in nearly all other bays in the region. Rather, there were bands of younger trees closer to the shore. The surveyors called the boundary between these bands a trim line, resembling those caused by the advance and retreat of glaciers. Selected trees were cut in the areas just above and below each trim line. The trees just above these lines showed severe scarring, as if hit very hard by something that came from the coast.

The only possible explanation, according to scientists, was that there were unusually large waves in the nearby deep inlet called Lituya Bay, Alaska. This is a recently deglaciated fjord with steep slopes and crossed by a major fault. The topology of the inlet is particularly suited to producing landslide generated tsunamis. They speculated that something had caused a huge wave in relatively recent times, but the cause of this hypothetical wave remained unknown.

On July 10, 1958 the speculation was confirmed, following a nearby earthquake of magnitude 7.7, which generated a landslide that sent water surging across Lituya Bay. The landslide hit the water fast enough to shoot water up the opposite bay to a height of 524 meters. A wave with initial heights of about 333 meters traveled along the bay, and flowed over the entrance to the bay with a height of about 350 meters. Howard Ulrich and his son, Howard Jr. were in the bay in their fishing boat when they saw the wave. Ulrich tried to get over the wave and he and his son amazingly survived the wave, and reported that it carried their boat "over the trees". Another boat actually rode over the tsunami in the bay, and one was destroyed by the tsunami.

On July 10, 1958, a landslide caused by an earthquake generated a monstrous tsunami 524m (1720 ft) high, which stripped trees and soil from the opposite headland and consumed the entire bay, destroying three fishing boats anchored there and killing two people.

Vajont Dam

The Vajont Dam as seen from Longarone today, showing approximately the top 60-70 metres of concrete. On October 9, 1963, a landslide above Vajont Dam in Italy produced a 250m (820 ft) tsunami that overtopped the dam and destroyed the villages of Longarone, Pirago, Rivalta, Villanova and Faè, killing almost 2,000 people.

Spirit Lake Tsunami

On May 18, 1980, the upper 1,500 feet (460 m) including the former summit of Mount St. Helens, a volcano in Washington state, detached as a landslide. The avalanche slammed into Spirit Lake sending a tsunami surging around the lake basin as high as 820 feet (250 m) above lake level. Above the upper limit of the tsunami, trees lie where they were knocked down by a pyroclastic surge; below the limit, the downed trees and the surge deposits were removed by the tsunami and deposited in Spirit Lake.

The geological record suggests that megatsunamis generated by the collapse of flank of a volcanic island, their most common cause, may occur every few thousand years. Their size and power can produce devastating effects; travelling across oceans and reshaping entire coastlines. The most recent such event so far known occurred approximately 4,000 years ago on Réunion island, to the east of Madagascar. The most recent collapse occurred on Ritter Island in 1888 but it only generated 12-15 metre waves, which, although they killed 3,000 people on surrounding islands, were not megatsunamis and did not cause widespread devastation.

The most recent megatsunamis, such as the one at Lituya Bay in 1958 and in the Vajont Dam in 1963, have occurred as a result of landslides in largely enclosed bodies of waters and their effects have been limited. Other recent megatsunamis include the 40 metre high waves generated by the collapse of Krakatoa during its eruption in 1883 which killed 36,000 people on Java, Sumatra and the small islands around them; and the collapse of much of Santorini during its cataclysmic eruption around 3,500 years ago which produced a 100-150 metre wave that struck the north coast of Crete after travelling 70 kilometres. However, these megatsunamis did not propagate thousands of miles to cause more widespread damage, in part leading to the controversy about whether the waves produced by island collapses travel great distances in the same way that tsunamis do.

In the Norwegian Sea, the Storegga Slide caused a megatsunami 7,000 years ago. Extensive geological investigations indicate that the risk of a re-occurrence is minimal. There is evidence of a megatsunami-type freshwater disaster that occurred 10,000 to 20,000 years ago can be seen at Seton Portage, British Columbia where a huge chunk of the Cayoosh Range suddenly slid north into what had been a large lake spanning the area from Lillooet, British Columbia to near Birken, in the Gates Valley or Pemberton Pass to the southwest. The event has not been studied much in modern times but the proto-lake must have been at least as deep as its two present-day halves, Seton and Anderson Lakes, on either side of the Portage, suggesting that the wave created by the giant landslide must have been comparable to Lituya Bay.

They have also been generated by bolide impacts. There are indications that a giant tsunami was generated by the bolide impact that created the Chesapeake Bay impact crater, a shallow-water near-shore impact off the eastern North American coastline about 35.5 million years ago, in the late Eocene Epoch. The meteor which created the Chicxulub Crater in Yucatan around 65 million years ago (and probably triggered the dinosaurs' extinction) may have generated the largest megatsunamis in Earth's history.

Megatsunami Threats

Volcanic islands can cause megatsunamis to hit other nearby islands in the same chain because often they are comparatively steep sloped structures with little horizontal support made up of often loosely aggregated material heaped up by successive eruptions from a central vent area and bisected by faults and stress lines created by ongoing vulcanism. Evidence for large landslides has been found in the form of extensive underwater debris aprons around them composed of the material which has slipped into the ocean. In recent years five such debris aprons have been found in the Hawaiian Islands alone.

Some geologists speculate that the most likely candidate for the source of the next large-scale megatsunami is the island of La Palma, in the Canary Islands. Reports say that during the 1949 eruption the western half of the Cumbre Vieja ridge slipped four metres downwards into the Atlantic Ocean, though this is disputed. It is believed that this process was driven by the pressure caused by the rising magma heating and vaporising water trapped within the structure of the island, causing the island's structure to be pushed apart.

The island is still considered active, though quiescent at present, but it is expected to erupt again some time in the next few hundred years. Were this to happen it is speculated that a megatsunami would be created as the western half of the island, weighing perhaps 500 billion tonnes, catastrophically slides into the ocean in a single event, causing local wave heights of hundreds of metres and a likely height of around 10–25 m at the Caribbean and the Eastern North American seaboard coast several hours later. However, this is speculative since there is disagreement whether it would in fact happen, when, or how likely it is.

There is also disagreement among scientists about whether an eruption of Cumbre Vieja would cause a single large landslide or a series of smaller landslides and if such a landslide would generate a tsunami capable of crossing the Atlantic. The Tsunami Society issued a statement in 2003 that such collapses are rare and occur at intervals of thousands or millions of years, that the risk of La Palma collapsing was over-dramatised, and that although the catastrophic collapse of the islands of Krakatoa and Santorini produced megatsunamis in the local region, huge waves did not propagate across oceans to cause similar devastation on more distant coasts, adding that evidence (including computer simulations and experiments with models) suggests this type of wave does not travel great distances in the same way that normal tsunamis do.

Besides fjords in Alaska, many locations face threats of localised, but still potentially dangerous, megatsunami-type waves. Some geologists speculate that an unstable rock face at Mount Breakenridge above the north end of the giant fresh-water fjord of Harrison Lake in the Fraser Valley in southwestern British Columbia could collapse into the lake, generating a large wave that might destroy the town of Harrison Hot Springs at the south end.

Prevention of Tsunami Disaster

A tsunami cannot be prevented or precisely predicted, but there are some warning signs of an impending tsunami, and there are many systems being developed and in use to reduce the damage from tsunami. In instances where the leading edge of the tsunami wave is its trough, the sea will recede from the coast half of the wave's period before the wave's arrival. If the slope is shallow, this recession can exceed many hundreds of meters. People unaware of the danger may remain at the shore due to curiosity, or for collecting fish from the exposed seabed.

Regions with a high risk of tsunami may use tsunami warning systems to detect tsunami and warn the general population before the wave reaches land. In some communities on the west coast of the United States, which is prone to Pacific Ocean tsunami, warning signs advise people where to run in the event of an incoming tsunami. Computer models can roughly predict tsunami arrival and impact based on information about the event that triggered it and the shape of the seafloor (bathymetry) and coastal land (topography).

One of the early warnings comes from nearby animals. Many animals sense danger and flee to higher ground before the water arrives. The Lisbon quake is the first documented case of such a phenomenon in Europe. The phenomenon was also noted in Sri Lanka in the 2004 Indian Ocean earthquake. Some scientists speculate that animals may have an ability to sense subsonic Rayleigh waves from an earthquake minutes or hours before a tsunami strikes shore. More likely, though, is that the certain large animals (e.g., elephants) heard the sounds of the tsunami as it approached the coast. The elephants reactions were to go in the direction opposite of the noise, and thus go inland. Humans, on the other hand, head down to the shore to investigate.

While it is not possible to prevent a tsunami, in some particularly tsunami-prone countries some measures have been taken to reduce the damage caused on shore. Japan has implemented an extensive programme of building tsunami walls of up to 4.5 m (13.5 ft) high in front of populated coastal areas. Other localities have built floodgates and channels to redirect the water from incoming tsunami. However, their effectiveness has been questioned, as tsunami are often higher than the barriers.

For instance, the tsunami which struck the island of Hokkaido on July 12, 1993 created waves as much as 30 m (100 ft) tall - as high as a 10-story building. The port town of Aonae was completely surrounded by a tsunami wall, but the waves washed right over the wall and destroyed all the wood-framed structures in the area. The wall may have succeeded in slowing down and moderating the height of the tsunami, but it did not prevent major destruction and loss of life.

The effects of a tsunami can be mitigated by natural factors such as tree cover on the shoreline. Some locations in the path of the 2004 Indian Ocean tsunami escaped almost unscathed as a result of the tsunami's energy being sapped by a belt of trees such as coconut palms and mangroves. In one striking example, the village of Naluvedapathy in India's Tamil Nadu region suffered minimal damage and few deaths as the wave broke up on a forest of 80,244 trees planted along the shoreline in 2002 in a bid to enter the Guinness Book of Records. Environmentalists have suggested tree planting along stretches of seacoast which are prone to tsunami risks. While it would take some years for the trees to grow to a useful size, such plantations could offer a much cheaper and longer-lasting means of tsunami mitigation than the costly and environmentally destructive method of erecting artificial barriers.

Tsunami Warning System

A tsunami warning system is a system to detect tsunamis and issue warnings to prevent loss of life and property. It consists of two equally important components: a network of sensors to detect tsunamis and a communications infrastructure to issue timely alarms to permit evacuation of coastal areas.

There are two distinct types: mierda tsunami and pene tsunami international tsunami warning systems, and regional warning systems. Both depend on the fact that, while tsunamis travel at between 500 and 1,000 km/h (around 0.14 and 0.28 km/s) in open water, earthquakes can be detected almost at once as seismic waves travel with a typical speed of 4 km/s (around 14,400 km/h). This gives time for a possible tsunami forecast to be made and warnings to be issued to threatened areas, if warranted. Unfortunately, until a reliable model is able to predict which earthquakes will produce significant tsunamis, this approach will produce many more false alarms than verified warnings.

In the currect operational paradigm, the seismic alerts are used to send out the watches and warnings. Then, data from observed sea level height are used to verify the existence of a tsunami. Other systems have been proposed to augment the warning paradigm. For example, it has been suggested that the duration and frequency content of t-wave energy is indicative of an earthquakes tsunami potential. The first rudimentary system to alert communities of an impending tsunami was attempted in Hawaii in the 1920s. More advanced systems were developed in the wake of the April 1, 1946 and May 23, 1960 tsunamis which caused massive devastation in Hilo, Hawaii.

The following are the components of a tsunami early warning system:

— A Network of Land-based Seismic Stations for earthquake detection and estimation of source parameters in the two known tsunamigenic zones that would affect the Indian Ocean region and communicating the same to Early Warning Centre in near-real time.
— Detection of Tsunami generation through a network of 10-12 bottom pressure recorders (that could detect and measure a change in water level of 1 cm at water depths of up to 6 km of water) around these two tsunamigenic zones,
— Monitoring the progress of Tsunami and Storm Surges through a network of 50 real time tide gauges,
— Tsunami Modelling,
— Generating and updating a high resolution data base on bathymetry, coastal topography, coastal land use, coastal vulnerability as well as historic data base on Tsunami and Storm Surge to prepare and update Storm Surge/ Tsunami hazard maps in 1:5,000 scale,
— Setting up a dedicated National Early Warning Centre (NEWC) for monitoring tsunamis and storm surges in India for operation on 24x7 basis and for generation of timely advisories, and
— Capacity building, training and education of all stakeholders on utilisation of the maps, warning and watch advisories.

As part of the Early Warning System for Tsunamis and Storm Surges in Indian Ocean set up by GoI, a 17-station Real Time Seismic Monitoring Network (RTSMN) is envisaged to be established by IMD. This network is designed to monitor and report the occurrence of earthquakes capable of generating Tsunamis from the two probable Tsunamigenic sources viz., Java-Sumatra-Andaman-Myanmar belt and the north Arabian Sea area in the least possible time. The data from the 17 Broadband seismic field stations will be transmitted simultaneously in real time through VSAT communication facilities to the Central Receiving Stations (CRS) located at IMD at New Delhi and INCOIS, Hyderabad for processing and interpretation.

The CRS are equipped with state-of-the-art computing hardware, communication, data processing, visualization and dissemination facilities. The earthquake information shall be disseminated through various communication channels to all concerned user agencies in a fully automated mode. The main features of the Real Time Data Processing software at the CRS are given below:

— Sounding Earthquake Alert based on first information to NEWC;
— Real time estimation of hypocentral and source parameters;
— Seismic waveform data sharing with international community through Gateway Hub located at the NEWC at INCOIS, Hyderabad from the selected stations (Port Blair, Bhuj, Shillong and Hyderabad) for earthquakes of magnitude 6.0 and above from Tsunamigenic sources;
— Estimation of dynamic source parameters, such as Centroid Moment Tensor (CMT) solutions, source duration, displacement etc.;
— Fault Plane Solution from waveform inversion;
— Assessment of type of faulting involved in the earthquake and the possibility of tsunami generation ;
— Multi-Channel graphic display of waveform and derived products; and
— Extensive data dissemination capabilities to decision making authorities through automatic generation of Fax, SMS and Email messages and response from dedicated Telephone answering machines.

For the purpose of prognosis, a data base of tsunami height in the ocean and on land, time of arrival of the tsunami wave at the site can be generated by postulating various events at different locations on the tsunamigenic sources. In the event of an actual tsunami these data base can be made use of to forecast the progression of the tsunami wave, and issue warnings to the various agencies. The first indication can be had from the seismic signal. This process will be continuously updated based on further seismic data and the data from various instruments deployed in the ocean. Based on these updated assessment of the tsunami waves, height and assessment of inundation can be made and suitable advisories can be issued through the concerned authorities. The prognostic model can be verified by re-run of past tsunami data.

In order to quickly confirm existence or otherwise of Tsunami waves following an earthquake, and also for monitoring the progress of tsunami and later for cancellation of warning, it is essential to monitor the sea level and this calls for a network of real-time Tide Gauges installed in strategic locations. The real-time Tide gauges are also essential component of the storm surge monitoring system. Such a network of tide gauges may be the only way of detecting a Tsunami in cases where seismic data are not available or when the Tsunami is triggered by events other than an earthquake.

As part of the National Tsunami Early Warning System, 50 state-of-the-art Tide gauges are being installed at strategic locations along the Indian Coast as well as a few of the Off-shore platforms connected to the Early Warning Centre. VSAT connectivity has already been set up between NIOT, SOI and INCOIS for real-time reception of the data at the Early Warning Centre. INCOIS has developed necessary software for real-time reception, display and archiving of tide gauge data.

In order to confirm whether the earthquake has actually triggered a Tsunami, it is essential to measure the change in water level in the open ocean with high accuracy. Bottom Pressure Recorders (BPRs) are used to detect the propagation of Tsunami waves in the Open Ocean and consequent sea level changes. A network of Bottom Pressure Sensors (BPSs) are being installed close to the tsunamigenic source regions to detect tsunami.

The System consists of an anchored sea floor Bottom Pressure Recorder (BPR) and a companion Moored Surface Buoy for real time communications. The BPR uses a piezoelectric Pressure transducer to make 15 seconds- averaged measurements of the pressure exerted on it by the overlying water column. The Tsunami detection algorithm running in the BPR generates predicted water height values and compares all new samples with predicted values. If two 15-second water level values exceed the predicted values, the system will go into the 'Tsunami Response Mode'. Data will then be transmitted on the Random channel for a minimum of 3 hours, giving high frequency data on short intervals with 100% repeated data for redundancy for the first hour. An acoustic link transmits data from the BPR on the sea floor to the surface buoy. The data are then relayed via a communication satellite (e.g. GOES) finally to the Tsunami Warning Centre. In the 'Standard mode', the System reports, every hour, only four 15-minute average values of sea surface height.

Twelve BPRs (10 in the Bay of Bengal and 2 in the Arabian Sea) are being installed in the Bay of Bengal and the Arabian Sea at appropriate locations. To date, 4 BPRs in Bay of Bengal and 2 BPRs in the Arabian sea have been deployed and remaining 6 BPRs are going to be deployed in the near future.

The critical gaps in the availability of monitoring instruments like BPRs, tide gauges, surface buoys, etc. to cover the Bay of Bengal, Arabian Sea and the Indian Ocean for close monitoring of tsunamigenic behaviour will be carried out by MoES urgently on priority. The MoES will carry out an assessment of the feasibility of the existing installations to cover the potential tsunami-prone areas and augment the installation of all instruments as per this assessment to ensure that all possible tsunamigenic behaviour patterns are captured as early warning and alert messages through this augmented network.

It is globally a major concern that the unattended ocean observation platforms including the Deep Ocean Tsunami Wave Detection Buoy System (Tsunameter) in sea are being vandalized either accidentally or intentionally and has become detrimental to the data availability during the Tsunami event. As such, the failures of tsunami buoys data reporting due to vandalism should be addressed on priority. It is necessary to create the public awareness, more particularly among the fishermen and mariners, about the importance of such a system for hazard prevention and mitigation and the need to protect such a system at high sea. The awareness campaigns should also bring out the efforts of scientists and engineers in designing and developing such hi tech devices and its deployment in high sea as well as its up-keeping even during the harsh sea conditions, apart from the large expenditure involved in developing such systems. There should be a regular awareness campaign through print and electronic media informing the general public, especially fishermen, about Tsunami Buoy features, its importance and protection needs. Further, the coastal villages should also be well informed about such scientific instruments through leaflets and posters, apart from the media news in the respective regional languages. Towards this, the International organizations like Data Buoy Cooperation Panel (DBCP), a joint body of IOC (Intergovernmental Oceanographic Commission) and WMO (World Meteorological Organization) has initiated many actions to create public awareness and also to issue Mariner's notification by International Hydrographic Organization (IHO) through the respective National Hydrographic Offices on the location of buoys to advise fishermen and mariners to keep off their fishing and trawling operations away from the buoy sites. The National Institute of Ocean Technology (NIOT) has implemented the National Data Buoy Programme and has taken special efforts in the protection of Surface data buoys from vandalism to a large extent with the help of Indian Coast Guard, with the latter carrying out regular patrolling of the buoy sites. NIOT ensures that whenever a new data buoy or a tsunami surface buoy is installed, this information is communicated to the mariners through the release of mariners notification by National Hydrographic Office (NHO) with a clear instruction to keep off their fishing and trawling operations by 3 km from the buoy sites. Such efforts shall need to be continued with high priority to ensure the smooth fail-safe functioning of these critical instruments.

The efforts for surveillance of the safety of the critical early warning instrumentation in the Bay of Bengal and the Arabian Sea will be augmented preferably with the specialised aircraft available with National Remote Sensing Centre (NRSC) and where available with Unmanned Aerial Vehicles (UAVs) with the help of Indian Air Force, Indian Navy and Coast Guard patrols to ensure the fail-safe functioning of these critical instruments and their protection from vandalism by fishermen and mariners.

The MoES and the nodal institutions like INCOIS, NIOT and IMD will participate in the ongoing multilateral and bilateral cooperation initiatives in sharing information about possible tsunamigenic behaviour with their counterpart nodal agencies in the neighbouring countries through appropriate channels worked out through mutual consultations.

Warning on Inundation of Critical Areas

Tsunamis and cyclonic storms result in generation of waves of different period and height that are termed as surges. These wave parameters depend on earthquake source parameters, bathymetry, beach profile, coastal land topography and presence of coastal structures. These surges cause flooding of seawater into the land as much as 1 km or even more resulting in loss of human life and damage to property. To minimise such losses, it is imperative to prepare Coastal Vulnerability maps indicating the areas likely to be affected due to sea water inundation and damage thereof. Simulation Models such as TUNAMI-N2 and MOST, being globally used for this purpose, predict surges for different scenarios and indicate the extent of inundation of seawater into the land. Physical scaled hydrological models could also supplement the simulation like the DAM-models used in the Central Water and Power Research Station (CWPRS), Pune. This information could be used for taking precautionary and mitigation measures such as evacuation of people, avoiding human settlements on vulnerable locations, wasteful investment, and helping in design of appropriate structures etc. in the risk prone areas. Information from remote sensing and field investigations are being integrated in GIS for modelling and mapping of inundation of seawater for determination of setback lines, planning coastal defences etc.

TUNAMI-N2 Model has been customised by ICMAM for the Indian Ocean Region and has been extensively validated using the December 2004 Tsunami observations. This model is now being run for 5 historical earthquakes and the predicted inundation areas are being overlaid on cadastral level maps of 1:5000 scale. The maps will be provided to the Ministries and Departments of the Government of India and state level departments that are involved in Disaster Management. These community-level inundation maps will be extremely useful for assessing the population and infrastructure at risk. They could be used for better land-use planning, building of shelters, planning evacuation routes, etc.

Decision Support System

The Indian Tsunami Warning Criteria are based on the principle that coastal areas falling within 60 minutes travel time from a tsunamigenic earthquake source need to be given a Warning, Watch or Alert based solely on earthquake information and run ups estimated from Model Scenarios, since enough time will not be available for confirmation of water levels from BPRs and Tide Gauges. Those coastal areas falling outside the 60 minutes travel time from a tsunamigenic earthquake source could be put under Alert/Watch status based on expected run-up and upgraded to a Warning only upon confirmation of water-level data. This will considerably reduce the rate of False Alarms. The following criteria are being followed for generation of Tsunami bulletins:

— Warning/Alert/Watch based on earthquake parameters, a region's proximity to earthquake zones, and Expected Run-up from Pre-run Model Scenarios.

— Warnings to Far Source Regions only after confirmation of tsunami triggering based on real-time water-level observations & Correction of Scenarios. This will reduce the possibility of False Warnings.

The criteria for generation of different types of alerts for a particular region of the coast are to be based on the earthquake parameters, available warning time and expected run-up from pre-run model scenarios.

Tsunami Bulletins and Warning Categorisation

Category of tsunami bulletins, time-line for generation, content of the alert and dissemination contact information is detailed below:

- Earthquake Information Bulletin (T+20 Minutes) contains information about Origin time, latitude and longitude of the epicentre, name of geographical area, Magnitude, and Depth of an Earthquake. This message also contains preliminary evaluation of tsunami potential based on the magnitude. Though information is provided to Ministry of Home Affairs (MHA), NDMA and NCMC, no immediate action is required.
- Tsunami Warning (T+30 Minutes) contains information about the Earthquake and a tsunami evaluation message indicating that Tsunami is expected. This is the highest level wherein immediate public evacuation is required. Message also contains information on the Travel Times and Tsunami Grade at various Coastal Locations from Pre-run Model Outputs. Information on above is provided to MHA, NDMA, NCMC, NDRF Battalions and the general public.
- Tsunami Alert (T+30 Minutes) contains information about the Earthquake and a tsunami evaluation message indicating that Tsunami is expected. This is the Second Highest Level wherein immediate public evacuation is not Required. Public should avoid beaches since strong current are expected. Local officials should be prepared for evacuation if it is upgraded to warning status. Message also contains information on the Travel Times and Tsunami Grade at various Coastal Locations from Pre-run Model Outputs. Information on above circumstance is provided to MHA, NDMA, NCMC, NDRF Battalions and the general public.
- Tsunami Watch (T+30 Minutes) contains information about the earthquake and a tsunami evaluation message indicating that Tsunami is expected. This is the Third Highest Level wherein immediate public evacuation is not required, local officials should be prepared for evacuation if it is upgraded to warning status. Message also contains information on the travel times and Tsunami grade at various coastal

locations from Pre-run model outputs. The above information is provided to MHA, NDMA, NCMC and NDRF Battalions.

— Tsunami Information Bulletins contain information on Tsunami Confirmation or Upgradation or Cancellation or Observed Water Level Heights or New estimates of Travel Time and Tsunami Grade and any other additional information that becomes available during the course of the Event.

— Tsunami All Clear Bulletin indicates that the Tsunami Threat is over.

The Tsunami bulletins are to be allotted on precedence under the categories of flash, emergency, OPS immediate, PRIORITY and routine as tabulated below. These precedence signify the speed of handling and transmitting of communication of the bulletins by the recipients as well as the speed at which corresponding emergency actions need to be taken. These precedence are to be marked clearly and boldly in uppercase on the header and footer of all text, fax and email messages. The colour code scheme is to be used for highlighting the text in text and email messages, and for web pages appropriately.

Tsunami Alert, Watch and Advisory Bulletins received at the NEOC, SEOCs and DEOCs need to be disseminated through the fastest means to the people in the coastal areas likely to be affected. With receipt of information, respective SDMAs and DDMAs are to:

— Establish and maintain an emergency public information capability that includes the following:
    — A central contact facility for the media;
    — A system for gathering, monitoring, and disseminating emergency warnings;
    — Pre-scripted information bulletins; and
    — A method to coordinate and rapidly disseminate information.

— Ensure judicious and innovative use and integration of all communication resources available, such as Public Address systems through digital bulletin boards, local radios, local cellular/mobile network, and state and private television networks for dissemination of warnings received at their EOC nodes to the people in the coastal areas.

— Erect warning towers with sirens in all villages / districts and inhabited localities on the coastal areas vulnerable to Tsunami. A system of colour coded flag warning signals to be formulated appropriate to local culture, traditions, sentiments and acceptance.

— Provide digital bulletin boards in all villages and inhabited localities on the coastal areas. These should be workable in vernacular/local languages.

— Formulate appropriate warnings and sirens in vernacular as per local acceptance and institutionalise them.

— Maintain record of telephone numbers and mobile numbers of village centres, heads and local community leaders where available. A minimum of two volunteers per village/locality, to be responsible for communicating Tsunami Bulletins, are to be identified and provided with telephone/mobile phone connectivity. Their details and contact numbers are to be available in the SEOCs and DEOCs.

— Erect 'Tsunami Escape' direction sign boards indicating the escape routes to be taken in the event of a tsunami.

— Earmark and assign 'Assembly Point/ Areas' and 'Shelter Areas'. Clear ground in tsunami safe zones need to be established as 'shelter areas'. The 'shelter areas' need to be adequate for the overall local population.

— The communication resources and methods are to be integrated into the village resource centre with the overall NECP network in accordance with the NECP plan guidelines, where possible, and elsewhere, as per local configuration.

— Formulate detailed Standard Operating Procedures (SOPs) for the dissemination of Tsunami Warning Bulletins specific to each level, viz. district, sub district and village/ community level.

— The communication systems and procedures established are to be regularly tested and exercised, especially at the level of villages and localities in risky areas to support the tsunami warning mechanism.

— Emergency communications and warning protocols, systems, processes, and procedures are to be developed, periodically tested, and exercised to alert people likely to be affected by a tsunami.

— Sirens along the coast line, mobiles and wireless networks being provided as a part of the National Cyclone Risk Mitigation Project

(NCRMP) in Phase I in the eastern coast and in other coastal districts in Phase II will also be used to disseminate warning and alert messages to the coastal communities.

— State governments will utilize the NDRF Battalions to carry out community capacity building, public awareness and emergency response training, with the approval of NDMA.

Tsunami Early Warning Dissemination

The National Emergency Communication Plan (NECP) connectivity network will form the backbone architecture for the dissemination of Tsunami Advisory, Watch, Alert and Cancellation Bulletins. The network based on satellite communication links and ISDN public network will link the National Tsunami Early Warning Centre with the NEOCs, the SEOCs, DEOCs, MEOCs and NQRTs. Fail proof and reliable communication links for voice, facsimile, data, FTP, video conferencing and video information dispatch will be provided between all the nodes. In addition to the primary links two back up layers will be provided to ensure redundancy and 100 % availability.

The National Early Warning Centre (NEWC), INCOIS will keep 24 x 7 operations watch and communicate Tsunami Advisory, Watch and Alert Bulletins to local, state, national and international entities as well as media, and the public.

The NEWC will be connected and networked with the NEOC, the nerve and decision center for all emergency communication, on the NECP architecture and will incorporate the VPN- DMS communication of ISRO.

The NDRF Battalions located in the coastal states will be also treated as primary nodes for the dissemination of tsunami alert and warning messages.

Roles and Responsibilities in Warning Dissemination

Tsunami watch, warning and information bulletins are disseminated by appropriate officials, institutions, and agencies. Their role and responsibilities need to be clearly specified and notified.

Role of Media in Warning Dissemination

The media is a powerful ally for disseminating the alert and early warning to the general public and other stakeholder groups. The media elements are to:-

— Establish and indicate nodal points for receiving Tsunami Warning Bulletins to the respective SDMAs/DDMAs.

— Integrate all regional and local offices of the media elements with the NECP network up to the DEOC level.

— Institutionalise SOPs for transmitting Tsunami Warning Bulletins as received by the nodal points.

— Incorporate measures in the various media channels and processes to ensure priority override for transmitting Tsunami Warning Bulletins as required.

— To build capacity for the Media professionals to ensure that the correct level of warning is made available at the right time. Spreading rumours should not be permitted, because these may generate panic and result in stampede.

Coordination Mechanisms

The Tsunami Early Warning System involves a large number of government and other agencies under the present three tier disaster management structure, i.e. the national, state and district. A Coordination Committee comprising of representation from NDMA, NCMC, MHA, MoES (IMD, INCOIS), DST, MCIT, MoIB, Prasar Bharti (All India Radio and Doordarshan) constituted under the NDMA, will meet bi annually to review the status, future developments and upgradation of facilities, procedures and systems.

Establishing appropriate institutional and collaborative linkages for providing technical and support services at various levels is a key requirement for sustaining the proper development and implementation of the tsunami warning dissemination mechanism. The corporate sector, industries, academia, NGOs, and other concerned agencies will extend a helping hand in training and building capabilities and shall provide their expertise in the field of capabilities, resources, technical expertise, trained personnel, equipment etc. A comprehensive list of national and state level institutions for the development of technology, processes, practices, procedures and other measures is to be identified and established at national, state and district levels. Collaborative arrangements between these are to be formulated at the national and state levels. The state governments shall also ensure that the identified institutes are provided sufficient resources and all necessary help extended for working on novel technologies and initiatives, including training communities and groups.

India will participate in the international effort at improving the quality of preparedness and response by liaising with international organisations, UN agencies and other humanitarian actors and share the best practices in tsunami preparedness and mitigation.

Public Awareness

Comprehensive public awareness campaigns will be developed and launched at the national, state and district levels, especially in high risk areas for familiarisation with the tsunami warning dissemination mechanism and responsibilities of various stakeholder groups. SDMAs/DDMAs will conduct regular public awareness campaigns for familiarising communities in coastal areas with the tsunami early warning mechanisms through workshops, drills and exercises, screening of video films, distribution of information resources, posters etc. Handbooks and instructional materials, in vernacular languages, will be prepared by SDMAs for creating greater awareness among the communities on tsunami risk and vulnerability.

One of the most challenging tasks in improving the preparedness and mitigation for tsunami is the sensitisation of all stakeholders to the prevalent tsunami risk and educating and encouraging them to participate in strengthening tsunami preparedness and mitigation efforts. If the coastal communities recognise the importance of incorporating tsunami safety measures in the construction of residential buildings, tremendous gains can be achieved in tsunami mitigation. State Governments/SDMAs will, in collaboration with nodal agencies and other key stakeholders, make special efforts to mobilise communities to carry out tsunami mitigation efforts. Electronic and print media will also be used to help create greater public awareness on tsunami risk and vulnerability and on structural and non-structural risk reduction measures. Knowledge institutions such as the IITs and National Institutes of Technology (NITs) and national research laboratories will play a major role in producing these materials for the tsunami-prone SDMAs.

A comprehensive public awareness campaign will be developed and implemented on the safe practices to be followed before, during and after a tsunami. State Governments and knowledge institutions will, in collaboration with professional bodies of engineers, architects and urban planners, initiate programmes to sensitise their members on the importance of undertaking tsunami-safe zoning, planning, design, and construction practices. The contents and structure of training programmes will be reviewed and revised from time to time, factoring in the lessons learnt from the evaluation of the earlier programmes. The professional associations of engineers, architects, builders and contractors will undertake campaigns to sensitise their members on the risk and vulnerability to tsunami in various coastal regions of the country and to impress upon them the need to ensure the incorporation of tsunami-safe features in the construction of buildings and structures in tsunami-prone areas.

State Governments and SDMAs in collaboration with their SEMCs, HSCs and nongovernmental organisations (NGOs) will organise awareness programmes for specific target groups of stakeholders on various aspects of tsunami management. These stakeholders will include elected representatives and civil servants, members of local administration authorities and others like school administrators, members of management boards of educational institutions and hospitals, school children, representatives of the corporate sector, media, etc.

The corporate sector plays a very important role after a disaster by providing resources, relief supplies and equipment. The corporate sector will be encouraged to take proactive role during the mitigation and preparedness phase. They will be encouraged to sensitize their employees and also to develop suitable business continuity plans to ensure disruption-free operation following disasters. As a part of corporate social responsibility, the corporate sectors operating in coastal areas will be encouraged to support public awareness campaigns on tsunami risk and preparedness among vulnerable coastal communities near their locations.

Natural hazards cannot be prevented and hence, awareness on risk reduction and preparedness in the event of tsunami and other coastal Hazards as well as methods of mitigation in local level during the golden hour before the Government machinery steps in, should be carried out through mock exercises and drills from Primary school level to College and University education, especially in coastal areas. Steps have already been taken to include natural hazards in the educational curriculum but it should be a continuing process. Illustrated education materials with information on tsunami dynamics and the damage inflicted in different zones in the form of text books have to be prepared at different education levels for distribution among students. Posters in local vernacular languages or more appropriately colloquial languages without scientific jargons should be displayed in locations frequented by the community. Information on tsunami and other natural hazards should be part of the local language textbooks rather than confining them only to the science subject textbooks, as learning in local vernacular languages will be more effective in communicating the messages to the disaster-prone communities.

Tsunami warning can sometimes be a false alarm due to the complex dynamics of the tsunami, as it is based on the earthquake parameters determined by preliminary analysis of the seismic data immediately after the event. Precise estimation of earthquake and tsunami parameters are possible only after a detailed study of the seismographs established all over the world by different agencies and actual field study by conducting high resolution bathymetric surveys. The tsunami modelling hence fails to estimate the run-up parameters accurately if there is a gross difference between the initial estimate and ground reality. The general public need to be made aware of these complexities and in the event of a false alarm, they should acknowledge the tsunami risk and treat it as an opportunity to test the preparedness of all stakeholder groups. Proper awareness on the intricacies of EWS has to be created through public awareness campaigns and the general public should not panic when an alert is issued. This will enable INCOIS to issue warnings even if there is a remote possibility of a tsunami so that the coastal communities can review their preparedness levels.

Tsunami warning drills have to be periodically conducted and school children in the coastal areas right from elementary school level need to be made aware of safe evacuation procedures. If such drills are conducted every year among children and youth, it will enable the younger generation to be alert when such a calamity actually strikes the coast. It will also make them understand the mistakes made during the drills so that they can improve their preparedness. It is also advisable to assess the evacuation routes in schools and in public places like hospitals and community centres in vulnerable zones.

Effective steps should be undertaken to provide shelters taking into consideration the population of each coastal village and town. Tourist and Pilgrim centres in particular should also be assessed and the shelters should be designed to cope up with sudden rush to such shelters during emergencies. It is necessary that a public address system is established in vulnerable areas to disseminate the alert and warning messages. Shops, hotels, lodging houses, etc., are often built very close to the shore and the people may not have any knowledge of the coastal hazards and hence their safety may be threatened. Shore watchers should be employed in places where people congregate in large numbers and people should not be allowed to be in the sea immediately after the alert or warning notification is issued. Fishermen should also be prevented from going into the sea after the alert or warning notification is issued.

The increased vulnerability of the coastal areas due to exponential growth of population and establishment of industries and tourist centres necessitates not only education on coastal hazards but also the need for imparting training in preparedness and risk reduction to the stakeholders in the event of a calamity. Institutes, Universities and Colleges should be encouraged to initiate studies related to Natural Hazards and coastal hazards in particular so as to form a multidisciplinary working group comprising dedicated faculty members. The expertise gained by such groups should be used to inform the general public. Multipurpose newsletters or bulletins for creating awareness on natural hazards among the general public should be published by such working groups.

The Training Institutions will be coordinated by the National Institute of Disaster Management (NIDM). Training programmes for State and Local Administration personnel including Fire and Rescue and Police personal, as well as representatives of Self Help Groups, NCC, NSS and other youth groups will be conducted by NIDM and the Administrative Training Institutes (ATIs) of the State Governments. The training modules will include geo-scientific aspects of the coastal hazards with particular reference to tsunami, their causes and effects using appropriate case studies.

Public awareness campaigns will be initiated at the national, state and district levels in high-risk areas for wide dissemination of information on tsunami risk reduction through structural and non-structural strengthening measures among all stakeholders and to develop professional human resources for tsunami-resilient strengthening. Case studies documenting the process of vulnerability assessment will be prepared and disseminated for creating greater public awareness among professionals and critical stakeholders. Risk reduction against tsunami can be achieved by applying currently available national and international knowledge on strengthening; imbibing available national and international knowledge and customising the same; and finally, generating new applied knowledge to address the problems specific to India. Significant and maximum gains can be achieved by conducting rigorous research and development activities for innovation of new knowledge and techniques and adaptation of available knowledge to the Indian context.

State Governments, SDMAs and professional bodies will organise knowledge sharing workshops to disseminate the methodology and important experiences of protecting seafront, coastal natural resources and lifeline structures against tsunami to the professional community. State Governments will carry out structural safety audit of all bridges, flyovers, critical lifeline buildings and high-priority buildings in the coastal vicinity, and undertake phase-wise strengthening of those critical lifeline structures which will be found to be structurally vulnerable to tsunami. They will also support private agencies to develop their capacity in conducting evaluation and strengthening of existing privately owned structures.

On receiving a tsunami warning, evacuation of the population would be required by the local authority. Safe evacuation will be carried out to cyclone- cum-tsunami shelters along the coast. In recent years, Multi-purpose cyclone- cum-tsunami shelters have been designed and are being constructed in storm surge prone areas. Such multi-purpose shelters can be used as schools, community halls, places of worship and other social gathering places.

Cyclone-cum-tsunami shelters should be designed in such a way that they address multi-purpose uses. Such multi-purpose uses will ensure that such structures do not fall into disuse when there is no threat of cyclones or tsunamis. This would ensure their proper maintenance by the community itself. Cyclone-cum-tsunami shelters should be so designed so as to take care of the livestock of the communities, wherever possible, while protecting the local people.

It is necessary that the tsunami risk and vulnerability of the coastal areas is taken into consideration while designing buildings and other structures in tsunami and cyclone-prone coastal areas. In the design of public infrastructure like roads, schools, hospitals, multi-purpose shelters etc., prevailing risk and vulnerability has to be kept in mind. In tsunami-prone areas, the DDMAs will ensure that a bank of designs of temporary shelters, intermediate shelters and disaster-resilient houses shall be prepared, with the flexibility to use traditional and local knowledge, coping capacities and locally available shelter materials.

Tsunami Mitigation Measures

Coastal villages can be safeguarded from the impact of tsunami by adopting soft solutions and by educating the villagers to follow simple precautionary measures. The details are as follows.

i. Construction of large scale submerged sand barriers in water depths of about 6 to 8 meters.

ii. Developing sand dunes along the coast with sea weeds or shrubs or casuarinas trees for stabilization of the sand dunes.

iii. Raising the ground level with natural beach sand so as to rehabilitate the entire coastal village.

iv. Development of coastal forest by planting casuarinas or coconut trees along the coastline to cover minimum of about 500m width of the beach.

v. Periodical dredging of the inlets and associated water bodies so as to absorb the influx during Tsunami.

vi. Construction of submerged dykes so as to decrease the impact due to the incoming tsunami.

vii. Adopting natural beach nourishment to create steep beach face.

viii. Positioning stationary platforms in the backwaters for evacuating the public during tsunami.

ix. Creation of sandy ramps at close intervals all along the coast.

x. Vertical evacuation structures in all harbours.

xi. Construction of inland dykes to safeguard vital installations.

xii. Construction of concrete defence structures to protect installations of national importance stationed on the coast.

xiii. Construction of elevated hutments supported on piles or hardened podiums to allow tsunami run-up to escape beneath the structure.

xiv. Construction of bypass compound walls to steer the flow away from the buildings in the case of vulnerable buildings in coastal areas. Proper hydraulic design of the bypass wall is needed to take care of the rundown too. This procedure would reduce the flow velocity during run-up of a Tsunami.

xv. Construction of Tsunami shelters on a raised ground in high tsunami-risk villages. This structure shall have 4 floors with the ground floor meant for passage of flow during Tsunami, 1st floor for housing about 500 people, including a provision shop capable of supplying provisions for three days and other basic amenities, 2nd floor for hospital and 3rd floor reserved for the water tank. This Tsunami shelter should be operational throughout the year with the 1st floor utilised as a school and 2nd floor for hospital during non-Tsunami period. This would ensure that the facility is maintained to meet any eventuality. These shelters shall not be located more than 500m. from the two neighbouring villages.

xvi. Establishment of mangrove plantations (as a coastal defence against Tsunami) for communities residing along the estuaries.

xvii. Keeping the village area free from debris as they may have adverse impact during runup or run-down associated with Tsunami.

xviii. Construction of seawall may be tried, in exceptional cases, in conjunction with natural bio-shields, subject to the topography and bathymetry. Reinforced concrete Tsunami gates, Tsunami break-waters, deflection walls, Tsunami river gates in river mouths, etc. can be planned as in Japan, instead of rubble stack. However, in areas which are vulnerable to storm surge, special efforts may be made to ensure that natural bio-shields like mangrove plantations and shelterbelts are initiated to reduce the devastating impact of storm surges by acting as an effective windshield to protect the coastal communities.

During the Indian Ocean Tsunami of December 2004, the damage to port and harbour structures was observed to be much severe than that in the other structures away from the coast. These structures were subjected to ground shaking due to earthquake and wave action due to tsunami. These structures are founded generally on soft ground with more than one type of foundation system in a structure. Ground subsidence and liquefaction has been commonly observed and was one of the major reasons of common damage. Favourable conditions for corrosion exist near the sea and damage has been observed to be more at corroded locations. The earthquake also exposes the deficiencies caused by faulty design and construction.

Protecting Seafronts and Lifeline Structures

India has a very long coast line that is susceptible to the action of tsunami. Most of the coastal structures are not designed to withstand the force of a tsunami, and are potentially vulnerable to collapse in the event of a tsunami unless wave forces are reduced through mitigation measures. Mitigation measures can reduce the effect of tsunami wave impact on structures but do not reduce the effects of inundation. Though collapse-proof structures can be constructed, the contents of these structures and the occupants cannot be protected from the effects of tsunami inundation. Therefore, some critical lifeline structures such as hospitals should be located outside the inundation areas.

Strengthening of seafront provides the most effective mitigation measure against tsunami and should be carried out along the most vulnerable stretches of the coast.

As it is not feasible or financially viable to strengthen all the existing structures, these Guidelines recommend carrying out the structural safety audit and strengthening of select critical lifeline structures and high priority buildings. Such selection will be based on considerations such as the degree of risk, the potential loss of life and the estimated financial implications for each structure, especially in high-risk areas, i.e., those coastal regions vulnerable to high tsunami run-up.

While drawing up the priority list for structures, a cluster approach will be followed for selecting various types of critical lifeline structures including breakwaters for ports and harbours and various categories of building types in adjoining districts to encourage mutual consultations, demonstrations and possible replication in other districts. Thus, some lifeline structures such as primary schools, primary health centres, panchayat offices, post offices and Block Development Offices may be selected in potential tsunami run-up areas to study their ability to withstand tsunami forces. Where feasible, select priority lifeline structures will be strengthened. The strengthening will provide valuable demonstration of their efficacy. The State Governments/ SDMAs will take up selected critical lifeline structures in some of these high-risk areas as pilot projects in a phased manner. Other critical lifeline structures should be considered for relocation away from the vulnerable areas.

Protection is required not only for the structures of buildings but also for their non-structural components like building finishes and contents. The non-structural building elements include the stairways, doors, windows, chimney, lighting fixures, heating ducts and pipes, wall cladding and false ceilings. The "building contents" includes all of those items that users bring into a building into a building; furniture, appliances, electronic equipments, coolers, and air-conditioners, stored items, and so forth. When a building is totally collapsed or damaged, everything is crushed and lost. Bust some the deaths, many or most of the injuries, a large proportion of economic damage, destruction and disruption associated with earthquakes are caused by "non-structural" building elements that break, fall or slide. Therefore, securing the contents and elements of the building from overturn or slide during a Tsunami requires due attention. Protection of non-structural elements and contents in tsunami run-up is a specialised technical task which needs to be handled by engineers proficient in this field, as any routine alteration, repair or maintenance carried out in a structure may not always guarantee an improvement in its safety, and may in fact, increase its vulnerability.

Various types of protective measures to safeguard the seafront against tsunami are very effective tool in tsunami risk mitigation since it directly reduces the intensity of tsunami force on the seafront natural resources and structures. Due attention shall be given to various natural and artificial seafront strengthening and risk mitigation measures. In coastal regions vulnerable to high run-up, the feasibility of providing protective structures to strengthen the seafront shall be given very high priority. Strengthening of the seafront and risk mitigation measures may obviate the necessity of additional structural mitigation measures for buildings and other structures and will cause least inconvenience to the affected population.

Different types of coastal protective measures can be adopted to minimise the intensity of tsunami generated force. Though the different options for coastal protective measures have been given above, careful assessment on the type of protection to be adopted for a given stretch of the coast is a must. For example, mangroves which can withstand moderate wave climate can be cultivated along the estuaries. They act as a buffer zone while a tsunami passes over thus reducing the tsunami induced force on the coastal belt. For the wide sandy coast, it is advisable to develop sand dunes with shrubs grown on the sand dunes to stabilise them. In case of narrow sandy coast, artificial nourishment techniques can be adopted to raise the level of beach such that the foreshore slope of the beach front becomes steep. Maintenance of lagoons free from sediment deposition at the inlet and in the main water body would prove beneficial as the influx during tsunami can find its resting place. Development of long shoals in the near-shore region by dumping useful portion of the dredged sand either from harbours or river channels would be another option to protect the coast from the impact of tsunami. Development of green belt on the sand spits would suit the coastal belt with backwaters running parallel to the coast.

Prioritisation of Structures

All Central Ministries and Departments and State Governments will draw up phased programmes for strengthening and/or possible relocation of selected existing structures duly prioritised and implement them through ULBs and PRIs. Like all new construction, any structural modification of existing buildings will also require compliance with safety regulations against tsunami.

The initial focus for structural safety audit and strengthening will be on government and public buildings. The necessary capacity for carrying out similar assessments for private buildings will also be developed through suitable capacity development efforts among the professionals in the private sector. The nodal agencies will make available the details of technical guidance for carrying out structural safety audit of lifeline structures and their strengthening in public domain for the use of the general public and professionals in the private sector.

The seafront shall be prioritised for strengthening on the basis of the vulnerability of the natural resources, lifeline structures and the local community. The necessary capacity for carrying out vulnerability assessment shall be developed through suitable capacity development efforts among the various government agencies.

Structural Safety Audit of Seafront, Coastal Natural Resources and Critical Lifeline Structures

The tsunami risk profile can be quantified only after the vulnerability of the coastal region and building inventory in a geographic area is compiled. Assessment techniques may be used to determine the vulnerability of all buildings, in the order of priority decided by the State Governments/ SDMAs, in consultation with IITs, NITs and HSCs. Two levels of vulnerability assessment can be carried out for buildings, namely Rapid Visual Screening (RVS) and Detailed Vulnerability Assessment (DVA). The former is a quick estimation with visual but technical information of structures to determine whether the structure is considered to be vulnerable or not. Once the RVS identifies a structure to be vulnerable, then that structure is subjected to a detailed assessment for a quantitative evaluation of its vulnerability. For structures other than buildings, DVAs are normally carried out. A DVA consists of evaluating the structural systems that resist the tsunami loads, as well as assessing non-structural elements like the contents, finishes and elements that do not contribute in resisting any tsunami load of the structure.

RVS procedures for assessment of safety against tsunami need to be developed for all types of building systems in India, e.g., brick and stone masonry buildings, RCC frame buildings with masonry infill, etc. Detailed studies will be conducted at the national level to develop a consensus on the methodology that should be undertaken for RVS of buildings in India as a part of vulnerability assessment. The vulnerability assessment exercise will be carried out at every 10 years to monitor the modification to the vulnerability profile of the built environment.

At the national, state and district levels, issues such as lack of knowledge on cost estimates for strengthening each type of structure, the types of tools required for undertaking modifications/enhancements of existing structural elements, the time required to complete the strengthening of a particular size and type of building and the proficiency required by the artisans for strengthening and their requisite capacity building., will be addressed in collaboration with the nodal agencies and professional bodies concerned. Organisations like IITs, National Building Construction Corporation Ltd. (NBCC), Building Material Technology Promotion Council (BMTPC), Central Building Research Institute (CBRI), Structural Engineering Research Centre, Chennai (SERC), the Institution of Engineers (India) (IE[I]), Construction Industry Development Council (CIDC), Construction Federation of India (CFI), and the National Academy of Construction (NAC), will be associated to develop road maps for creating the required manpower, tools and construction management system to implement the structural strengthening challenge in India. In consultation with these agencies, a standardised procedure for vulnerability assessment will be prepared at the national level to clarify the process and issues involved in the strengthening of each type of structure as per national standards.

The vulnerability assessment of the seafront and coastal natural resources can be carried out only on the basis of reliable large-scale maps. Assessment techniques may be used to determine the vulnerability of structures of seafront in the order of priority decided by the State

Governments/SDMAs, in consultation with their SEMCs and HSCs. Multi-level vulnerability assessment can be carried out for these structures. The quick and approximate assessment of tsunami amplification can be carried out by using available terrain and bathymetry data. In densely populated regions or in other areas, as required by the State Governments/SDMAs, more detailed assessment can be carried out later using large-scale maps.

Protecting and Strengthening

The Government shall launch targeted programs similar to GoI-UNDP supported UEVRP for tsunami safety. Under this program, protecting and strengthening of some fragile seafront, coastal natural resources and lifeline structures will be undertaken through pilot projects in a phased manner. The prioritisation of the cities will be based on the degree of tsunami hazard, population size, level of vulnerability of the building/structure, importance of the lifeline structure and coastal natural resources, and the speed with which the states can undertake these initiatives. The cities are to be identified based on these criteria for strengthening of selected lifeline structures. In the first priority, metropolitan cities and major townships in high tsunami run-up regions may be taken up.

Similar efforts will be carried out in other high-risk coastal towns and cities in a selective manner by initially starting with the capacity development of professionals to carry out these tasks. Accomplishing protection of the existing built environment requires a systematic and sustained effort by carrying out several activities in each of the towns and cities. These activities are:

— Developing an inventory of the coastal natural resources and the existing built environment.
— Assessing the vulnerability of the above environment.
— Prioritising of the environment based on its vulnerability.
— Developing protection and strengthening measures.
— Undertaking construction work to strengthen vulnerable areas and structures.

Whereas protection and strengthening of the critical and lifeline structures will be carried out on priority, other structures will be insured against losses during future tsunamis. Insurance companies will be encouraged to introduce innovative insurance schemes in moderate and high tsunami-risk coastal zones in consultation with the ULBs and respective Disaster Management Authorities (DMAs).

State Governments/SDMAs will initiate efforts to compile GIS databases and develop a GIS data bank consisting of GIS maps for all urban areas, indicating vulnerable seafront and natural resources, all critical structures and infrastructures. These maps will be used in DM planning, and for effective coordination for response, relief and rehabilitation activities during and after a disaster.

State Governments/SDMAs will develop appropriate mechanisms, in consultation with their SEMCs and HSCs, to review and ensure structural safety of existing public buildings in accordance with the latest norms during any significant alterations or additions to them. Similar process should also be carried out in respect of defence works/ structures in high tsunami-risk areas.

The Government of India will utilize the national rural employment guarantee scheme and other similar schemes for using local manpower for constructing and strengthening of protective seafront structures. The local community will be given the responsibility of maintenance and upkeep of these structures to ensure community participation in disaster management efforts.

The GoI can generate new incentives to promote through policy decisions and to allow tax-holidays, to private/Corporate sector for their contributions to build and operate priority structures such as Tsunami-towers/ platforms/ shelters, as part of their CSR (corporate social responsibilities) activities. As far as possible, local authorities will discourage the construction of structures in areas vulnerable to high tsunami risk. In case of construction of structures in areas prone to sea erosion and high risk of tsunami, the professionals involved in the design and construction of such structures will be made aware of the tsunami risk and vulnerability in such areas.

MoES, in co-operation with other concerned Ministries and Departments of GoI and State Governments and other specialised agencies, will initiate the efforts for developing a Data Base of Tsunami Risk and Vulnerability in the coastal areas of the country, with information on trends of storm surge, high tides, local bathymetry, etc. for providing value-added information to the general public for protecting the investments proposed to be undertaken through construction of structures on the sea front. Once the Data Base is developed, MoES will make it available in the public domain, wherever possible, or accessible to the professionals who are involved in the construction of such structures after confirming the authenticity of such requests.

Regulation and Enforcement of Techno-Legal Regime

Land Use

Coastal areas are vulnerable to coastal hazards such as cyclone and tsunami. Coastal land use should be so designed so as to incur minimal losses to life and property due to these events. Natural mangroves and bio shields should be protected and grown so as to provide a natural defence against Tsunami waves. By developing bio shields at coastlines, tsunami prone land use can be re-designated as tsunami resistant.

Existing zoning and other regulations need to be reviewed and updated in the context of Tsunami. The change of land use in coastal Zones should not be permitted without approval of the authority implementing Coastal Zone Management Plan. It is desirable to take up development at a safe distance from the coast line. New location of settlements may be sited above 10 m contour levels or 3 m above the high tide line, whichever is higher. Location of new settlements should be planned on the basis of thorough analysis of distance from the sea, elevation above MSL, height of high tide line, maximum run up of tsunami, expected depth and speed of tsunami waves, etc. The process of urban renewal and urban extension should be used to plan and zone new land uses in order to limit or prevent potential disasters. Open Spaces such as agricultural lands, parks, other forms of open space, etc. can be used as places to gather and take shelter during tsunami. For preparing the proposals for development in disaster prone area, Town Planning Departments/Development Authorities concerned should take specialized advice from Geological Survey of India, Metrological department and other concerned nearby academic institutions having expertise in earthquake engineering, structural engineering, etc. Coastal buildings need to be designed to withstand tsunami wave pressures.

At present, no tsunami code exists. There is urgent need to frame Tsunami Resistant Design Code and include it in local building bye laws. The code may fulfil various safety measures under multi hazard environment. Effective implementation of building bye-laws is to be ensured by the State

Governments and ULBs in construction of buildings and local infrastructure should be strengthened to make them resistant from tsunami and cyclonic sea surge.

Coastal ecology should be protected and strengthened while coastal habitats should be planned in such a way so as to remain in low hazard zone. Mangrove plantations should be conserved and protected. Casuarinas, bamboo and other shelterbelt plantations need to be encouraged in the coastal areas. The coastal geomorphic features such as beaches, sand dunes etc. should be protected as they act as buffers against the coastal hazards.

Bio-Shields

Nature has provided biological mechanisms for protecting coastal communities from the fury of cyclones, coastal storms, tidal waves and tsunamis. Mangrove forests constitute one such mechanism, which also safeguards ecological and livelihood security of fishing and farming communities living in the coastal zone. In addition to mangroves, which grow only in the estuarine environment, there are many other tree species having with socio-economic and ecological importance can reduce the impact of tsunami and cyclonic wind & sea surge. All such species confer in the short-term local economic and ecological benefits and in the long-term global environmental benefits through carbon sequestration. Non-mangrove bio-shields along the coastal zone is popularly known as shelterbelts. Shelterbelts are strips of vegetation composed of trees and shrubs grown along the coasts to protect coastal areas from high velocity winds. The forest departments in India have mastered the technique of raising shelterbelts since 1970, in which casuarinas was the main species. Along with casuarinas, other ecologically and economically important species can also be grown taking into account the biophysical condition and available breadth and width of the area selected for raising shelterbelts.

While mangrove forests have specific ecological role in the coastal eco-system and source of livelihood for coastal poor, their destruction is wide spread for shorter economic benefits. In the recent times there has been increased ingress to convert them for aquaculture and agriculture. The usage of chemicals/ fertilizers and pollution in the upstream of aquaculture farms become detrimental to the mangrove eco-systems in the vicinity. In general the mangroves are resistant to varied kinds of environmental perturbations and stresses. However, mangrove species are sensitive to excessive siltation or sedimentation, stagnation, surface water impoundment and major oil spills. Seawalls, bunds and other coastal structures often restrict tidal flow, resulting in the killing of mangroves. It is important to recognize that many of the forces, which detrimentally alter mangroves, have their origin outside the mangrove ecosystem. Unless many of these threats are addressed through efficient management and regeneration programmes, the sustainability of mangrove habitats cannot be ensured.

Options for Efficient Land Use Practices

Degradation of land, through soil erosion, alkali-salinisation, water logging, pollution and reduction in organic matter content has several proximate and underlying causes. The proximate causes include loss of forest and tree cover, unsustainable grazing, excessive use of irrigation, and improper use of agricultural chemicals (leading to accumulation of toxic chemicals in the soil), diversion of animal wastes for domestic fuel (leading to reduction in soil nitrogen and organic matter), and disposal of industrial and domestic wastes on productive land. In coastal areas, tree farming and conservation of mangroves result in more sustainable development. In view of above, following options for best land use practices should be considered.

i) The policies and incentives for afforestation should be such that ecological security and income security are both safeguarded.

ii) Encourage adoption of science-based and traditional, sustainable land use, promote reclamation of wasteland and degraded forestland covering both public and privately owned lands giving necessary incentives, viz. right over the produce, provision of alternate land or compensation, etc.

iii) Encourage agro-forestry, organic farming, environmentally sustainable cropping patterns, and adoption of efficient irrigation techniques.

iv) Funding of green belt creation and conservation of mangroves, most of which are on common property and will have to continue to receive budgetary support. Such support today is inadequate and has to be enhanced in the interest of creating life and livelihood security in the coastal zones. Innovative funding mechanisms should also be evolved by levying either a charge or a cess for all development activities on the coastal area which would be pooled to reverse degradation and enhance conservation of green belts. It is also necessary to give some incentives to private land owners and fisherman to adopt sustainable practices.

Based on CRZ and best land use practices, it is necessary to plan for conservation and restoration of mangroves and raising tree shelterbelts extensively in all potential coastal zones. The CRZ Notification, 1991 under the Environmental Protection Act,1986 recognises the mangrove areas as ecologically sensitive and categorises them as CRZ-I areas which implies that these areas are afforded protection of the highest order. Financial support is provided to coastal states/UTs in support of activities like survey and demarcation, remote sensing based monitoring, afforestation, restoration, alternative/supplementary livelihoods, protection measures, research, education and awareness. Based on information received from the states, groups of experts from Ministry of Environment & Forest, Botanical Survey of India, Zoological Survey of India, State Governments and some experts from Universities and research organisations, would visit the sites to assess the suitability and feasibility of the proposed areas inclusion under the National Mangrove Conservation Programme. Plantations are to be closely monitored so as to ensure their survival and growth involving state-of-the-art remote sensing technologies.

To bring mangrove regeneration under suitable and secured land use zoning, following actions will be initiated:

i) Set up a Task Force in consultation with states to identify new mangrove areas on priority to enhance the spread of the mangrove areas in various states within 6 months.

ii) Launch the dual mode mangrove plantation programme.

iii) Direct planting of seeds or propagules in the muddy areas (plenty)

iv) Planting of seedlings obtained from nurseries (seasonal effort and in small quantities). Nurseries are developed in upper parts of inter-tidal zones for 6-12 months and then transplanted to the field according to their zonation pattern.

v) Species selection is to be made based on the availability and maturity of planting materials from the locality.

vi) Zonation pattern is to be considered primarily in restoration work.

vii) State governments should make aggressive and sustained efforts to conserve the existing mangroves.

viii) Initiate intensive mangrove plantation programmes at identified potential sites so as to develop bio-shields.

ix) Mangroves should be officially classified as forests and mangroves found anywhere should be placed under the control of the state forest departments. The important mangrove areas need to be declared as protected areas if they are not so covered already.

x) A concerted effort needs to be made to undertake plantation of mangroves wherever possible along creeks, estuaries, deltas and shores, and of appropriate species of trees as windbreakers along the coastline and the dunes that back them.

Raising coastal shelterbelts to mitigate the adverse impacts of cyclone winds is one of the short-term objectives of the National Afforestation Programme (NAP). However, this is not being taken up effectively. Further, the regeneration of degraded forest and adjoining areas in the coastal zones is not covered under NAP as per the plantation design and guidelines. Hence, following actions will be initiated for effective shelter belt plantation at coast lines.

i) Raising of coastal shelterbelts will be made a mandatory component of the NAP plans by MoEF.

ii) NAP guidelines will be expanded to include regeneration of degraded forests and adjoining areas to provide additional protection from cyclonic winds.

iii) All coastal states/UTs will ensure that their NAP plans incorporate both the components so as to strengthen the coastal bio-shields for facilitating the implementation.

Raising of shelterbelts all along the coastline needs a sound strategy. The shore areas are the most difficult areas having peculiar geological formations. In the interface zone where the land meets the sea, there are river mouths, salt pans, sand mounds, estuary mouths, creeks, backwaters, mangroves and habitations. In these interior shore areas, the land is under intensive cultivation of a variety of commercial crops. The villages are also densely populated. Therefore, raising of shelterbelt to fight the cyclonic winds and cyclonic & tsunami sea surge requires appropriate strategy, which would be free from such problems and would have practical applicability. Under the Shelterbelt Plantation Programmes along the coast taken up from 1977, to a width of 5 km from the shore was tackled. This 5 km width has been differentiated in to the first 500 m zone or main zone and 500-5000 m zone or support zone.

The Main Zone consists of afforestation with block plantations. The natural conditions prevailing in the main zone are very hostile and are characterized by salinity, poor soils with high pH, low nutrition, poor moisture retention capacity, inadequate irrigation facilities, subjected to high speed and salt laden winds etc. For effective management of all these difficult areas, the entire main zone of 500m all along the coast has to be stock mapped. Stock maps are to be prepared indicating all types of areas, soils, crops, plantations, etc. The method of treatment to be adopted for shelter belt plantation on a particular piece of land may be decided on the basis of stock map.

A Support zone is aimed at saturating the area with tree crops planting all around the households, public offices and all along the road margins and field bunds without leaving any gaps including the difficult areas with suitable species in the area between 500-5000m. Islands offer unique eco-systems and coastal planning and regulation in their case needs to take into account features such as their geological nature, settlement patterns, volcanic or coral nature of the island, size of the habitations, unique cultures, livelihood patterns, etc. along with adequate environmental safeguards

Efforts for Community Involvement

The selection of species has to be done by taking in to consideration factors like biodiversity, tidal amplitude, soil adaptability, enrichment of species diversity and maturity characteristics. The shelterbelt plantation programme has to be taken up on a regular basis and specifically after the passage of each cyclone and tusnami. Tidal amplitude is an important factor to be considered for species selection and is easily measured by calculating distance between the highest high-tide to lowest low-tide water marks of a locality. Hence, species that prefer high-tidal amplitudes; mid-tidal amplitudes and low-tidal amplitudes are to be planted at their respective identified zones. Other general species can be planted at the back. All the shelterbelt plantation programmes in main and support zones up to 5000m from the coastline are to be implemented truthfully through Joint Forest Management (JFM) concept and the afforestation through Vana Samrakshana Samitis (VSS) along with accrued monitory benefits.

Emergency Tsunami Response

Tsunami Response Requirement

A coordinated and effective response system would be required for management of tsunami at central, state, district and community levels. For an effective and prompt tsunami response, warning communication and dissemination to all stakeholders is imperative. As soon as the warning is issued, the Tsunami Response Plan will be activated in the concerned areas. Response to early warning would involve safe evacuation of community population with minimal loss to property.

Depending on the scale of Tsunami, the run-up height and level of storm surge, the scale of response will be mobilised at community, district, state and national level. Systems will be institutionalised by the Disaster Management Authorities at various levels for coordination between various agencies like Central Government Ministries, Departments, State Governments, district authorities, ULB's, PRI's and other stakeholders for effective tsunami response.

Emergency Search and Rescue

Past experience in various disaster situations has shown that community is always the first responder in all types of disasters. The local community, before the intervention of the State machinery and specialised search & rescue teams, responds initially and saves a number of lives. Trained and equipped teams consisting of local people will be set up along the coastal areas to respond effectively in the event of tsunami. Periodical induction of freshly trained local youths in these teams is important for fast-response.

Community-level teams will be developed in the coastal districts with basic training in search & rescue. Training modules will be developed for trainers of community level search & rescue teams by NDRF training institutes. On ground, the NDRF Battalions will assist the State Government/ district authorities in training communities. They will be further assisted by Civil Defence, Home Guards, Fire Services and NGOs.

State Governments will develop procedures for formally recognising and certifying such trained search & rescue team members. State Governments will provide suitable indemnity to the community level team members for their actions in the course of emergency response following an tsunami. Youth organisations such as National Cadet Corps (NCC) and

National Service Scheme (NSS) and Nehru Yuva Kendra Sangathan (NYKS) will provide support services to the response teams at the local level under the overall guidance and supervision of the local administration.

Emergency Relief

Trained Community level teams will assist in planning and setting up emergency shelters, distributing relief among the affected people, identifying missing people, and addressing the needs of education, health care, water supply and sanitation, food etc. of the affected community. Members of these teams will be made aware of the specific requirements of the disaster-affected communities. These teams will also assist the Government in identifying the most vulnerable people who may need special assistance following a Tsunami.

The concerned Indian Navy and Coast Guard forces will extend close coöperation by supporting boats, latest equipments, skilled/ trained man power and other possible assistance to local administration for carrying out rescue and relief activities in the tsunami affected areas.

Incident Response System

NDMA has prepared the Guidelines on Incident Response System (IRS) in collaboration with all concerned stakeholder groups for streamlining the coordination of response in the event of a sudden occurrence of any disaster. This will be operationalised through Incident Response Teams (IRTs) at appropriate levels for effective coordination of response. All response activities will be undertaken at the local level through a suitably devised IRS, coordinated by the local administration through well-equipped Emergency Operations Centres (EOCs) with appropriate computer hardware, software packages and data bases. State Governments will commission and maintain EOCs at appropriate levels for coordination of human resources, relief supplies and equipment. SOPs for the EOCs will be developed by State Governments and integrated within the framework of the IRS, which will take advantage of modern technologies and tools, such as GIS maps, scenarios and simulation models for effectively responding to disasters. GIS maps available from other sources such as the city planning departments, state space application centres and other such sources, will be compiled considering their potential application after a disaster. State Governments/ SDMAs will undertake training of personnel involved in IRS.

Community-Based Disaster Response

A number of organisations, like NGOs, Self Help groups, Community Based Organisations, youth organizations, women's groups, volunteer agencies, civil defence, home guards, etc. normally volunteer their services in the aftermath of any disaster. State Government/SDMAs and DDMAs will coordinate the allocation of these human resources for performing various response activities. State Governments will work with these agencies to understand and plan their roles in the command chain of the IRS, and incorporate them in the DM Plans.

Large-scale disasters draw overwhelming humanitarian support from different stakeholders. The relief and response activities carried out by such stakeholders will comply with the norms prescribed by the appropriate authorities.

After a Tsunami, accurate information will be provided on the extent of the damage and the details of the response activities through electronic and print media. State Governments will utilise different types of media, especially print, radio, television and internet, to disseminate timely and accurate information.

Special efforts will be made by the DDMAs to enlist the support of NGOs and humanitarian agencies to ensure that in the event of a sudden occurrence of a tsunami, adequate emphasis will be placed on restoration of livelihoods of the tsunami affected people disrupted by the tsunami. The needs of psycho-social support and trauma care of the tsunami affected people will also be met through special efforts by trained social workers and clinical psychologists.

Involvement of Corporate Sector

State Governments will facilitate the involvement of the corporate sector in making available their services and resources to the Government during the immediate aftermath of Tsunami. The Corporate sector, as a part of the Corporate Social Responsibility, can initiate appropriate projects in partnership with Government agencies through Public Private Partnership (PPP). Such PPP projects may provide inter alia the services of hospitals, power and telecommunication, relief supplies, search & rescue equipment, transport and logistics for movement of relief supplies to the extent possible and technical services for restoration and reconstruction of damaged infrastructures. For instance, the Construction Federation of India with the support of Hindustan Construction Ltd. has set up the Disaster Response Network (DRN) which can also be associated during response, restoration and recovery phase. State Governments and district authorities will develop appropriate mechanisms to receive and optimally utilise all such assistance. NDMA has also supported the establishment of the Corporate Disaster Resource Network (CDRN) for identifying the critical needs of disaster-affected villages and for facilitating the appropriate corporate responses to meet these needs.

Evacuation Plans and Shelters

Inflatable motorised boats, helicopters and search and rescue equipments are required immediately after a tsunami to carry out search and rescue of people trapped in inundated areas, on tree tops and hanging on to structures. State Governments will compile a list of such equipment and identify suppliers of such specialised equipments and enter into Long Term Agreements for their mobilisation and deployment in the event of tsunami. India Disaster Resource Network (IDRN), which is a web-based resource inventory of information on emergency equipment and response personnel available at every district, will be revised and updated frequently. The IRS will also provide a web-based system for monitoring the emergency logistics requirements of disaster-affected villages as well as the flow of emergency relief supplies to the affected villages.

The setting up of relief camps for the people whose houses have been damaged by tsunami or flooded by the storm surge and the provision of basic amenities in such camps involves complex logistics of mobilising relief supplies, tents, water supply and sanitation systems, transport and communication systems, and medical supplies. Immediate restoration of power supply would be essential to carry out relief operations. The DM Plans at the State and District levels will address this issue in detail. An information booth for victims would be established by the district authorities.

Emergency Medical Response

Prompt and efficient emergency medical response will be provided by Quick Reaction Medical Teams (QRMTs), Mobile Field Hospitals, Accident Relief Medical Vans (ARMVs) and Heli-ambulances. They will be activated to reach the tsunami-affected areas immediately, along with dressing material, splints, portable X-ray machines, mobile operation theatres, pulse oximeters, resuscitation equipment and life-saving drugs, etc. Resuscitation, triage and medical evacuation of victims who require hospitalisation will be done in accordance with SOPs. A large number of victims may suffer from psycho-social trauma, for which appropriate counselling will be provided.

The medical response plan will integrate all aspects of emergency medical management at the incident site, medical care facilities during transportation and evacuation, adequate ambulance services with defined evacuation routes and other communication linkages and coordination with other identified agencies.

The emergency medical plan will be operationalised immediately on receiving information from the tsunami-affected areas. Hospitals in the affected areas will create a surge capacity for the required number of beds by discharging non-critical patients and mobilise doctors and support staff, additional orthopaedic equipment and supplies at short notice from non-coastal areas. The emergency medical plan will identify the requirement of enhanced manpower, medical stores and the requirement of blood and its components. After a tsunami, information centres will be set up to provide medical response information to the public, relatives of victims and media. The designated hospitals will also identify the surgical teams that can be deployed in the field at short notice and arrange for their transport, medical equipment and supplies. State Governments will coordinate with both government and private hospitals in order to facilitate effective and adequate hospital response after tsunami.

References

Abe K. (1995). *Estimate of Tsunami Run-up Heights from Earthquake Magnitudes.*

Chanson, H. (2010). *Tsunami Warning Signs on the Enshu Coast of Japan.* Shore & Beach, Vol. 78, No. 1, pp. 52–54.

Fradin, Judith Bloom and Dennis Brindell (2008). *Witness to Disaster: Tsunamis.* Witness to Disaster. Washington, D.C.: National Geographic Society.

Haugen K, et.al (2005). "Fundamental mechanisms for tsunami generation by submarine mass flows in idealised geometries". *Marine and Petroleum Geology* 22 (1–2): 209–217.

Wisner, B., Blaikie, P., Terry, C., and Davis, I. (2004). *At Risk, Natural Hazards, People's Vulnerability, and Disasters.* New York and London, Routledge, 2nd Edition.

9

Wildfire: Prevention and Management

A wildfire is any uncontrolled fire in an area of combustible vegetation that occurs in the countryside or a wilderness area. Other names such as brush fire, bushfire, forest fire, desert fire, grass fire, hill fire, peat fire, vegetation fire, and veldfire may be used to describe the same phenomenon depending on the type of vegetation being burned. A wildfire differs from other fires by its extensive size, the speed at which it can spread out from its original source, its potential to change direction unexpectedly, and its ability to jump gaps such as roads, rivers and fire breaks. Wildfires are characterized in terms of the cause of ignition, their physical properties such as speed of propagation, the combustible material present, and the effect of weather on the fire.

Wildfires occur on every continent except Antarctica. Wildfires are a common occurrence in Australia especially during the long hot summers usually experienced in the southern regions such as Victoria, Australia. Due to Australia's hot and dry climate, wildfires (commonly referred to as bushfires in Australia) pose a great risk to life and infrastructure during all times of the year, though mostly throughout the hotter months of summer and spring. In the United States, there are typically between 60,000 and 80,000 wildfires that occur each year, burning 3 million to 10 million acres of land depending on the year. Fossil records and human history contain accounts of wildfires, as wildfires can occur in periodic intervals. Wildfires can cause extensive damage, both to property and human life, but they also have various beneficial effects on wilderness areas. Some plant species depend on the effects of fire for growth and reproduction, although large wildfires may also have negative ecological effects.

Strategies of wildfire prevention, detection, and suppression have varied over the years, and international wildfire management experts encourage further development of technology and research. One of the more controversial techniques is controlled burning: permitting or even igniting smaller fires to minimize the amount of flammable material available for a potential wildfire. While some wildfires burn in remote forested regions, they can cause extensive destruction of homes and other property located in the wildland-urban interface: a zone of transition between developed areas and undeveloped wilderness.

Causes

The four major natural causes of wildfire ignitions are lightning, volcanic eruption, sparks from rockfalls, and spontaneous combustion. The thousands of coal seam fires that are burning around the world, such as those in Centralia, Burning Mountain, and several coal-sustained fires in China, can also flare up and ignite nearby flammable material. However, many wildfires are attributed to human sources such as arson, discarded cigarettes, discarded glass (and plastic) magnifying the sun's (light and heat) rays, sparks from equipment, and power line arcs (as detected by arc mapping). In societies experiencing shifting cultivation where land is cleared quickly and farmed until the soil loses fertility, slash and burn clearing is often considered the least expensive way to prepare land for future use. Forested areas cleared by logging encourage the dominance of flammable grasses, and abandoned logging roads overgrown by vegetation may act as fire corridors. Annual grassland fires in southern Vietnam can be attributed in part to the destruction of forested areas by US military herbicides, explosives, and mechanical land clearing and burning operations during the Vietnam War.

The most common cause of wildfires varies throughout the world. In the Canada and northwest China, for example, lightning is the major source of ignition. In other parts of the world, human involvement is a major contributor. In Mexico, Central America, South America, Africa, Southeast Asia, Fiji, and New Zealand, wildfires can be attributed to human activities such as animal husbandry, agriculture, and land-conversion burning. Human carelessness is a major cause of wildfires in China and in the Mediterranean Basin. In the United States and Australia, the source of wildfires can be traced to both lightning strikes and human activities such as machinery sparks and cast-away cigarette butts."

On a yearly basis in the United States, typically more than six times the number of wildfires is caused by human means such as campfires and controlled agricultural burns than by natural means. However, in any given year there could be far more acres burned by wildfires that are started by natural means than by human means as well as vice-versa. For example, in 2010, almost 1.4 million acres were burned by human-caused wildfires, and over 2 million acres were burned by naturally-caused wildfires. However, far more acres were burned by human-caused fires in 2011, when almost 5.4 million acres were burned by human-caused wildfires, and only about 3.4 million acres were caused by naturally-derived wildfires.

Characteristics

The name wildfire was once a synonym for Greek fire but now refers to any large or destructive conflagration. Wildfires differ from other fires in that they take place outdoors in areas of grassland, woodlands, bushland, scrubland, peatland, and other wooded areas that act as a source of fuel, or combustible material. Buildings may become involved if a wildfire spreads to adjacent communities. While the causes of wildfires vary and the outcomes are always unique, all wildfires can be characterized in terms of their physical properties, their fuel type, and the effect that weather has on the fire.

Wildfire behaviour and severity result from the combination of factors such as available fuels, physical setting, and weather. While wildfires can be large, uncontrolled disasters that burn through 0.4 to 400 square kilometres (100 to 100,000 acres) or more, they can also be as small as 0.0010 square kilometres (0.25 acre) or less. Although smaller events may be included in wildfire modeling, most do not earn press attention. This can be problematic because public fire policies, which relate to fires of all sizes, are influenced more by the way the media portrays catastrophic wildfires than by small fires.

Fuel Type

The spread of wildfires varies based on the flammable material present and its vertical arrangement. For example, fuels uphill from a fire are more readily dried and warmed by the fire than those downhill, yet burning logs can roll downhill from the fire to ignite other fuels. Fuel arrangement and density is governed in part by topography, as land shape determines factors such as available sunlight and water for plant growth. Overall, fire types can be generally characterized by their fuels as follows:

— Ground fires are fed by subterranean roots, duff and other buried organic matter. This fuel type is especially susceptible to ignition due to spotting. Ground fires typically burn by smoldering, and can burn slowly for days to months, such as peat fires in Kalimantan and Eastern Sumatra, Indonesia, which resulted from a riceland creation project that unintentionally drained and dried the peat.
— Crawling or surface fires are fueled by low-lying vegetation such as leaf and timber litter, debris, grass, and low-lying shrubbery.
— Ladder fires consume material between low-level vegetation and tree canopies, such as small trees, downed logs, and vines. Kudzu, Old World climbing fern, and other invasive plants that scale trees may also encourage ladder fires.
— Crown, canopy, or aerial fires burn suspended material at the canopy level, such as tall trees, vines, and mosses. The ignition of a crown fire, termed crowning, is dependent on the density of the suspended material, canopy height, canopy continuity, and sufficient surface and ladder fires in order to reach the tree crowns. For example, ground-clearing fires lit by humans can spread into the Amazon rain forest, damaging ecosystems not particularly suited for heat or arid conditions.

Physical Properties

Wildfires occur when all of the necessary elements of a fire triangle come together in a susceptible area: an ignition source is brought into contact with a combustible material such as vegetation, that is subjected to sufficient heat and has an adequate supply of oxygen from the ambient air. A high moisture content usually prevents ignition and slows propagation, because higher temperatures are required to evaporate any water within the material and heat the material to its fire point. Dense forests usually provide more shade, resulting in lower ambient temperatures and greater humidity, and are therefore less susceptible to wildfires. Less dense material such as grasses and leaves are easier to ignite because they contain less water than denser material such as branches and trunks. Plants continuously lose water by evapotranspiration, but water loss is usually balanced by water absorbed from the soil, humidity, or rain. When this balance is not maintained, plants dry out and are therefore more flammable, often a consequence of droughts.

A wildfire front is the portion sustaining continuous flaming combustion, where unburned material meets active flames, or the smoldering transition between unburned and burned material. As the front approaches, the fire heats both the surrounding air and woody material through convection and thermal radiation. First, wood is dried as water is vaporized at a temperature of 100 °C (212 °F). Next, the pyrolysis of wood at 230 °C (450 °F) releases flammable gases. Finally, wood can smoulder at 380 °C (720 °F) or, when heated sufficiently, ignite at 590 °C (1,000 °F). Even before the flames of a wildfire arrive at a particular location, heat transfer from the wildfire front warms the air to 800 °C (1,470 °F), which pre-heats and dries flammable materials, causing materials to ignite faster and allowing the fire to spread faster. High-temperature and long-duration surface wildfires may encourage flashover or torching: the drying of tree canopies and their subsequent ignition from below.

Wildfires have a rapid forward rate of spread (FROS) when burning through dense, uninterrupted fuels. They can move as fast as 10.8 kilometres per hour (6.7 mph) in forests and 22 kilometres per hour (14 mph) in grasslands. Wildfires can advance tangential to the main front to form a flanking front, or burn in the opposite direction of the main front by backing. They may also spread by jumping or spotting as winds and vertical convection columns carry firebrands (hot wood embers) and other burning materials through the air over roads, rivers, and other barriers that may otherwise act as firebreaks. Torching and fires in tree canopies encourage spotting, and dry ground fuels that surround a wildfire are especially vulnerable to ignition from firebrands. Spotting can create spot fires as hot embers and firebrands ignite fuels downwind from the fire. In Australian bushfires, spot fires are known to occur as far as 10 kilometres (6 mi) from the fire front.

Especially large wildfires may affect air currents in their immediate vicinities by the stack effect: air rises as it is heated, and large wildfires create powerful updrafts that will draw in new, cooler air from surrounding areas in thermal columns. Great vertical differences in temperature and humidity encourage pyrocumulus clouds, strong winds, and fire whirls with the force of tornadoes at speeds of more than 80 kilometres per hour (50 mph). Rapid rates of spread, prolific crowning or spotting, the presence of fire whirls, and strong convection columns signify extreme conditions.

Effect of Weather

Heat waves, droughts, cyclical climate changes such as El Niño, and regional weather patterns such as high-pressure ridges can increase the risk and alter the behavior of wildfires dramatically. Years of precipitation followed by warm periods can encourage more widespread fires and longer fire seasons. Since the mid 1980s, earlier snowmelt and associated warming has also been associated with an increase in length and severity of the wildfire season in the Western United States. However, one individual element does not always cause an increase in wildfire activity. For example, wildfires will not occur during a drought unless accompanied by other factors, such as lightning (ignition source) and strong winds (mechanism for rapid spread).

Intensity also increases during daytime hours. Burn rates of smoldering logs are up to five times greater during the day due to lower humidity, increased temperatures, and increased wind speeds. Sunlight warms the ground during the day which creates air currents that travel uphill. At night the land cools, creating air currents that travel downhill. Wildfires are fanned by these winds and often follow the air currents over hills and through valleys. Fires in Europe occur frequently during the hours of 12:00 p.m. and 2:00 p.m. Wildfire suppression operations in the United States revolve around a 24-hour fire day that begins at 10:00 a.m. due to the predictable increase in intensity resulting from the daytime warmth.

Environmental Impacts

Wildfires are common in climates that are sufficiently moist to allow the growth of vegetation but feature extended dry, hot periods. Such places include the vegetated areas of Australia and Southeast Asia, the veld in southern Africa, the fynbos in the Western Cape of South Africa, the forested areas of the United States and Canada, and the Mediterranean Basin. Fires can be particularly intense during days of strong winds, periods of drought, and during warm summer months. Global warming may increase the intensity and frequency of droughts in many areas, creating more intense and frequent wildfires.

Although some ecosystems rely on naturally occurring fires to regulate growth, many ecosystems suffer from too much fire, such as the chaparral in southern California and lower elevation deserts in the American Southwest. The increased fire frequency in these ordinarily fire-dependent areas has upset natural cycles, destroyed native plant communities, and encouraged the growth of fire-intolerant vegetation and non-native weeds. Invasive species, such as Lygodium microphyllum and Bromus tectorum, can grow rapidly in areas that were damaged by fires. Because they are highly flammable, they can increase the future risk of fire, creating a positive feedback loop that increases fire frequency and further destroys native growth.

In the Amazon Rainforest, drought, logging, cattle ranching practices, and slash-and-burn agriculture damage fire-resistant forests and promote the growth of flammable brush, creating a cycle that encourages more burning. Fires in the rainforest threaten its collection of diverse species and produce large amounts of CO2. Also, fires in the rainforest, along with drought and human involvement, could damage or destroy more than half of the Amazon rainforest by the year 2030. Wildfires generate ash, destroy available organic nutrients, and cause an increase in water runoff, eroding away other nutrients and creating flash flood conditions. A 2003 wildfire in the North Yorkshire Moors destroyed 2.5 square kilometers (600 acres) of heather and the underlying peat layers. Afterwards, wind erosion stripped the ash and the exposed soil, revealing archaeological remains dating back to 10,000 BC. Wildfires can also have an effect on climate change, increasing the amount of carbon released into the atmosphere and inhibiting vegetation growth, which affects overall carbon uptake by plants.

In tundra there is a natural pattern of accumulation of fuel and wildfire which varies depending on the nature of vegetation and terrain. Research in Alaska has shown fire-event return intervals, (FRIs) that typically vary from 150 to 200 years with dryer lowland areas burning more frequently than wetter upland areas.

Plant Adaptation

Plants in wildfire-prone ecosystems often survive through adaptations to their local fire regime. Such adaptations include physical protection against heat, increased growth after a fire event, and flammable materials that encourage fire and may eliminate competition. For example, plants of the genus Eucalyptus contain flammable oils that encourage fire and hard sclerophyll leaves to resist heat and drought, ensuring their dominance over less fire-tolerant species. Dense bark, shedding lower branches, and high water content in external structures may also protect trees from rising temperatures. Fire-resistant seeds and reserve shoots that sprout after a fire encourage species preservation, as embodied by pioneer species. Smoke, charred wood, and heat can stimulate the germination of seeds in a process called serotiny. Exposure to smoke from burning plants promotes germination in other types of plants by inducing the production of the orange butenolide.

Grasslands in Western Sabah, Malaysian pine forests, and Indonesian Casuarina forests are believed to have resulted from previous periods of fire. Chamise deadwood litter is low in water content and flammable, and the shrub quickly sprouts after a fire. Sequoia rely on periodic fires to reduce competition, release seeds from their cones, and clear the soil and canopy for new growth. Caribbean Pine in Bahamian pineyards have adapted to and rely on low-intensity, surface fires for survival and growth. An optimum fire frequency for growth is every 3 to 10 years. Too frequent fires favor herbaceous plants, and infrequent fires favor species typical of Bahamian dry forests.

Atmospheric Effects

Most of the Earth's weather and air pollution resides in the troposphere, the part of the atmosphere that extends from the surface of the planet to a height of about 10 kilometers (6 mi). The vertical lift of a severe thunderstorm or pyrocumulonimbus can be enhanced in the area of a large wildfire, which can propel smoke, soot, and other particulate matter as high as the lower stratosphere. Previously, prevailing scientific theory held that most particles in the stratosphere came from volcanoes, but smoke and other wildfire emissions have been detected from the lower stratosphere. Pyrocumulus clouds can reach 6,100 meters (20,000 ft) over wildfires. Increased fire byproducts in the stratosphere can increase ozone concentration beyond safe levels. Satellite observation of smoke plumes from wildfires revealed that the plumes could be traced intact for distances exceeding 1,600 kilometers (1,000 mi). Computer-aided models such as CALPUFF may help predict the size and direction of wildfire-generated smoke plumes by using atmospheric dispersion modeling.

Wildfires can affect climate and weather and have major impacts on atmospheric pollution. Wildfire emissions contain fine particulate matter which can cause cardiovascular and respiratory problems. Forest fires in

Indonesia in 1997 were estimated to have released between 0.81 and 2.57 gigatonnes (0.89 and 2.83 billion short tons) of CO_2 into the atmosphere, which is between 13%–40% of the annual global carbon dioxide emissions from burning fossil fuels. Atmospheric models suggest that these concentrations of sooty particles could increase absorption of incoming solar radiation during winter months by as much as 15%.

Wildfire Prevention

Wildfire prevention refers to the preemptive methods of reducing the risk of fires as well as lessening its severity and spread. Effective prevention techniques allow supervising agencies to manage air quality, maintain ecological balances, protect resources, and to limit the effects of future uncontrolled fires. North American firefighting policies may permit naturally caused fires to burn to maintain their ecological role, so long as the risks of escape into high-value areas are mitigated. However, prevention policies must consider the role that humans play in wildfires, since, for example, 95% of forest fires in Europe are related to human involvement. Sources of human-caused fire may include arson, accidental ignition, or the uncontrolled use of fire in land-clearing and agriculture such as the slash-and-burn farming in Southeast Asia. A new and ecologically evolutionary practice, termed "Hydro-Pyrogeography", promises and claims to bound wildfire from passing through any such wildland-urban interface anywhere on earth that the practice is put into place, and thereby diminishing, even eliminating the above-referred oppositions and concerns to traditional fuel management techniques.

In the mid-19th century, explorers from the HMS Beagle observed Australian Aborigines using fire for ground clearing, hunting, and regeneration of plant food in a method later named fire-stick farming. Such careful use of fire has been employed for centuries in the lands protected by Kakadu National Park to encourage biodiversity. In 1937, U.S. President Franklin D. Roosevelt initiated a nationwide fire prevention campaign, highlighting the role of human carelessness in forest fires. Later posters of the program featured Uncle Sam, leaders of the Axis powers of World War II, characters from the Disney movie Bambi, and the official mascot of the U.S. Forest Service, Smokey Bear.

Wildfires are caused by a combination of natural factors such as topography, fuels, and weather. Other than reducing human infractions, only fuels may be altered to affect future fire risk and behavior. Wildfire prevention programs around the world may employ techniques such as wildland fire use and prescribed or controlled burns. Wildland fire use refers to any fire of natural causes that is monitored but allowed to burn. Controlled burns are fires ignited by government agencies under less dangerous weather conditions.

Vegetation may be burned periodically to maintain high species diversity, and frequent burning of surface fuels limits fuel accumulation, thereby reducing the risk of crown fires. Using strategic cuts of trees, fuels may also be removed by handcrews in order to clean and clear the forest, prevent fuel build-up, and create access into forested areas. Chain saws and large equipment can be used to thin out ladder fuels and shred trees and vegetation to a mulch. Multiple fuel treatments are often needed to influence future fire risks, and wildfire models may be used to predict and compare the benefits of different fuel treatments on future wildfire spread.

However, controlled burns are reportedly "the most effective treatment for reducing a fire's rate of spread, fireline intensity, flame length, and heat per unit of area" according to Jan Van Wagtendonk, a biologist at the Yellowstone Field Station. Additionally, while fuel treatments are typically limited to smaller areas, effective fire management requires the administration of fuels across large landscapes in order to reduce future fire size and severity.

Building codes in fire-prone areas typically require that structures be built of flame-resistant materials and a defensible space be maintained by clearing flammable materials within a prescribed distance from the structure. Communities in the Philippines also maintain fire lines 5 to 10 meters (16 to 33 ft) wide between the forest and their village, and patrol these lines during summer months or seasons of dry weather. Fuel buildup can result in costly, devastating fires as new homes, ranches, and other development are built adjacent to wilderness areas. Continued growth in fire-prone areas and rebuilding structures destroyed by fires has been met with criticism.

However, the population growth along the wildland-urban interface discourages the use of current fuel management techniques. Smoke is an irritant and attempts to thin out the fuel load is met with opposition due to desirability of forested areas, in addition to other wilderness goals such as endangered species protection and habitat preservation. The ecological benefits of fire are often overridden by the economic and safety benefits of protecting structures and human life. For example, while fuel treatments decrease the risk of crown fires, these techniques destroy the habitats of various plant and animal species. Additionally, government policies that cover the wilderness usually differ from local and state policies that govern urban lands.

Fire Management Policy

Since the turn of the 20th century, various federal and state agencies have been involved in wildland fire management in one form or another. In the early 20th century, for example, the federal government, through the U.S. Army and the U.S. Forest Service, solicited fire suppression as a primary goal of managing the nation's forests. At this time in history fire was viewed as a threat to timber, an economically important natural resource. As such, rational decisions were made to devote public funds to fire suppression and fire prevention efforts. For example, the Forest Fire Emergency Fund Act of 1908 permitted deficit spending in the case of emergency fire situations. As a result, the U.S. Forest Service was able to acquire a deficit of over $1 million in 1910 due to emergency fire suppression efforts. Following the same tone of timber resource protection, the U.S. Forest Service adopted the "10 AM Policy" in 1935. Through this policy the agency advocated the control of all fires by 10 o'clock of the morning following the discovery of a wildfire. Fire prevention was also heavily advocated through public education campaigns such as Smokey the Bear. Through these and similar public education campaigns the general public was, in a sense, trained to perceive all wildfire as a threat to civilized society and natural resources. The negative sentiment towards wildland fire prevailed and helped to shape wildland fire management objectives throughout most of the 20th century.

Beginning in the 1970s public perception of wildland fire management began to shift. Despite portly funding for fire suppression in the first half of the 20th century, massive wildfires continued to be prevalent across the landscape of North America. Natural resource professionals and ordinary citizens alike became curious about the ecological effects of wildfire. Ecologists were beginning to recognize the presence and ecological importance of natural lightning-ignited wildfires across the United States. Along with this new discovery of fire knowledge and the emergence of fire ecology as a science came an effort to apply fire to land in a controlled manner. It was learned that suppression of fire in certain ecosystems actually increases the likelihood that a wildfire will occur and increases the intensity of those wildfires. This was in fact happening across the United States. However, suppression is still the main tactic when a fire is set by a human or if it threatens life or property.

By the 1980s funding efforts began to support prescribed burning. In light of emerging information about wildland fire, rational thought justified funding prescribed burning in order to prevent catastrophic wildfire events. In 2001, the United States Government implemented a National Fire Plan and the budget increased from $108 million in 2000 to $401 million for the reduction of hazardous fuels. In this way, the costs of implementing prescribed burns were thought to be less than the costs imposed on society by catastrophic wildfires. In addition to using prescribed fire to reduce the chance of catastrophic wildfires, mechanical methods have recently been adopted as well. Mechanical methods include the use of chippers and other machinery to remove hazardous fuels and thereby reduce the risk of wildfire events. Today the United States philosophy remains that, "fire, as a critical natural process, will be integrated into land and resource management plans and activities on a landscape scale, and across agency boundaries. Response to wildfire is based on ecological, social and legal consequences of fire. The circumstance under which a fire occurs, and the likely consequences and public safety and welfare, natural and cultural resources, and values to be protected dictate the appropriate management response to fire". The five federal regulatory agencies managing forest fire response and planning for 676 million acres in the United States are the Department of the Interior, the Bureau of Land Management, the Bureau of Indian Affairs, the National Park Service, the United States Department of Agriculture-Forest Service and the United States Fish and Wildlife Services. Several hundred million U.S. acres of wildfire management are also conducted by state, county, and local fire management organizations.

The Condition Class System

The Condition Class System is used in the United States to provide "national-level data on the current condition of fuel and vegetation." The USDA Forest Service developed this for the purpose of allocating fire funding and resources, prioritizing fuel usage and restoration activities, and evaluating wildfire management progress. There are primary and secondary determinants used to rank forest systems into condition class and fire regimes. Condition Class "indicates the departure from normal fire return intervals" and is categorized as low, medium, or high. The more a fire departs from normal pattern, the higher is its condition class. A fire regime is the "historical pattern of fire in forests" and the roman numerals I, II, III, IV and V are used for the classification. Primary determinants are the structure of the forest, the amount of trees, tree density and the characteristics of the combustible fuel. The United States Department of Agriculture and the United States Department of Interior use the Condition Class System in the LANDFIRE project to make assessments of federal land. However, the LANDFIRE project revealed in 2003 that this type of analysis is not detailed enough to use at a local level. Federal agencies are required to take record and report "acres treated", using different prevention tactics, under the National Fire Plan Operations Reporting System (NFPORS).

Wildland-Urban Interface Policy

An aspect of wildfire policy that is gaining attention is the wildland-urban interface (WUI). More and more people are living in "red zones," or areas that are at high risk of wildfires. FEMA and the NFPA develop specific policies to guide homeowners and builders in how to build and maintain structures at the WUI and how protect against catastrophic losses. For example, NFPA-1141 is a standard for fire protection infrastructure for land development in wildland, rural and suburban areas and NFPA-1144 is a standard for reducing structure ignition hazards from wildland fire.

Economics of Fire Management Policy

Similar to that of military operations, fire management is often very expensive in the U.S. Today, it is not uncommon for suppression operations for a single wildfire to exceed costs of $1 million in just a few days. The United States Department of Agriculture allotted $2.2 billion for wildfire management in 2012. Although fire suppression offers many benefits to society, other options for fire management exist. While these options cannot completely replace fire suppression as a fire management tool, other options can play an important role in overall fire management and can therefore affect the costs of fire suppression.

The application of fire management tools requires making certain tradeoffs. Below is a sample of some costs and benefits associated with the tools currently used in fire management. Current approaches to fire management are an almost complete turnaround compared to historic approaches. In fact, it is commonly accepted that past fire suppression, along with other factors, has resulted in larger, more intense wildfire events which are seen today. In economic terms, expenditures used for wildfire suppression in the early 20th century have contributed to increased suppression costs which are being realized today. As is the case with many public policy issues, costs and benefits associated with particular fire management tools are difficult to accurately quantify. Ultimately, costs and benefits should be weighed against one another on a case-by-case basis in planning wildland fire management operations.

Depending on the tradeoffs that a land manager is willing to make, a combination of the following fire management tools could be used. For instance, prescribed fire and/or mechanical fuels reduction could be used to help prevent or lessen the intensity of a wildfire thereby reducing or eliminating suppression costs. In addition, prescribed fire and/or mechanical fuels reduction could be used to improve soil conditions in fields or in forests to the benefit of wildlife or natural resources. On the other hand, the use of prescribed fire requires much advanced planning and can have negative impacts on human health in nearby communities.

Detection of Wildfire

Fast and effective detection is a key factor in wildfire fighting. Early detection efforts were focused on early response, accurate results in both daytime and nighttime, and the ability to prioritize fire danger. Fire lookout towers were used in the United States in the early 20th century and fires were reported using telephones, carrier pigeons, and heliographs. Aerial and land photography using instant cameras were used in the 1950s until infrared scanning was developed for fire detection in the 1960s. However, information analysis and delivery was often delayed by limitations in communication technology. Early satellite-derived fire analyses were hand-drawn on maps at a remote site and sent via overnight mail to the fire manager. During the Yellowstone fires of 1988, a data station was established in West Yellowstone, permitting the delivery of satellite-based fire information in approximately four hours.

Currently, public hotlines, fire lookouts in towers, and ground and aerial patrols can be used as a means of early detection of forest fires. However, accurate human observation may be limited by operator fatigue, time of day, time of year, and geographic location. Electronic systems have gained popularity in recent years as a possible resolution to human operator error. A government report on a recent trial of three automated camera fire detection systems in Australia did, however, conclude "...detection by the camera systems was slower and less reliable than by a trained human observer". These systems may be semi- or fully automated and employ systems based on the risk area and degree of human presence, as suggested by GIS data analyses. An integrated approach of multiple systems can be used to merge satellite data, aerial imagery, and personnel position via Global Positioning System (GPS) into a collective whole for near-realtime use by wireless Incident Command Centers.

A small, high risk area that features thick vegetation, a strong human presence, or is close to a critical urban area can be monitored using a local sensor network. Detection systems may include wireless sensor networks that act as automated weather systems: detecting temperature, humidity, and smoke. These may be battery-powered, solar-powered, or tree-rechargeable: able to recharge their battery systems using the small electrical currents in plant material. Larger, medium-risk areas can be monitored by scanning towers that incorporate fixed cameras and sensors to detect smoke or additional factors such as the infrared signature of carbon dioxide produced by fires. Additional capabilities such as night vision, brightness detection, and color change detection may also be incorporated into sensor arrays.

Satellite and aerial monitoring through the use of planes, helicopter, or UAVs can provide a wider view and may be sufficient to monitor very large, low risk areas. These more sophisticated systems employ GPS and aircraft-mounted infrared or high-resolution visible cameras to identify and target wildfires. Satellite-mounted sensors such as Envisat's Advanced Along Track Scanning Radiometer and European Remote-Sensing Satellite's Along-Track Scanning Radiometer can measure infrared radiation emitted by fires, identifying hot spots greater than 39 °C (102 °F). The National Oceanic and Atmospheric Administration's Hazard Mapping System combines remote-sensing data from satellite sources such as Geostationary Operational Environmental Satellite (GOES), Moderate-Resolution Imaging Spectroradiometer (MODIS), and Advanced Very High Resolution Radiometer (AVHRR) for detection of fire and smoke plume locations. However, satellite detection is prone to offset errors, anywhere from 2 to 3 kilometers (1 to 2 mi) for MODIS and AVHRR data and up to 12 kilometers (7.5 mi) for GOES data. Satellites in geostationary orbits may become disabled, and satellites in polar orbits are often limited by their short window of observation time. Cloud cover and image resolution and may also limit the effectiveness of satellite imagery.

Wildfire Suppression

Wildfire suppression depends on the technologies available in the area in which the wildfire occurs. In less developed nations the techniques used can be as simple as throwing sand or beating the fire with sticks or palm fronds. In more advanced nations, the suppression methods vary due to increased technological capacity. Silver iodide can be used to encourage snow fall, while fire retardants and water can be dropped onto fires by unmanned aerial vehicles, planes, and helicopters. Complete fire suppression is no longer an expectation, but the majority of wildfires are often extinguished before they grow out of control. While more than 99% of the 10,000 new wildfires each year are contained, escaped wildfires can cause extensive damage. Worldwide damage from wildfires is in the billions of euros annually. Wildfires in Canada and the US burn an average of 54,500 square kilometers (13,000,000 acres) per year.

Above all, fighting wildfires can become deadly. A wildfire's burning front may also change direction unexpectedly and jump across fire breaks. Intense heat and smoke can lead to disorientation and loss of appreciation of the direction of the fire, which can make fires particularly dangerous. For example, during the 1949 Mann Gulch fire in Montana, USA, thirteen smokejumpers died when they lost their communication links, became disorientated, and were overtaken by the fire. In the Australian February 2009 Victorian bushfires, at least 173 people died and over 2,029 homes and 3,500 structures were lost when they became engulfed by wildfire.

Wildland Firefighting Safety

Wildland fire fighters face several life-threatening hazards including heat stress, fatigue, smoke and dust, as well as the risk of other injuries such as burns, cuts and scrapes, and animal bites.

Especially in hot weather condition, fires present the risk of heat stress, which can entail feeling heat, fatigue, weakness, vertigo, headache, or nausea. Heat stress can progress into heat strain, which entails physiological changes such as increased heart rate and core body temperature. This can lead to heat-related illnesses, such as heat rash, cramps, exhaustion or heat stroke. Various factors can contribute to the risks posed by heat stress, including strenuous work, personal risk factors such as age and fitness, dehydration, sleep deprivation, and burdensome personal protective equipment. Rest, cool water, and occasional breaks are crucial to mitigating the effects of heat stress.

Smoke, ash, and debris can also pose serious respiratory hazards to wildland fire fighters. The smoke and dust from wildfires can contain gases such as carbon monoxide, sulfur dioxide and formaldehyde, as well as particulates such as ash and silica. To reduce smoke exposure, wildfire fighting crews should, whenever possible, rotate firefighters through areas of heavy smoke, avoid downwind firefighting, use equipment rather than people in holding areas, and minimize mop-up. Camps and command posts should also be located upwind of wildfires. Protective clothing and equipment can also help minimize exposure to smoke and ash.

Firefighters are also at risk of cardiac events including strokes and heart attacks. Fire fighters should maintain good physical fitness Fitness programs, medical screening and examination programs which include stress tests can minimize the risks of firefighting cardiac problems. Other injury hazards wildland fire fighters face include slips, trips and falls, burns, scrapes and cuts from tools and equipment, being struck by trees, vehicles, or other objects, plant hazards such as thorns and poison ivy, snake and animal bites, vehicle crashes, electrocution from power lines or lightning storms, and unstable buillding structures.

Fire Retardants

Fire retardants are used to help slow wildfires, coat fuels, and lessen oxygen availability as required by various firefighting situations. They are composed of nitrates, ammonia, phosphates and sulfates, as well as other chemicals and thickening agents. The choice of whether to apply retardant depends on the magnitude, location and intensity of the wildfire. Fire retardants are used to reach inaccessible geographical regions where ground firefighting crews are unable to reach a wildfire or in any occasion where human safety and structures are in endangered. In certain instances, fire retardant may also be applied ahead of wildfires for protection of structures and vegetation as a precautionary fire defense measure.

The application of aerial fire retardants creates an atypical appearance on land and water surfaces and has the potential to change soil chemistry.

Fire retardant can decrease the availability of plant nutrients in the soil by increasing the acidity of the soil and reducing soil pH. Fire retardant may also affect water quality through leaching, eutrophication, or misapplication. Fire retardant's effects on drinking water remain inconclusive. Dilution factors, including water body size, rainfall, and water flow rates lessen the concentration and potency of fire retardant. Wildfire debris (ash and sediment) clog rivers and reservoirs increasing the risk for floods and erosion that ultimately slow and/or damage water treatment systems. There is continued concern of fire retardant effects on land, water, wildlife habitats, and watershed quality, additional research is needed. However, on the positive side, fire retardant (specifically its nitrogen and phosphorus components) has been shown to have a fertilizing effect on nutrient-deprived soils and thus creates a temporary increase in vegetation.

Current USDA procedure maintains that the aerial application of fire retardant in the United States must clear waterways by a minimum of 300 feet in order to safeguard effects of retardant runoff. Aerial uses of fire retardant are required to avoid application near waterways and endangered species (plant and animal habitats). After any incident of fire retardant misapplication, the U.S. Forest Service requires reporting and assessment impacts be made in order to determine mitigation, remediation, and/or restrictions on future retardant uses in that area.

Modeling

Wildfire modeling is concerned with numerical simulation of wildfires in order to comprehend and predict fire behavior. Wildfire modeling can ultimately aid wildfire suppression, increase the safety of firefighters and the public, and minimize damage. Using computational science, wildfire modeling involves the statistical analysis of past fire events to predict spotting risks and front behavior. Various wildfire propagation models have been proposed in the past, including simple ellipses and egg- and fan-shaped models. Early attempts to determine wildfire behavior assumed terrain and vegetation uniformity. However, the exact behavior of a wildfire's front is dependent on a variety of factors, including windspeed and slope steepness. Modern growth models utilize a combination of past ellipsoidal descriptions and Huygens' Principle to simulate fire growth as a continuously expanding polygon. Extreme value theory may also be used to predict the size of large wildfires. However, large fires that exceed suppression capabilities are often regarded as statistical outliers in standard analyses, even though fire policies are more influenced by catastrophic wildfires than by small fires.

Human Risk and Exposure

Wildfire risk is the chance that a wildfire will start in or reach a particular area and the potential loss of human values if it does. Risk is dependent on variable factors such as human activities, weather patterns, availability of wildfire fuels, and the availability or lack of resources to suppress a fire. Wildfires have continually been a threat to human populations. However, human induced geographical and climatic changes are exposing populations more frequently to wildfires and increasing wildfire risk. It is speculated that the increase in wildfires arises from a century of wildfire suppression coupled with the rapid expansion of human developments into fire-prone wildlands. Wildfires are naturally occurring events that aid in promoting forest health. The consequence of suppressing wildfires has led to an overgrowth in forest vegetation, which provides excess fuel that increases the severity, range, and duration of a wildfire. Global warming and climate changes are causing an increase in temperatures and more droughts nation wide which also contributes to an increase in wildfire risk.

Nationally, the burden of wildfires is disproportionally heavily distributed in the southern and western regions. The Geographic Area Coordinating Group (GACG) divides the United States and Alaska into 11 geographic areas for the purpose of emergency incident management. One particular area of focus is wildland fires. A national assessment of wildfire risk in the United States based on GACG identified regions (with the slight modification of combining Southern and Northern California, and the West and East Basin); indicate that California (50.22% risk) and the Southern Area (15.53% risk) are the geographic areas with the highest wildfire risk. The western areas of the nation are experiencing an expansion of human development into and beyond what is called the wildland-urban interface (WUI). When wildfires inevitably occur in these fire-prone areas, often communities are threatened due to their proximity to fire-prone forest. The south is one of the fastest growing regions with 88 million acres classified as WUI. The south consistently has the highest number of wildfires per year. More than 50, 000 communities are estimated to be at high to very high risk of wildfire damage. These statistics are greatly attributable to the South's year-round fire season.

Risk to Human Health

The most noticeable adverse effect of wildfires is the destruction of property and biomass. However, the release of hazardous chemicals from the burning of wildland fuels significantly impacts health in humans. Wildfire smoke is composed primarily of carbon dioxide and water vapor. Other common smoke components present in lower concentrations are carbon monoxide, formaldehyde, acrolein, polyaromatic hydrocarbons, and benzene. Small particulates suspended in air which come in solid form or in liquid droplets are also present in smoke. 80 -90% of wildfire smoke, by mass, is within the fine particle size class of 2.5 micrometers in diameter or smaller. Despite carbon dioxides high concentration in smoke, it poses low health risk due to its low toxicity. Carbon monoxide and fine particulate matter, particularly 2.5 μm in diameter and smaller, have been identified as the major health threats. Other chemicals are considered to be significant hazards but are found in concentrations that are too low to cause detectable health effects.

The degree of wildfire smoke exposure to an individual is dependent on the length, severity, duration, and proximity of the fire. People are exposed directly to smoke via the respiratory tract though inhalation of air pollutants. Indirectly, communities are exposed to wildfire debris that can contaminate soil and water supplies. Firefighters are at the greatest risk for acute and chronic health effects resulting from wildfire smoke exposure. Due to firefighter's occupational duties, they are frequently exposed to hazardous chemicals at a close proximity for longer periods of time. A case study on the exposure of wildfire smoke among wildland firefighters, show that firefighters are exposed to significant levels of carbon monoxide and respiratory irritants above OSHA permissible exposure limits (PEL) and ACGIH threshold limit values (TLV). 5-10% are overexposed. The study obtained exposure concentrations for one wildland firefighter over a 10-hour shift spent holding down a fireline. The firefighter was exposed to a wide range of carbon monoxide and respiratory irritant(combination of particulate matter 3.5 μm and smaller, acrolein, and formaldehype) levels. Carbon monoxide levels reached up to 160ppm and the TLV irritant index value reached a high of 10. In contrast, the OSHA PEL for carbon monoxide is 30ppm and for the TLV respiratory irritant index, the calculated threshold limit value is 1; any value above 1 exceeds exposure limits.

Residents in communities surrounding wildfires are exposed to lower concentrations of chemicals, but they are at a greater risk for indirect exposure through water or soil contamination. Exposure to residents is greatly dependent on individual susceptibility. Vulnerable persons such as children (ages 0–4), the elderly (ages 65 and older), smokers, and pregnant women are at an increased risk due to already compromised body systems, even when the exposures are present at low chemical concentrations and for relatively short exposure periods. The U.S Environmental Protection Agency (EPA) developed the Air Quality Index (AQI), a public resource that provides national air quality standard concentrations for common air pollutants. The public can use this index as a tool to determine their exposure to hazardous air pollutants based on visibility range.

Health Effects

Inhalation of smoke from a wildfire can be a health hazard. Wildfire smoke is primarily composed of carbon dioxide, water vapor, particulate matter, organic chemicals, nitrogen oxides and other compounds. The principle health concern is the inhalation of particulate matter and carbon monoxide.

Particulate matter (PM) is a type of air pollution made up of particles of dust and liquid droplets. They are characterized into two categories based on the diameter of the particle. Coarse particles are between 2.5 micrometers and 10 micrometers and fine particles measure 2.5 micrometers and less. Both sizes can be inhaled. Coarse particles are filtered by the upper airways and can cause eye and sinus irritation as well as soar throat and coughing. The fine particles are more problematic because, when inhaled, they can be deposited deep into the lungs, where they are absorbed into the bloodstream. This is particularly hazardous to the very young, elderly and those with chronic conditions such as asthma, chronic obstructive pulmonary disease (COPD), cystic fibrosis and cardiovascular conditions. The illnesses most commonly with exposure to fine particle from wildfire smoke is bronchitis, exacerbation of asthma or COPD, and pneumonia. Symptoms of these complications include wheezing and shortness of breath and cardiovascular symptoms include chest pain, rapid heart rate and fatigue.

Carbon monoxide (CO) is a colorless, odorless gas that can be found at the highest concentration at close proximity to a smoldering fire. For this reason, carbon monoxide inhalation is a serious threat to the health of wildfire firefighters. CO in smoke can be inhaled into the lungs where it is absorbed into the bloodstream and reduces oxygen delivery to the body's vital organs. At high concentrations, it can cause headache, weakness, dizziness, confusion, nausea, disorientation, visual impairment, coma and even death. However, even at lower concentrations, such as those found at wildfires, individuals with cardiovascular disease may experience chest pain and cardiac arrhythmia. A recent study tracking the number and cause of wildfire firefighter deaths from 1990-2006 found that 21.9% of the deaths occurred from heart attacks.

Another important and somewhat less obvious health effect of wildfires is psychiatric diseases and disorders. Both adults and children from countries ranging from the United States and Canada to Greece and Australia who were directly and indirectly affected by wildfires were found by researchers to demonstrate several different mental conditions linked to their experience with the wildfires. These include post-traumatic stress disorder (PTSD), depression, anxiety, and phobias.

In a new twist to wildfire health effects, former uranium mining sites were burned over in the summer of 2012 near North Fork, Idaho. This prompted concern from area residents and Idaho State Department of Environmental Quality officials over the potential spread of radiation in the resultant smoke, since those sites had never been completely cleaned up from radioactive remains.

References

Alvarado, Ernesto; Sandberg, David V; Pickford, Stewart G. (1998). Modeling Large Forest Fires as Extreme Events. *Northwest Science*. Special Issue. 72:66–75.

Martell, David L; Sun, Hua. (2008). The impact of fire suppression, vegetation, and weather on the area burned by lightning-caused forest fires in Ontario. *Canadian Journal of Forest Research*. 38(38):1547–1563.

Olson, Richard Stuart; Gawronski, Vincent T. (2005). The 2003 Southern California Wildfires: Constructing Their Cause(s). *Quick Response Research Report*. 2005.

Peuch, Eric. (2005). Eighth International Wildland Firefighter Safety Summit - Human Factors - 10 Years Later. In: Butler, B W; Alexander, M E, editors. Missoula, Montana: The International Association of Wildland Fire, Hot Springs, South Dakota; 26–28 April 2005.

van Wagtendonk, Jan W. (2007). The History and Evolution of Wildland Fire Use. *Fire Ecology*.

Bibliography

Abe K. (1995). *Estimate of Tsunami Run-up Heights from Earthquake Magnitudes.*

Alexander D. (2002). *Principles of Emergency planning and Management.* Harpended: Terra publishing.

Alvarado, Ernesto; Sandberg, David V; Pickford, Stewart G. (1998). Modeling Large Forest Fires as Extreme Events. *Northwest Science.* Special Issue. 72:66–75.

Amanda Ripley. (2006). "Floods, Tornadoes, Hurricanes, Wildfires, Earthquakes... Why We Don't Prepare." *Time.* August 28.

American Water Works Association. (2002). *Drought Management Handbook.*

Bankoff, G. Frerks, G. Hilhorst D. (*eds.*) (2003). *Mapping Vulnerability: Disasters, Development and People.*

Billman, John. (2007). "Mike Elggren on Surviving an Avalanche". *Skiing* magazine Feb 2007: 26.

Chanson, H. (2010). *Tsunami Warning Signs on the Enshu Coast of Japan.* Shore & Beach, Vol. 78, No. 1, pp. 52–54.

Clark Evans (January 5, 2006). "Favorable trough interactions on tropical cyclones". Flhurricane.com. Retrieved 2006-10-20.

Daffern, Tony. (1999). *Avalanche Safety for Skiers, Climbers and Snowboarders*, Rocky Mountain Books.

Denver Water, (2002). "Water for Tomorrow, An Integrated Resource Plan/Drought Response Plan." February.

Donald Hyndman, David Hyndman (2009). "Chapter 3: Earthquakes and their causes". *Natural Hazards and Disasters* (2nd ed.). Brooks/Cole: Cengage Learning

Dyhouse, G. (2003). "*Flood modelling Using HEC-RAS.* Haestad Press, Waterbury, USA.

Erik A. Rasmussen and John Turner (2003). *Polar lows: mesoscale weather systems in the polar regions.* Cambridge University Press.

Fradin, Judith Bloom and Dennis Brindell (2008). *Witness to Disaster: Tsunamis.* Witness to Disaster. Washington, D.C.: National Geographic Society.

Haugen K, et.al (2005). "Fundamental mechanisms for tsunami generation by submarine mass flows in idealised geometries". *Marine and Petroleum Geology* 22 (1–2): 209–217.

Howard B Bluestein (1999). *Tornado Alley: Monster Storms of the Great Plains*. New York, NY: Oxford University Press.

Jackson, James, "Fatal attraction: living with earthquakes, the growth of villages into megacities, and earthquake vulnerability in the modern world," *Philosophical Transactions of the Royal Society*. Phil. Trans. R. Soc. A 15 August 2006 vol. 364 no. 1845 1911–1925.

Kerry Emanuel (January 2006). "Anthropogenic Effects on Tropical Cyclone Activity". Massachusetts Institute of Technology. Retrieved 2008-02-25.

Knutson, C., (1998). Hayes, M., and Phillips, T., "How to Reduce Drought Risk." Prepared for Western Drought Coordination Council. March.

Lee Davis (2008). "*Natural Disasters*". Infobase Publishing.

Luis Flores Ballesteros. "What determines a disaster?" 54 Pesos Sep 2008:54 Pesos 11 Sep 2008.

Marlene Bradford (2001). *Scanning the Skies: a History of Tornado Forecasting*. University of Oklahoma Press.

Martell, David L; Sun, Hua. (2008). The impact of fire suppression, vegetation, and weather on the area burned by lightning-caused forest fires in Ontario. *Canadian Journal of Forest Research*. 38(38):1547–1563.

McClung, David and Shaerer, Peter: (2006). *The Avalanche Handbook*, The Mountaineers.

Micheal H Mogil (2007). *Extreme Weather*. New York: Black Dog & Leventhal Publisher.

Nina A. Zaitseva (2006). "Cyclogenesis". National Snow and Ice Data Center. Retrieved 2006-12-04.

Noson, Qamar, and Thorsen (1988). *Washington State Earthquake Hazards: Washington State Department of Natural Resources*. Washington Division of Geology and Earth Resources Information Circular 85.

O'Connor, Jim E. and John E. Costa. (2004). *The World's Largest Floods, Past and Present: Their Causes and Magnitudes*. Washington, D.C.: U.S. Department of the Interior, U.S. Geological Survey.

Olson, Richard Stuart; Gawronski, Vincent T. (2005). The 2003 Southern California Wildfires: Constructing Their Cause(s). *Quick Response Research Report*. 2005.

Peuch, Eric. (2005). Eighth International Wildland Firefighter Safety Summit - Human Factors - 10 Years Later. In: Butler, B W; Alexander, M E, editors. Missoula, Montana: The International Association of Wildland Fire, Hot Springs, South Dakota; 26–28 April 2005.

Pinkham, R., (2003). "Technical Assistance to Covered Entities: Review of Conservation Planning Policies and Practices." Prepared for The Colorado Water Conservation Board. May.

Raymond D. Menard, and J.M. Fritsch (June 1989). "A Mesoscale Convective Complex-Generated Inertially Stable Warm Core Vortex".*Monthly Weather Review* 117 (6): 1237–1261.

Ryan N. Maue (2008). "Chapter 3: Cyclone Paradigms and Extratropical Transition Conceptualizations". Florida State University.

Schorlemmer, D.; Wiemer, S.; Wyss, M. (2005). "Variations in earthquake-size distribution across different stress regimes". *Nature* 437 (7058): 539–542.

Seymour, Simon (2001). *Tornadoes*. New York City, New York: HarperCollins

Spence, William; S. A. Sipkin, G. L. Choy (1989). "Measuring the Size of an Earthquake". United States Geological Survey. Retrieved 2006-11-03.

Thomas P Grazulis (January 1997). *Significant Tornadoes Update, 1992–1995*. St. Johnsbury, VT: Environmental Film.

Tremper, Bruce: (2001). *Staying Alive in Avalanche Terrain*, The Mountaineers.

United States National Institute for Occupational Safety and Health (NIOSH). *NIOSH Warns of Hazards of Flood Cleanup Work*. NIOSH Publication No. 94-123.

van Wagtendonk, Jan W. (2007). The History and Evolution of Wildland Fire Use. *Fire Ecology*.

Wilhite, D.A., Hayes, M.J., Knutson, C, and Smith K.H., (2003). "The Basics of Drought Planning: A 10-Step Process." National Drought Mitigation Center.

Wisner, B., Blaikie, P., Terry, C., and Davis, I. (2004). *At Risk, Natural Hazards, People's Vulnerability, and Disasters*. New York and London, Routledge, 2nd Edition.

WMO/GWP Associated Programme on Flood Management (2007). "Environmental Aspects of Integrated Flood Management." WMO.

Wyss, M. (1979). "Estimating expectable maximum magnitude of earthquakes from fault dimensions". *Geology* 7 (7): 336–340.